Lesbian, Gay, Bisexual and Transgender Christians

Also available from Bloomsbury

The Bloomsbury Reader in Religion, Sexuality and Gender, edited by Donald
L. Boisvert and Carly Daniel-Hughes
The Crisis of Islamic Masculinities, Amanullah De Sondy
Sex, Death and Witchcraft, Douglas Ezzy

Lesbian, Gay, Bisexual and Transgender Christians

Queer Christians, Authentic Selves

Bronwyn Fielder and Douglas Ezzy

Bloomsbury Academic
An imprint of Bloomsbury Publishing Plc

B L O O M S B U R Y
LONDON · OXFORD · NEW YORK · NEW DELHI · SYDNEY

Bloomsbury Academic

An imprint of Bloomsbury Publishing Plc

50 Bedford Square
London
WC1B 3DP
UK

1385 Broadway
New York
NY 10018
USA

www.bloomsbury.com

BLOOMSBURY and the Diana logo are trademarks of Bloomsbury Publishing Plc

First published 2018

British Library Cataloguing-in-Publication Data
A catalogue record for this book is available from the British Library.

ISBN: HB: 978-1-3500-3002-2
ePDF: 978-1-3500-3003-9
ePub: 978-1-3500-3004-6

Library of Congress Cataloging-in-Publication Data
Names: Fielder, Bronwyn, author.
Title: Lesbian, gay, bisexual, and transgender Christians : queer Christians,
authentic selves / Bronwyn Fielder and Douglas Ezzy.
Description: 1 [edition]. | New York : Bloomsbury Academic, 2017. |
Includes bibliographical references and index.
Identifiers: LCCN 2017036897 | ISBN 9781350030022 (hardback) |
ISBN 9781350030046 (epub)
Subjects: LCSH: Christian sexual minorities–Religious life.
Classification: LCC BV4596.G38 F54 2017 | DDC 261.8/35766–dc23
LC record available at https://lccn.loc.gov/2017036897

Typeset by Newgen KnowledgeWorks Pvt. Ltd., Chennai, India
Printed and bound in Great Britain

Contents

Illustrations

Figures

Photographs

Acknowledgements

This book would not have been possible without the participation of the interviewees, including members of the congregations of the Metropolitan Community Churches in Melbourne and Sydney, and some participants from the Uniting Church, who welcomed Bronwyn generously and with open arms. We thank you all for giving of yourselves and sharing a part of your lives. The following dedication is for you.

> Whatever knowledge gained in the interactions and time spent with the participants of this study and imparted in the following chapters is in some way fleeting, a minute facet of the whole moving history – the ebb and flow of lives and loves. It is as fleeting as a perfect spider web in the morning dew, or the song of a bird. Knowing just a little awakened in me, and will hopefully awaken in the reader, a wonder, an awe at the vague momentary imprint of the lives of others, and despite realizing how imperfect and transitory the imprint is, I rejoice in both the sharing and the mystery, the knowing and not knowing, and take with me the honour and privilege that I have been able to take part in that moment. (Bronwyn Fielder)

Thank you also to Kristin Natalier, who played a key role in guiding the development of the project, and to Nick Hookway whose assistance with some of the finer points was invaluable.

1

Introduction

Luke describes the day 'he lost everything', the day members of his evangelical church discovered he was same-sex attracted:

> We had this massive traumatic break and very emotional, very traumatic, over the top, screaming at people, all this sort of stuff. One day I was youth leader of my church, leading a youth group, leading Bible study, and the next day I was just gone [motions that he was swept aside]. Yeah, and for me that was one of the hardest times of my life. I lost everything. That was not just my church world; that was my whole world. That was the house that I lived in, all the friends that I had. It was my family: my parents were pastor of the church that I was at. So, to an extent, for a few years, my relationship with my family was gone; we didn't even talk very much. I just lost everything at once. I was twenty.

Luke's life changed from that moment. His central story, initially one of loss, is a story that is duplicated across Australia and across continents, at times leading to heartbreaking loss of life, more often to loss of faith. The stories in this book do not dwell on loss. However, Luke's story of loss is important because it illustrates the centrality of Christianity to the lives of many lesbian, gay, bisexual and transgendered (LGBT) people.[1] Loss has also been recognized as 'the springboard for religious transformation' (Ritter and O'Neill 1996: 12) and is the beginning point for the journey of many LGBT Christians.

The book examines how committed LGBT Christians understand their lives and their faith, how they rebuild and transform their faith, exerting agency and creating conditions of belief that allow the coexistence of their sexuality and religious worldview. This transformation is effected in ways that on one hand remain tightly interwoven with Christian normative thought, expressed in the desire to live authentically – loving God, loving Jesus, loving others. On the other hand, this transformation is intricately connected to a disruption of Christian normative spaces, a 'queering' of Christian practices that enables LGBT Christians to live the authentic lives they desire, true to their faith and true to their sexuality.

Luke, for example, is now a pastor in a newly formed church, where, as an openly gay man, he inspires others who are facing similar struggles, preaching a message of inclusivity but still within the bounds of Christianity.

This book is centred on identities – queer identities, Christian identities, authentic identities. Using qualitative methods to investigate and describe how LGBT Christians integrate their faith and sexuality, we argue that the LGBT Christians are guided by an 'ethic of authenticity' (Taylor 1991). They desire to be ethically authentic through the expression of their 'true' sexual, gendered and religious selves. This desire is magnified by their religiosity which frames their sexuality and gender as 'God given'. This is illustrated beautifully by the words of one transgender participant: 'God has been the driver of my transitioning'.

In the pursuit of their desire to live authentic lives, true to their sexual, gendered and religious selves, many LGBT Christians struggle emotionally and psychologically due to the religious habitus of their upbringing. This book investigates the nature of these internal struggles. We argue that the religious habitus is based upon internalized dispositions, feelings and cognitions (Bourdieu 1977). Change to this habitus occurs over time through working with emotions, changed relationships, understandings, and religious practices. Individuals transform their religious habitus, exerting agency to break free of structural constraints in the patriarchal and heteronormative spaces and practices of Christianity. The book maps the processes that LGBT Christians go through to integrate their sexuality, gender and religiosity.

A form of 'queer Christianity' is the product of the desire to live authentic sexual and religious lives. Queer practices and relationships unsettle the heteronormative order and permeate borders that historically and culturally have contained Christian practice. In enacting these practices and building new relationships, a new religious habitus is created.

This research also questions the extent to which spaces and practices are transformed, and in what ways macro normative processes are reproduced or resisted and 'queered', and to what extent Christianity and 'queer' can be reconciled. Is it the case that, as Ken Plummer (1995: 148) asserts: 'queer fundamentalists have no way of reconciling differences with Christian fundamentalists'? Are there irreconcilable differences between queer and Christianity, or is 'fundamentalist' the operative word? Queer theorists might charge that LGBT Christians are living according to a 'homonormative' order, where 'hetero' is merely replaced by 'homo', and all restraining conditions remain the same. However, we argue that queering does occur, but is irregular and inconsistent, according to individual contingencies and demographic factors. We conclude that queering only occurs as individual agency is exerted in the discovery and expression of the authentic self and that the institution of Christianity remains relatively untroubled.

In the following section we introduce the 'problem' of alternative sexualities and genders for religion – the 'social problem' which this book addresses. We then briefly sketch the historical and sociological background of the problem faced by LGBT Christians in the contemporary world, followed by a summary of the nature and extent of the contemporary societal and religious tensions between Christianity and same-sex attraction. The final section is a summary of the book chapters.

Irreconcilable differences?

For many people, the concepts of religion and homosexuality are irreconcilable. This is the case for those of both religious and non-religious backgrounds and those of the wider non-heterosexual community. The homosexual Christian is scarcely considered possible (Comstock and Henking 1997; Rycenga 2004; Thumma and Gray 2005; Walton 2006). However, the lived reality is that LGBT individuals are born into religious families and communities, where their faith is inextricably connected to their individual and cultural identity. Further, many LGBT individuals choose to turn to faith at some point in their lives (Primiano 2005). Many mainline and conservative religious groups incorporate religious ritual into everyday life, and it is through these everyday rituals that those born into religious families learn what is acceptable and what is not. For some, this religious self is driven 'deeply into the bone' (Grimes 2000: 124) and not easily abandoned.

Some Christians who find themselves same-sex attracted are faced with a seemingly insoluble problem. Most conservative Christian groups believe and teach that homosexuality is a sin and that such sinful desires are temptations of the devil. Homosexual lifestyles will inevitably lead to divine retribution and damnation (Hansen and Lambert 2011). In the United States, in 2009 as many as 72 per cent of all Christian denominations opposed same-sex sexuality (Rodriguez 2009), although this number is fast declining (Murphy 2015).

The tragedy for LGBTIQ Christians is that not only do a large majority of Christian churches do not accept them as they are but often the wider LGBTIQ community shun them as well, because they understand Christianity to be hostile to non-heteronormative sexuality (Comstock and Henking 1997; O'Brien 2004; Wilcox 2007). The conflicts that arise are deep and often seemingly irreconcilable. While a minority negotiate their religious and sexual identities in ways to find acceptable personal solutions, many remain stymied by their conflicting identities, withdrawing from religion altogether (Rodriguez and Ouellette 2000; Couch et al. 2008).

According to the Private Lives study carried out in Australia in 2005, of the 72.8 per cent LGBTIQ population that were brought up within a Christian denomination, only 14.8 per cent are currently practising (Couch et al. 2008). Moreover, when compared with the general Australian population (ABS 2013), the LGBTIQ participants in the online survey were over three times more likely to report no religion and three times less likely to be Christian. In addition, LGBTIQ individuals are slightly more likely to affiliate with a non-Christian faith (Couch et al. 2008). A range of survey research also suggests that the tensions between same-sex attracted individuals and the tenets of the Christian faith are the catalyst for those people leaving the religion of their youth (Mahaffy 1996; Morrow 2003; Hillier, Turner and Mitchell 2004; Couch et al. 2008).

Lynne Hillier and her associates (1998; 2004; 2010) have conducted three national surveys investigating the experiences of same-sex attracted and gender-questioning young people in Australia. One unexpected outcome from their 2004 survey was the surprisingly high number of young people who identified as religious but who found extreme difficulty in the coexistence of their sexual and religious identities (Hillier, Mitchell and Mulcare 2008).

There are serious negative health effects for LGBTIQ young people as a result of the hostility and alienation from families and church communities as well as the wider LGBTIQ community (Hillier, Turner and Mitchell 2004). For example, LGBTIQ youth who are religiously affiliated feel worse about their lives and are more likely to think about, or succeed in, self-harm than those not from religious families (Hillier, Mitchell and Mulcare 2008). While the majority of LGBT Christians choose to reject either their sexual identity or their religious identity (Rodriguez and Ouellette 2000), the present study concentrates on the small percentage that remain faithful to their religion of birth – in this study, Christianity – or those who became converts at some point in their lives.

In this book we describe and seek to understand the lived experience of committed LGBT Christians, including their aspirations and struggles. We identify why they maintain their faith even in the context of Christian hostility towards LGBT people. The book explores and maps the strategies that both the pastors and members of their congregations employ in negotiating their religious, gendered and sexual identities, drawing on sociological theory to interpret these processes. This encompasses cognitive, relational and emotional aspects of individuals' lives, focusing on relationships, ritual and emotion as core meaning-making, empowering, and possibly vital processes, to facilitate identity transformation. The analysis extends existing research on identity negotiation of LGBT Christians to focus on the importance of the moral dimension as a motivating factor in the process of identity negotiation and transformation.

Qualitative sociological research conducted on the intersection of same-sex attraction and religion in Australia is sparse. Alison Kirkman (2001), in New Zealand, develops a sociological account of the sexual and religious identities of lesbians. Luke Gahan and Tiffany Jones (2013) open the conversation with their diverse collection of contributions exploring the intersection of religion and spirituality in Australia. In addition, a recent dissertation by Curtis Dickson (2012) investigates issues of identity and belonging among active LGBT Christians in Sydney, Australia. The present study adds to these small data sets, describing the lived experience of LGBT Christians in four congregations in Melbourne and Sydney. According to Andrew Yip (2010: 45): 'the importance of the documentation of the lived experiences cannot be underestimated ... for while theology often grapples with what ought to be, empirical work focuses on what is, amidst the messiness of life as lived'.

This book addresses the lack of mainstream acceptance of the legitimacy of active LGBT Christians. Their legitimacy is contested by the general LGBTIQ community, the Christian community or the community at large (Comstock and Henking 1997; Rycenga 2004; McKinney and Tolbert 2005; Thumma and Gray 2005; Wilcox 2007). While the last decade has seen 'a paradigm shift' (Rodriguez 2009: 8) in the recognition of same-sex attracted individuals as legitimate religious and spiritual beings, the process is far from complete. Without developing academic and social discourse around the intersection of sexuality and religion, in this case more specifically same-sex attracted individuals and Christianity, the issue remains relatively unexamined and unaddressed. According to Nancy Tosh (2001), only with this step of naming can legitimacy be gained and the history of erasure repaired.

The book also has a critical agenda. We explore whether the structural constraints of patriarchy and heteronormativity are produced and reproduced within the LGBT congregations and how these structural constraints are experienced, if at all, by the participants. Gender, for example, is a significant factor in understanding the Christian experience due to Christianity's patriarchal foundations (Morrow 2003). The book questions to what extent and in what ways heteronormativity and patriarchy are constructed and reproduced in the lives and religious practice of LGBT Christians.

Same-sex attraction and Christianity

The experience of the LGBT Christians is profoundly shaped by a long history of conflict between alternative sexuality and Christianity. Christian opposition to LGBT sexuality is often portrayed as having biblical sources. However, various studies demonstrate it has broader social sources in the confession box, the medicalization of sexuality, the decline of traditional Christianity, neoliberal economics, and the politics of fear. The experiences of lesbian, gay, bisexual and transgender Christians described in this book are profoundly shaped by these broader historical and cultural processes.

The claim that homosexuality is 'immoral and unnatural' is the defining characteristic of contemporary Western opposition to homosexuality, which primarily refers to male homosexuality in most historical research (Boswell 2009: 324). This charge is grounded predominantly in religious statutes – in this case Christian writings and beliefs (Baunach 2011; Whitehead 2010). However, the argument that homosexuality is immoral is a relatively recent one within Christianity. According to John Boswell (1979), early Christians did not hold homosexuality to be morally unacceptable, although for practical reasons they did hold a certain hostility to non-procreative sexuality. There was a profound change of attitudes to homosexuality around the late 12th to 13th centuries (Boswell 1979). European society that was previously tolerant to not only homosexual behaviour, but also Jews, Muslims, witches and women became, in a short space of time, rigid, intolerant and punitive. Jews were executed in the street if they questioned the Christian faith, women were expelled from universities in which they had previously been enrolled and laws were passed in many European countries that outlawed homosexual acts and prescribed the death penalty (Boswell 1979).

According to Boswell, this popular demonization of homosexuality influenced the Christian church. Homosexuality, which had previously been accepted or at worst tolerated as comparable to heterosexual fornication, began to be portrayed as one of the most despicable sins. Boswell argues that the repression and hatred of homosexuality came about due to 'popular misunderstandings of the Christian theology, not from faithful implementation of Church policy' (1992: 96). Derrick Bailey's book *Homosexuality and the Western Christian Tradition* (1955) was an important turning point for contemporary LGBT-friendly biblical scholars. Many have supported his claims, for example, that the biblical story of Sodom and other biblical verses have been wrongly interpreted, mistranslated and often taken out of context (Bullough 1976). Bailey (in

Bullough 1976: 353) explains that the church was complicit in the process of the demonization of homosexuality, stating that 'the Christian church cannot be entirely exonerated from all responsibility for hostility toward homosexuality'. For the purposes of this summary it is not necessary to specify each biblical reference; suffice to say that according to Bailey, Boswell and others, 'the objections to homosexuality are not biblical, they are not consistent and not part of Jesus' teachings, nor are they fundamentally Christian' (Boswell 1979: 5).

The idea that homosexuality is unnatural is a deeply ingrained attitude that pervades Christianity and contemporary society more broadly (Iyer 2014). This is despite the many theologians who have refuted the argument that homosexuality is immoral, arguing for different interpretations of the biblical references to homosexuality (Spong 1991; Heyward 1999; Edser 2012). The unnaturalness of homosexuality is based upon the argument that the dichotomous masculine and feminine characteristics are biblically ordained or naturally occurring. According to this understanding of Christianity, 'natural' relations are between a man and a woman (Rom. 1.27),[2] and God created Adam and Eve to populate the world (Gen. 1.28). This tension between same-sex attraction and the Christian worldview is deeply ingrained and has a powerful impact upon many of the LGBT Christians. In order to understand this tension, we turn to historical and sociological accounts.

The strange transformation from neutral to hostile attitudes towards homosexuality has clear social sources. Foucault's (1990) landmark study of sexuality, *The History of Sexuality* (1976/1990), sheds light upon the forces of power at work since the 17th century. The hostility towards homosexuality was created through the medicalization of sexuality and the conceptualization of homosexuality as a sin as part of the practice of confession. Medicalization is the process by which more and more of social life becomes subject to advice from doctors and medical experts. The early medical profession conceptualized homosexuality as a condition that could be treated (Foucault 1990). This marginalized homosexuality as an illegitimate identity. The Christian practice of confession, in a similar way, transformed homoerotic thoughts, feelings and sexual acts into a sinful 'homosexual identity' (Foucault 1990).

In the early church, sexual and other sins were relatively undifferentiated, according to Foucauldian scholar Mark Jordan (1997). However, during medieval times some sexual acts gained greater status (Armour 2010). In his book *The Invention of Sodomy in Christian Theology*, Jordan traces the emergence of 'sodomy' as a particularly 'problematic' sin which over time is stabilized as an irredeemable identity, 'the sodomite' (Jordan 1997: 57, 123, 162). Ellen Armour also argues that the 'invention' of sodomy is a pivotal point in the emergence of '*scientia sexualis*' or science of sexuality (Armour 2010: 116). The *scientia sexualis* cemented, at least, the male homosexual's identity as an aberration, an unnatural, abnormal condition.

These social and historical processes created the person defined by his/her sexuality (Foucault 1990; Jagose 1996). With the 'birth' of the homosexual identity, and the increasing individualization of late modernity, in particular since the 1960s, came the political move from the private to the public sphere, where previously marginal identities asserted their claim to legitimacy. For the LGBT community, the 'coming out discourse' became paramount (Wilcox 2010: 251; Baunach 2011: 349).

The emerging homosexual identity was, and is, perceived as a threat by the dominant heteronormative discourse and practice. These power relations hold the key to tensions that exist today. According to Raewyn Connell and Gary Dowsett (1992: 2), sexuality is 'inherently a domain of power relations' between women and men, or heterosexuals and LGBTIQ individuals. Power relations are particularly relevant in conservative Christianity, a predominantly patriarchal and heterosexist institution. The Christian churches have sought to control many aspects of sexuality throughout the modern era (Comstock 1993). Christians often celebrate their influence on collective morality. Frame (2007), for example, bemoans the slide to hedonism that afflicts secular Australia as he recognizes the waning belief and attendance at Christian churches in contemporary Australia. They seem blind, however, to the suffering and trauma caused by Christian attitudes towards sexuality.

Christianity today

Attendance at traditional mainstream Christian churches has declined, sometimes catastrophically. However, at the same time, other forms of religion have grown, driven by immigration and alternative and 'New Age' forms of spirituality (Heelas and Woodhead 2005; Bouma 2006). Australia, for example, has seen a growth in Islam, Buddhism and Hinduism, mainly as a consequence of migration. This migration has also resulted in ethnically diverse forms of Christianity, while Christianity itself has splintered into liberal, charismatic, conservative and fundamentalist forms (Bouma 2006). At the same time, alternative forms of spirituality, such as Witchcraft and Paganism, have become increasingly popular (Berger and Ezzy 2007).

In this environment of uncertainty, in the United States and to a lesser degree in Australia, white Protestant conservatives have been able to assert cultural dominance. This has manifested in 'virtuous crusades' which seek to define what is acceptable and what is deviant, promoting destruction of 'evil people, wicked institutions and practices' (Adam 2003: 263). Despite the late modern move towards difference and a greater respect for human rights, Protestant conservatives have clearly placed same-sex attracted individuals in the camp of the wicked. Homosexuality has been successfully framed within the religious field as a symptom of 'moral decline'.

Politicization of marriage equality

Moral crusades based on the demonization of homosexuality have brought religious values back into the public political sphere (Bouma 2006). This is partly as a response to the increasing marginalization of the church, and partly as a consequence of its revitalization. Traditionally, fundamentalist and conservative evangelicals emphasized 'conversion of the human heart' (van Geest 2007: 202). In the last forty years, however, the Christian right has voiced increasingly shrill moral positions on issues such as abortion, women's rights and homosexuality.

Although Australia differs from the United States in that it does not have an overtly religious voter base, religion has influenced Australian politics in the last two decades. 'Family values' – the catch phrase of the 21st century – was unknown in Australian politics in 1975. John Howard's prime ministership marked the beginning of the transformation of Australian politics. According to Marion Maddox (2005), in the 2004 federal election campaign, 'religion seemed to spring out of nowhere to take centre stage'. Howard 'broke the truce between religion and politics' in Australia (Maddox 2011). This emphasis on the political significance of religiously framed 'moral' issues has had the effect of polarizing believers into conservative or progressive positions, both *within* and *between* faith groups (van Geest 2007: 202). Chris Dowd (2011) sees, for example, the LGBT issue as central to a type of cultural war between conservative and progressive factions of the Christian church worldwide, a war he sees as unwinnable and divisive.

The politicization of a Christian right morality is demonstrated in the polarized and contested arguments for and against same-sex marriage worldwide. The first gay male activists agitated for the right to marry in the United States as early as 1970, a move that led to the banning of same-sex marriages US-wide by 1994. Since that time, the Christian right has grown in strength as has the strength of the opposition. Although same-sex marriage in the United States is now federally recognized on the basis of equality (Supreme Court of the United States 2015), those who oppose it remain a powerful force. The recent battle between the state of Alabama and the US Supreme Court is an example of this polarization, with the state-endorsed Christian right moral agenda at odds with the federal ruling in support of equality (Holpuch 2015). Similarly, the call to allow legal refusal of service to LGBT individuals in Northern Ireland is a reminder of the power of conservative Christian morality at work in the public sphere (Strudwick 2014).

Northern Europe led the way in the recognition of same-sex partnerships, with mainstream churches adopting attitudes towards homosexuality that reflected their acceptance among the general population. According to Brown and Woodhead (2016), the state churches of Denmark, Norway and Sweden retain more public trust than, for example, the Church of England in the United Kingdom. These Scandinavian countries recognized civil same-sex unions legally in 1989 (Denmark), and, in early 2000s, same-sex marriages (2009 Norway and Sweden; 2012 Denmark). Although participation levels remain very low, the state churches in Scandinavia remain culturally relevant to the people, who, on the whole, supported marriage equality (Jakobsson, Kotsdam and Jakobsson 2013).

In Holland, the Dutch Protestant church, the 'Remonstrants', performed the first civil unions in 1986, and performed the first same-sex marriages in 2004, after same-sex marriages were legalized in 2001 (Andries 2007). Spain (2005), and France (2013), both led by socialist parties at the time, voted for marriage equality, with strong opposition from the Catholic Church (Erlanger 2013). Both have weathered legal challenges from the Catholic Church and right wing political parties (Digoix et al. 2016). Opposition came in United Kingdom from the two largest church organizations, the Catholic Church and the Church of England. Despite this opposition, marriage equality was introduced in 2014, partly as the church became largely powerless and alienated from the population (Brown and Woodhead 2016).

In Australia, conservative attitudes within both Protestant and Catholic churches have converged. In particular, disaffected Presbyterians have joined forces with the conservative Sydney Anglican enclave, some Pentecostals and factions of the Catholic Church (Thompson 1994; Frame 2007) to publicly oppose same-sex marriage. The political agenda is driven by a very powerful, conservative and overtly political group, the Australian Christian Lobby (ACL), which is profoundly influential in the federal capital, Canberra. Both Labor and Liberal prime ministers, including Howard, Rudd and Abbott, have spoken at ACL conferences. In 2004, the conservative Howard government amended the Marriage Act of 1961, to define marriage as 'the union of a man and a woman, to the exclusion of all others' (Marriage Amendment Act 2004). Despite more than ten years of challenges from states and territories, the 2004 amendment remains unchanged at this time. The conservative right argues that not only the institution of marriage, but the very fabric of society, is under threat (Gillies 2003).

In the context of a polarizing world of growing threats and economic insecurity, it is attractive for conservative Christian political operatives to focus on the threat posed by the LGBTIQ 'other' as a way of diverting attention from political, economic and environmental sources of insecurity. Over the last few decades, a nostalgic sense of a safe and secure past entered the political sphere in Australia and elsewhere. Nostalgia is bound up with a longing for so-called historical Christian values, the historial reality of which is debatable. This nostalgia is closely tied to the malaise generated by the rise of neoliberalism, growing economic inequality. By the 1990s, religious fundamentalism and evangelical Christianity had become a 'refuge for victims of economic recession and the vicissitudes of rapid social change' (Thompson 1994: 140).

In addition, the growing threat of global terrorism since 2001 has had a deeply polarizing effect worldwide, with the successful framing of Christians in the West as 'us' and Muslims as 'them'. These broad social trends are important because they play into the demonization of LGBTIQ sexuality by conservative Christians. LGBTIQ individuals are held up by conservative Christians as a focus for the fear and uncertainty generated by these broad social processes, even though LGBTIQ individuals play no part in the creation of these dangers. These societal and cultural discourses surrounding same-sex attraction profoundly influence the way same-sex attracted Christians negotiate and experience their religious identity.

Chapter summaries

This book gives a voice to a group of lesbian, gay, bisexual and transgender Christians, telling their story in their words. The book begins with a chapter that argues for the importance of the theoretical concepts of authenticity, emotion and habitus for understanding the experience of LGBT Christians. This is followed by chapters that empirically describe the changing lives of same-sex attracted and gender questioning Christians. In the final chapter we return to the broader social context to situate our findings.

Chapter 2 outlines the theories that are employed to describe and analyse the experience of the LGBT Christians and the institution of Christianity. Charles Taylor's (1991) concept of the 'ethic of authenticity' focuses our attention on the moral dimension of LGBT Christians' lives as they strive to express their 'true' or 'authentic' sexuality and gender within the context of their religiosity. Pursuing an authentic self produces a 'queer' Christianity. We use the concept of 'queer' in a particular way to describe, for example, how Christian heteronormative boundaries are subverted through queer Christian practices. Emotion (Ahmed 2004) plays a key role in the human interactions and power relations that make this queering possible. We underline how religion is fundamentally emotional and experiential (Riis and Woodhead 2010). Bourdieu's (1977) theory of practice and the concept of habitus is woven through these conceptualizations of religion, queer Christianity and practices of authenticity.

Chapters 3–7 describe the experiences of the LGBT Christians drawing on interviews and observations. Chapter 3 sets the stage with comparative descriptions of each congregation of the Metropolitan Community Church (MCC) that participated in the research. We describe the institutional structure, the church space, its people and its practices. These accounts are based upon Bronwyn's observations, the interviews and supporting literature. The MCC is experienced by participants as a safe and inclusive space. For example, inclusive practices such as communion are common to all congregations and are pivotal to the queering and transforming of these spaces. There are important differences between each congregation and some tensions exist to a greater or lesser degree in each congregation. For example, practices that queer Christianity are often in tension with attitudes based upon the Christian patriarchal normative tradition. Chapter 3 describes the congregations in general terms. The following chapters focus on the experiences of individuals in those congregations.

Chapter 4 describes the desire of the participants to live an authentic life and what this entails. The LGBT Christians understand their sexuality and gender, in the case of the transgendered participants, as essential, as a gift from God. A central life goal is to live authentically with their sexuality and gender in the context of Christianity. The 'ethic of authenticity' describes the moral framework that shapes how participants seek to live their lives. The performative act of coming out, for example, is central to the attainment of authenticity, as is living a good life, following the example of Jesus.

Chapters 5 and 6 focus on the transformation of identities – how authentic identities are achieved and how queer identities and Christian identities deal with conflict and reach a state of integration. Chapter 5 maps a five-stage process that individuals move through when faced with tension between their same-sex attraction and religious worldview. This chapter builds on earlier descriptions of the process of transformation experienced by LGBT Christians (Levy and Reeves 2011) to provide a more nuanced understanding of this process.

Catalytic moments are often experienced by LGBT Christians, and these are described in Chapter 6. Catalytic moments enable and empower LGBT Christians to move forward to begin a process of resolution. Catalytic moments are primarily emotional and relational experiences, and only sometimes informed by changes in cognitive understandings of beliefs or theology. Catalytic moments are followed by a stage of positive rebuilding. Ritual practices aid the realization of peaceful integration of sexual and gendered identity and religious worldview. These practices can also be described as queered practices, practices that unsettle heteronormative constraints and are most effectively practised in safe spaces, such as the MCC. The lived religion of LGBT Christians is an integrally emotional and relational experience, alongside their beliefs.

Chapter 7 analyses the tension between queerness and authenticity – two concepts that at first glance appear diametrically opposed. Striving to live an authentic life is aided by the queering of practices. The two work together in tension, at times in tandem, in the relational dynamics and practices of the LGBT Christians in this study. This tension is exposed by the gender dynamics of the MCC congregations and attitudes to bisexuality and responses to transgendered Christians. While MCC queers Christianity in terms of resisting heteronormative constraints, the patriarchal institution of Christianity as expressed in MCC remains untroubled. There remains a profound resistance to queering in everyday life.

The central argument of the book, summarized in Chapter 8, is that LGBT Christians have found a way to live according to an ethic of authenticity, true to their sexual, gendered and religious selves. The transformation of their identities to make this authenticity possible is effected through emotional and relational factors, through religious practices that are often, but not always, underpinned by changes in cognitive beliefs and understandings.

2

Queer Authentic Christian Lives

My sermon was entitled, 'Be True to You.' It was actually inspired by Polonius' advice to his son, Laertes, when the young man was about to leave. It's early in Shakespeare's play, Hamlet, and it's from those lines that go: 'This above all: To thine own self be true, And it must follow, as the night the day, Thou canst not then be false to any man.' (Perry 2004: 1)

Introduction

At first glance, the pursuit of authenticity and queer practices appear diametrically opposed. The pursuit of 'authenticity' assumes an essential unchanging self, while a queer self is a continually created and transformed self. In this sense 'queer' is anti-identitarian, in which the self is never crystallized. Despite this, these two practices do coexist in the lives of LGBT Christians. This is clearly illustrated in the quotation above from Troy Perry. Perry was the founder of the Metropolitan Community Church and the above quotation comes from his first sermon to that church in 1968. The MCC is led by gay and lesbian Christians and is discussed in more detail in Chapter 3.

The participants in this study strive to live an authentic existence, which entails expressing sexualities and/or gendered identities by transgressing, or queering, normative boundaries. The participants thus enact a queer Christianity. LGBT Christians also unsettle traditional theoretical understandings of religion that emphasize belief. While belief and theology do have a role, the experiential and emotional aspects of religious practice are much more central to the lives of LGBT Christians. The queer concept of 'performativity' links elegantly with this: being an LGBT Christian is primarily about the doing of religion. This chapter begins with a discussion of Charles Taylor's concept of the 'ethic of authenticity', is followed by a consideration of how queer theory helps us understand the lives of the LGBT Christians, and concludes with a discussion of emotional and performative aspects of being religious.

Photo 2.1 Altar at Metropolitan Community Church, Melbourne. The altar cloth is a rainbow flag, a key symbol of LGBT pride. Photo by Douglas Ezzy

The ethic of authenticity

LGBT Christians in this study strive to live authentically by expressing their sexualities and/or gender. Individualistic freedom characteristic of contemporary society enables this. At the same time the pursuit of authenticity troubles conservatives who view LGBT individuals as 'choosing' to live a certain lifestyle, a lifestyle they see as an immoral. Some conservatives express alarm at the perceived moral decline associated with the postmodern 'slide into relativism' and the subsequent breaking loose from moral norms that they think leads to narcissistic and hedonistic lifestyles.

Some sociological studies have argued that the contemporary 'self' oriented culture of authenticity is narcissistic and denies individuals higher or expanded meaning beyond themselves (Bell 1976; Lasch 1979; Lipovetsky 1989/2005). Contemporary lives, they say, are narrowed and flattened. In contrast, Charles Taylor (1991) argues that authenticity can be a workable moral framework that draws people into meaningful and significant relationships: 'an ethic of authenticity' (Taylor 1991: 15). For the LGBT Christians in this study, their authentic self is an expression of a God-given sexuality and gender, which they feel morally obliged to reflect, and which draws them into meaningful relationships and ways of living.

Taylor (1991) argues that the moral landscape of modern Western society is far from hedonistic and meaningless but is rather complex and nuanced. He acknowledges the problem and reality of moral relativism, but argues that critics do not recognize the other aspects of contemporary morality that exist alongside this relativism. Taylor observes that many individuals express a 'moral ideal' of being 'true to oneself' (Taylor 1991: 15, 35; 2007: 475) that leads to a 'culture of authenticity'. The culture of authenticity initially emerged from romantic expressionism in the late 18th century and holds that everyone has their own unique way of being and of realizing humanity. The modern rationalized 'buffered self' (Taylor 2007: 476) that evolved from this did separate individuals off from one another, 'buffering' them in a disengaged form of self-discipline. In response to the malaise generated by this disengaged individualism, Taylor discerns the development of an 'ethic of authenticity' as individuals seek creative ways of engaging with each other. This results in a form of morality that pursues a unique self in the context of meaningful relationships.

The 'ethnic of authenticity' is clearly manifest in the desire of the LGBTIQ community to 'come out' and be open about their sexuality and/or gender, and to resist conformity to an ideal imposed from outside. In this way, desire, morality and sense of integrity come together with the insistence that it is wrong to hide, and that they have a moral obligation to realize the true self (Taylor 2007).

The ethic of authenticity is by its very nature dialogical, constrained by shared frameworks of meaning and common moral precepts (Taylor 1991: 37). Taylor describes these backgrounds as 'horizons of significance', or shared understandings of what constitutes a moral life, that are necessarily relational. Taylor's argument is based upon an understanding of the social sources of the self, from which our sense of self emerges and develops. Understanding identity as integrally dialogical and social addresses the misunderstandings about the ethic of authenticity of early commentators and conservative critics who overemphasize the so-called 'slide to subjectivity' or moral abyss, and ignore the moral and social dimensions of authenticity.

Identity and the sense of self were primarily defined by social class and status in earlier historical periods. In contemporary Western society, individuals are much more likely to construct and define themselves reflexively and individually (Giddens 1992). The desire to be an individual, to do things 'my way', to be true to oneself, developed through this new sense of reflexive self-definition (Taylor 1991: 29). Despite this new sense of self-determining freedom and choice, no individual is free of external influences. Identity, for example, is formed in significant relationships (Taylor 1991). George Herbert Mead (1934) similarly articulates that individuals define themselves 'dialogically' in relation to others, whether in resistance to, or in accordance with, others.

Taylor maintains that late modern theories on free-floating reflexivity and liquidity ignore the dialogic nature of identity and sense of self. Significant relationships, those with significant others who 'matter enough to effect change in self-definition' (Sullivan 1940: 34) contribute to identity development and life-long transformation, even when this is an unconscious occurrence. Significant relationships can be with family members, partners and peers, other persons in positions of authority, as well as spiritual entities, more specifically God or Jesus. The crux of this discussion is the connection of identity to the ethic of authenticity and horizons of significance.

The freedom to define the self is constrained within the boundaries of how others define and respond to us. Taylor (1991: 33–36) identifies how relationships with others form 'inescapable horizons' or 'horizons of significance'. These horizons of significance are conditions that cannot be decided arbitrarily; what is significant is not determined by the self. When an individual chooses self-fulfilment without regard to (a) 'the demands of [the] ties with others, and (b) the demands of something more or other than human desires' the conditions for realizing authenticity are undermined (Taylor 1991: 35).

Denying the past or ignorance of others beyond the self both form conditions that 'collapse horizons of significance' (Taylor 1991: 22, 39). Choice, as an end in itself, does not confer authenticity. Choice is rather the means to an end, and what is done with the choice matters. Whether a person lives according to horizons of significance determines what constitutes an authentic life. Horizons of significance could be determined through those close to the self, through partners and family, or through more broad relations with others and society, religious beliefs or connections to nature.

> I can define my identity only against things that matter … only if I exist in a world in which history, or the demand of nature, or the needs of my fellow human beings, or the duties of citizenship, or the call of God, or something else of this order matters crucially, can I define my identity for myself that is not trivial. (Taylor 1991: 40–41)

Taylor maintains that some narcissist choices are indeed shallow, not because of the culture of authenticity but because they go against it. Horizons of significance provide individuals with connections to causes and social relations beyond the self and are intrinsically tied to the creation of an authentic sense of self. The desire to live an authentic life, although an individual project, is intimately connected to others. Relationships with significant others determine what constitutes a meaningful life. The pursuit of authenticity is also contextualized by relationships with broader society.

A belief in God is one of the key horizons of significance that contextualize the pursuit of authenticity for LGBT Christians. Belief in God is central to living ethically, in particular as this belief shapes the realm of love and intimacy, which Taylor understands as the 'prime loci' (Taylor 1991: 47) of self-fulfilment and self-discovery. This is the nub of the dilemma that confronts many LGBT Christians.

Recognition by others is an integral part of identity creation and self-fulfilment (Taylor 1991). This is more pronounced in the contemporary world where identity is a negotiated reflexive process rather than a given. It is particularly relevant to same-sex attracted individuals for whom, for example, 'coming out', proclaiming publicly the 'true' sexual or gendered self, is central to the notion of living authentically. Coming out is understood as a moral mandate driven by the relationship with God and Jesus. For LGBT Christians, an authentic existence necessarily means actively resisting normative expectations of sexuality and gendered identity and doing Christianity differently. This can be understood as a queer life.

Queer theory

Queer analysis resists normative understandings of sexuality and gender, such as those that are inherent in some of Taylor's concepts. Many see queer theory as offering a solution for those who experience identities as constraining. Multiple identities are not resolved into a consistent whole. Rather, queer allows 'the maintenance of identity and difference in tension' (Epstein 1994: 197). The most useful conceptual tools borrowed from queer theorists to understand and analyse the religious experience of the LGBT Christians are the concepts of heteronormativity and performativity.

'Heteronormativity' describes a key aspect of the social and cultural context that frames the struggles of LGBT Christians. Queer analysis interrogates traditional understandings of the binary distinctions of heterosexuality and non-heterosexuality, questioning the 'natural' nature of heterosexuality. Heteronormativity (Warner 1991) describes how heterosexuality has been assumed as the 'norm' when understanding gender and sexuality. The assumption that heterosexuality is the norm may or may not be conscious. The concept of heteronormativity also points to the political and social consequences of normalizing heterosexuality, in this case within the institution of Christianity.

If gender is constructed in an ongoing process, does this mean that an individual is free to choose to become or not to become a certain gender? Both Judith Butler (1990) and Eve Kosofsky Sedgwick (1990), influenced by Foucault's idea of discourse, conclude that a person is not a free agent but already constrained within discursive limits that have been set by a 'heterosexual matrix of power' (Salih 2007: 48). This is similar to the concept of 'compulsory heterosexuality' coined by Adrienne Rich (1980). She likens institutional patriarchy to a matrix of power which constrains and limits multiple expressions of sexuality. The work of queer theory destablizes this matrix of power. Gender and heterosexuality become more fluid when people begin to recognize and name the heterosexual normative framework of gendered existence, and question the legitimacy of this framework (Butler 1990). However, in most places this framework has remained dominant.

The dominance of the hetero/homosexual binary in contemporary Western culture is constraining and oppressive (Kosofsky Sedgewick 1990). Kosofsky Sedgewick asserts that since the turn of the 20th century, every individual is assigned summarily, with all its implications, as being not only of a certain gender but also of being either hetero- or homosexual. Through the 20th century, sexuality gained an increasingly 'privileged' position in the discourse of identity formation (Foucault in Kosofsky Sedgwick 1990: 3). It is deeply problematic that among all the multiple manifestations of sexuality, this binary categorization of gender and sexual desire has become the central categorizing feature. Similar to Butler, Kosofsky Sedgwick is motivated by the humanist desire to combat a deeply ingrained homophobia in contemporary Western society:

To alienate conclusively, definitionally, from anyone on any theoretical ground the authority to describe and name their own sexual desire is a terribly consequential seizure. In this century, in which sexuality has been made expressive of the essence of both identity and knowledge, it may represent the most intimate violence. (Kosofsky Sedgwick, in Masterson 2006: 26)

Queer theorists provide three key critiques of heteronormativity. The first is that it creates a binary between heterosexual and non-heterosexual in which one is regarded as natural or normal, and the other unnatural and abnormal. Second, in the process of promulgating this binary, it groups all non-heterosexual identities into one essentialized entity which reinforces the binary (Munoz 1999, in Abes and Kasch 2007). Third, queer theorists expose the way heterosexuality is privileged and thus reproduces a power imbalance.

Queer theory instigates a radical disruption and transformation of the heteronormative order (Butler 1990; Warner 1991). It is not assimilationist but radical. Thus, for example, the majority of queer theorists currently oppose the recent push for marriage equality, deeming that issue an acknowledgement of the legitimacy of the dominant hierarchical structures.

A second central tenet of queer theory is performativity (Butler 1990). Butler proposes that gender and sexuality are constructed through performativity – the everyday actions of individuals. Performativity challenges that idea that individuals have a fixed identity that can be clearly defined and categorized (Plummer 2005; Lovaas, Elia and Yep 2007). Performativity proposes that the sense of self is created as part of an ongoing performance. Gender, for example, is not something a person has, but something a person 'does'. Performativity emphasises the non-binary and contested nature of identities. Butler (1990) proposes that both gender and sexuality are not essential entities that one has or is, but come about by doing, through multiple performative behaviours. Furthermore, these behaviours are not reflective of identity but create it.

In a clear departure from the essentialist understanding of the 'true self', Butler proposes there is no 'being' behind the 'doing', no pre-existing gendered or sexual subject, but one that creates itself through what Butler (1990) calls 'performative acts'. In this way the subject is not first created and then performed, rather subjectivity is the ritualized performance of norms that creates a temporal subject that is 'not determined fully in advance' (Butler 1993: 95). Sexuality and gender do not exist prior to performative actions, and are therefore subject to change. Thus, dominant social construction can be resisted (though with difficulty), and identity can be altered with repeated actions or citations (Butler

1990). Butler primarily concentrated upon the sex/gender binary and asserted that a person does not have a gender, but '*does*' gender (Butler 1990: 25).

Performativity can be used to understand both what people do, and what enables change. In the everyday performance of doing (but never becoming), the subject can transgress constraining heteronormative values and thus queer space. Transgressive embodied practices can be liberating and empowering. Within the religious context, such practices might involve rituals or prayers that transform understandings and experiences of sexuality and gender. Through performative and repetitive actions, the subject can be deconstructed, reconstructed, and seemingly contradictory facets of identity can coexist.

Performativity helps understand the dynamic of change – how individuals exert agency and transgress normative boundaries of sexuality and/or gender, a process they engage in when seeking to express the authentic self. In doing so, individuals queer space (Browne, Munt and Yip 2010) and arguably, in the case of the participants in this study, queer Christianity (Shore-Goss 2013). These concepts – performativity and heteronormativity – are particularly relevant to this study. Doing religion through embodied performances has the potential to transform space, resisting heteronormative constraints (Roseneil 2000; Paris and Anderson 2001; Browne 2010).

While both queer theory and Taylor's ethic of authenticity articulate the individualistic desire to exist as a multifaceted being free from structural constraints, Taylor's (1991) emphasis on horizons of significance marks a clear departure from the tenets of queer. Queer impulses delight in subverting the normative tenets upon which the horizons of significance are based. Both recognize the boundaries and limits imposed upon the individual – the normative constraints – and both recognize the dialogic nature of identity development. Yet the queer desire to subvert through performativity is in direct opposition to Taylor's insistence that identity can only be defined in a meaningful way within the bounds of, for example, 'history, nature, society'. Perhaps for queer individuals the subversion is indeed a 'horizon of significance' that gives meaning beyond the self.

Further, Taylor's description of the desire to seek and discover an authentic and true self, though constructed relationally, intimates that an essential self is there to be discovered. Queer maintains the self is in continual creation, a self that can be consciously created and recreated iteratively once heteronormative structural constraints are uncovered. The stories of the LGBT Christians in this study highlights these tensions as they both challenge the normative order, while, at the same time, individuals consciously seek to live an authentic personal life and abide by higher moral order.

Until recently there has been little mention of religion within queer studies, and vice versa. The two fields seem at odds with each other (Wilcox 2007). In queer studies, religion appears to be curiously disregarded, considering the role of religion in the maintenance of normative order. Religious attitudes towards sexuality and gender also remain, in some respects, staunchly resistant to change. In particular, Christianity is usually branded as an oppressive heteronormative patriarchal institution (O'Brien 2004; Wilcox 2007). One source of divergence and tension between religious discourses and queer is apparent precisely in the field of identity. For example, religious arguments in favour of the acceptance of LGBT sexuality draw on essentialism, or more specifically the belief in the intrinsic nature of sexuality. In contrast, queer theorists argue for the transgression and queering of space through transgressing the normative order within the religious field. Queer theorists see essentialist understandings of sexuality as creating a new heteronormative space: a white middle-class male (Wilcox 2007) bound by middle-class values such as monogamy and creating a good gay and bad gay mentality. The experiences of LGBT Christians in the following chapters examine the extent to which the normative order is resisted, transgressed or reproduced in LGBT Christian experience.

While individuals and space are queered, there is a paradoxical recreation of new definitions of legitimacy. While norms are resisted, new conditions of legitimacy are created that exclude other bodies. In everyday life, repetitive performances solidify the new identifications, as pointed out by Moon (2005) in her focus on LGBT identifications among Christians. She describes how individuals legitimate their worldviews through repetitive testimony (Moon 2005). The majority of the participants in her study hold that lesbian and gay identities are fixed. They hold that gays and lesbians are born 'the way that God made them – just as He wanted them' (Warner 2005: 183). In this manner, linguistic and bodily performance legitimate a worldview that holds an essential understanding of identity. A new intelligible legitimate subject is defined (Butler 1993). Although there were a few exceptions to this view.

The Christians argument that the LGBT identity is 'good' and essential carries with it implications that define a way of life, thus recreating a dichotomous opposed 'abject or unthinkable subject' (Butler 1993: 3). Using the example of LGBT Christians, the abject or unthinkable subjects, those who do not conform, could be bisexuals or those who live a promiscuous lifestyle. This form of social power exercised in the name of heteronormativity is often termed symbolic violence (Moon 2005; Brady and Shirato 2011). When redeployed, often unintentionally, in the definition of alternate sexualities, it is sometimes termed 'homo-normativity' (Duggan 2002; *Positive Space Network Resource Person Manual* 2010: 26). This is the fundamental tension inherent in the relationship between queer and LGBT Christianity; in fact queer itself remains in a continual state of tension. In order to understand these tensions, we now turn to a more detailed account of the nature of religious experience.

Religion – relational, experiential and emotional

Academic studies of religion have concentrated on cognition, with belief as central to the understanding of religion. Relational, experiential and emotional factors have been neglected (Riis and Woodhead 2010, Harvey 2013). Understanding religious experience as relational and emotional provides a much clearer account of the conflict some LGBT Christians go through in integrating their seemingly disparate identities. Bourdieu's (1977) concept of habitus, and particularly the concept of a religious habitus, is useful in understanding the often deeply internalized struggle of LGBT Christians.

The concept of habitus, elaborated and made familiar by Bourdieu (1990: 54) describes how 'the pre-structured is everywhere' and how this 'pre-structured' shapes our thinking, our emotions, our predispositions *without our ever being aware of this*. He calls these 'residual dispositions' (Bourdieu 1990: 53), which reproduce of ways of 'thinking, feeling and acting'. All subjects are predisposed to act in a certain ways and respond to certain symbolic stimuli, in thought and emotion, perceptions and cognition, which forms a subjective lifeworld that is all encompassing, rendering critical reflection extremely difficult (Crossley 2005). As habitus is largely unconscious, individuals are often complicit in upholding the dominant order (and resistance to change). Beliefs are formed as part of certain religious habitus (Berlinerblau 1999). Bourdieu names these beliefs 'doxa', a 'realm of implicit and unstated beliefs' (Wacquant 1995: 185). Doxa also refers to the dominant worldview or 'common beliefs' or discourse (O'Brien 2004; Rey 2008; Yip 2010).

The concepts of habitus and doxa are particularly useful in understanding the internal conflict often experienced by the LGBT Christians in this study. Through the imposition of religious habitus, pious individuals can impose their worldview on other people, justifying acts of physical and symbolic violence as 'God's will' (Rey 2008). Symbolic violence is often perpetrated upon LGBT Christians who are deemed a 'marked other' (Goffman 1974; Bourdieu 2000).

The religious habitus governs and reproduces distinct worldviews, practices and behaviours that are oppressive. Such worldviews – doxa – are often unproblematically accepted, without conscious reflection, and experienced as natural and taken for granted (Bourdieu 1990). The church holds a powerful influence over taken for granted, or normative, worldviews. This is not a neutral process. Power inequalities occur and reoccur as stigmatized identities are distinguished in contrast to dominant normative identities. These inequalities are perpetuated due to the conscious and unconscious valorization of the dominant ways of thinking and associated values. Thus the borders between 'Us' and 'Them' are continually reproduced, as Ahmed (2004) describes, through emotional reactions to the 'Other'.

The religious habitus is also rewarding and attractive. The religious habitus cannot be easily cast aside. Religious understandings of the world are developed and strongly influenced by those we are related to and trust, within the family, church or school. The religious experience is embodied as memory (Connerton 1989) and as a deeply embedded aspect of identity (Taylor 1991; Ysseldyk, Matheson and Anisman 2010). Similarly religious beliefs are a 'corporal nexis' – a bodily state rather than just a thought process (Bourdieu 1977, in Rey 2008). Religious adherence is part of some people's dispositions, performatively, relationally and emotionally grounded, rather than derived from disembodied cognitive readings of the Bible or understanding of theology.

Being religious is an experience, a world of experiences, a whole 'context of understanding, both explicit and implicit which distinguishes the believer from the secular, the unbeliever' (Taylor 2007: 3). Taylor argues that the focus of faith is a sense of living a moral and spiritual life, based upon lived experiences, not simply theological belief. Many Christian believers seek a reality outside their everyday existence, a 'fuller, richer, deeper and more worthwhile, more admirable reality' (Taylor 2007: 5).

Some LGBT individuals find Christian religious practice rewarding because the relationships, performances and emotional repertoires it provides draw them into a rewarding and fulfilling sense of their lives. This Christian religious habitus is not something that is easily changed or abandoned. This understanding combines Taylor's arguments about the value of religious experience with Bourdieu's conception of religious habitus.

Emotions and cognitions

Historically, the body has been associated with emotion and the mind with reason. Biblical references to the body abound. In most cases, the body is seen as the weak vessel of the mind; the mind aims to be inhabited by the Holy Spirit, and thus purified. Paul in his letter to the Romans (Rom. 6:5) emphasized that the sinful body should be subjugated by a mind strengthened by faith in the sinless Christ. René Descartes (1641, in Woo 2013) similarly placed the body in a subordinate position. In his philosophical thesis *Meditations*, he proposed a dualistic union of mind and body in which the weak body was to be subjugated by a strong mind: the mind guided by reason, the body by passion (Descartes 1968, in Crossley 2005). The reasonable mind which dominates natural impulses becomes equated with culture; the body, however, remains ruled by nature (MacCormack 1980). The dualism between emotions and cognitions is also gendered. The male is often understood as more closely associated with the reasonable, cultured mind (Durkheim 1897b: 215, in Adams and Sydie 2002: 106). Women, on the other hand, are understood as more closely associated with emotions and nature.

Contemporary postmodern philosophers have challenged this dichotomous understanding of the mind and body, in particular post-war French philosophers such as Merleau-Ponty (1962). Merleau-Ponty, an existentialist phenomenologist, asserts that the mind is embodied and thus 'always based upon corporeal and sensual relations' (Grosz 1994: 86). The body is not guided by a 'pure and knowing subject' (Merleau-Ponty 1962: 3). Our body touches and sees the world, interacts with space, 'haunts space' (Merleau-Ponty 1962: 5). 'It is an embodied subject that occupies a perspective on objects ... this perspective dictates that modes of access to space are always partial or fragmentary' (Grosz 1994: 91).

Emotion is central to all cognitive thought. This understanding stands in contrast to the typical assumption that emotion is subordinate to cognition, 'relegated to the margins' and even deemed absent from cognitive thought altogether (Ahmed 2004: 4). Emotion had been understood as a 'weakness', that by being emotional an individual is 'soft', allowing another to impinge upon them, a person thus is shaped by others (Ahmed 2004: 3). Strength, on the other hand, is seen as being hard, unemotional and unshaped by others, being one's 'own person'. However, according to Ahmed's model, 'hardness' is not the absence of emotion, but rather an alternative 'emotional orientation to others' (Ahmed 2004: 4). Ignoring the central role of emotion results in a hierarchical 'cultural politics of emotion'. Emotion, when seen as softness and passivity, has been 'gendered as feminine' (Ahmed 2004: 3). Additionally, certain emotions have been recognized as legitimate (such as righteous anger) and guided by reasonable cognitive thought, while other emotions are a sign of weakness, and unreasonable.

Cognition is thus always embodied, emotional and influenced by past experiences, impressions and unconscious assumptions about reality. There is no superior mind cognitively guiding the weak emotionally laden body, but a fusion of embodied cognitive thought and emotion. Each individual is a body that has been etched and formed historically and culturally, a socially embodied subject – a lived body. According to Grosz (1994), the body is 'acted' upon and acts, from without and within, through repetitive normative behaviours. Bodies are marked and inscribed upon, both voluntarily and involuntarily, violently or more subtly, but no less coercively through the dominant norms and values of a given society. Through the inscriptions – which she refers to as 'scarification' or 'discursive etchings of the body' (Grosz 1994: 142) – individuals are bound to each other according to race, class, sex, sexuality, culture, age and other social positions. Discursive etchings could be deportment or other bodily forms or movements, manner or speech, or as mundane (but no less powerful) as makeup, clothing or hair styles. In this way, for example, we 'do' gender, race, class, sexuality or religion. Such inscribed bodies respond cognitively according to embodied experience, which cannot be divorced from emotion. Cognition is thus deeply entwined with emotion. Cognition and emotion both originate in the body, are lived in the body and expressed through the body.

Riis and Woodhead (2010: 5) analyse emotion as being 'constructed in the interplay between agents and structures'. Unlike the theories of emotion which represent emotion as either originating inside and being expressed outside (psychological theory) or as originating outside and being apprehended inside (Durkheim 1963), both Riis and Woodhead (2010) and Ahmed (2004) propose that emotions operate in relations between agents, objects and contexts. Emotion does not exist as a private internal 'feeling' but operates as movement between inside and private, and outside and social; between the personal and relational (Riis and Woodhead 2010). Emotions are not something we 'have' and are not 'in' bodies, but, in a similar vein to queer theory, we 'do' emotions (Ahmed 2004). For these theorists, movement is the critical conceptualization. The word e-*motion* encapsulates movement, and it is through emotion that actions and interactions are initiated (Ahmed 2004: 11; Riis and Woodhead 2010: 20).

Emotions create orientations to bodies and objects and occur in relationships to objects or bodies, whether visible or invisible (Ahmed 2004). The movement of emotion averts or attracts a subject away from or to an object. Ahmed (2004: 8–12) terms this 'the sociality of emotion'. Ahmed proposes that signs, words and symbols are 'sticky with emotion', causing emotional attraction or aversion according to the subjective position and relation to the person or object. Objects or bodies are transformed into objects of feeling. In this study, for example, the word 'homosexual' elicits an emotional response, one of attraction or aversion, and is rarely neutral. The word is 'sticky' in that clustered around it are multiple emotional responses over time, emotional responses that are guided by normative thought, and exclude certain ways of being (Ahmed 2004: 10). The emotional responses are produced and reproduced repetitively, a concept closely related to Butler's (1990) concept of performativity. Emotions are thus integral to the maintenance of hierarchical order (Ahmed 2004: 12). Emotion in this respect is both socially constructed and socially productive. It is not power neutral.

The 'stickiness' of words, metaphors and signs relates to social norms, some of which are valorized over others. To use another example, the word 'family' is saturated with meaning eliciting emotion which excludes relationships that do not conform with the ideal. Those who do not 'inhabit the norm' feel discomfort as they fail to reproduce the script. In Ahmed's words, the stickiness or repetitiveness of certain citations or words leads to emotional 'attachment to the object of ... subordination' (Ahmed 2004: 12). In this way, power relations are enacted in the recognition that some emotions and bodies enacting them are appropriate and legitimate and others not.

When religion is understood as relational, emotional and performed, the experience of individuals such as those in this study can be better understood. LGBT Christians, in seeking to express their God-given sexuality and/or gender, seek ways to remain true to their religious selves. They actively resist heteronormative constraints through entering a process of transformation of religious habitus.

Transformation of religious habitus

Religious ritual opens the possibility of personal and group transformation (Driver 1991). Theorists such as Thomas Csordas (1990), Tom Driver (1991) and Catherine Bell (1992) have described the transformative power and emotional impact of ritual. Ritual performance in Christian worship can encompass a variety of actions. Ritual can simply be attending a service regularly, meaning that once a week the individual enters a 'liminal' space, a place with much transformative potential. Ritual performance is both the 'doing' and the 'showing' (Driver 1991: 88, 91, 120). It includes giving or hearing testimony or service, receiving or serving at the altar, and hearing or singing the hymns. Ritual forms the link between symbols and bodily actions, where action is the primary initiator (Driver 1991).

Rituals are also profoundly integrative and function to maintain order, stability and foster community (Driver 1991). Rituals are sharing, communicative, group activities (Kertzer 1988). There need be no conscious acknowledgement of beliefs; indeed according to Bell (in Rey 2008: 112), ritual is 'lodged beyond the grasp of consciousness and articulation'. Through ritual, therefore, unconscious and unarticulated beliefs, or doxa, form worldviews which can be strengthened and reproduced. In this way, ritual is a mechanism of the reproduction of normative order. These two functions of ritual can work dialectically. The transformative function can enable identity change, while the normative function can enable a strengthening of the transformed state of being, a new habitus.

A ritual practice in itself is not necessarily a moral practice (Driver 1991). However, some forms of ritual – that Driver terms the 'confessional mode' and the 'ethical mode' – consciously direct activity to a moral end (Driver 1991: 112). The confessional mode changes an individual's relation to his/herself and the world, a movement that 'gives birth to the ethical mode'. This is particularly pertinent to the creation of positive emotional orientations to the self, for example the 'coming out' of LGBT individuals and communities. The Stonewall riots may be understood as confessional in that the performance was public and aimed at the legitimation of self and the community (Driver 1991: 118).

This book is a case study of the process of change, transformation and breaking free of structural constraints. The connecting thread between the theoretical approaches outlined above is the power of repetitive practice. Each theoretical approach, though focused on diverse fields and approaching from different angles, emphasizes the embodied and relational nature of human interactions. They all concentrate on repetitive actions through which both normative expectations are enacted and transformation occurs. Transformation occurs through, first, awareness of injustice; second, recognition of alternatives; third, an emotional response; and finally, *bodily practices* in *social fields* that enable and empower.

Performative repetitive actions have individual and spatial consequences. They form the basis for the continual doing of, for example, gender, a concept that opens the way for fluidity and multiplicity of identity. As articulated by Abes and Kasch (2007), the transgressing, liminal subject is created, opening the way for transformation. Embodied enactments, or ritual, are central to the creation of community, stability and transformation of both individuals and spaces (Kertzer 1988; Driver 1991). According to Browne (2010), for example, places of worship are transfigured through religious practices, relationships and interactions, and are effectively 'queered' (Paris and Anderson 2001; Munt 2010). Iterative performatives, whether linguistic or embodied enactments such as singing, prayer and practices of worship such as communion, change the space in which they are practised (Atkinson and Delamont 2008). The space becomes liminal (Abes and Kasch 2007), or 'anti-structural' (Yang 2000: 383). This, according to queer theory, is a space which continually resists heteronormative constraint. In this sense, the institution of Christianity is queered. Through ritual the places of worship gain texture and take on the characteristics of the people who inhabit them (Bell and Binnie 2004; Maliepaard 2015).

Transformation of religious habitus and worldview is driven by emotion, ritual practice, relationships and self-understandings. Emotion is 'the catalyst through which individual transformation occurs and new ideas are embraced' (Robnett 1997: 34). The religious experience is lived and practised through relationships and ritual. These form a fertile ground for change. Understanding the centrality of emotion to religious belief and experience explains the deeply ingrained nature of religious worldviews. While change is both an extremely difficult and often painful process, it can also be extremely rewarding and liberating, as reflected in the stories recorded in the following chapters.

Conclusion

LGBT Christianity seems to many to be inherently contradictory. We argue that understanding religious experience as experiential, relational and emotional leads to a better understanding of the experience of religion, explaining how apparent contradictions can be integrated and how the dynamics of transformation works in individual lives. The remainder of the book demonstrates that LGBT Christians act according to an 'ethic of authenticity' driven by a desire to express their 'true' sexual, gendered and religious selves. To do so they necessarily queer practices and spaces. Through relationships, emotions and performative ritual practices, individuals transform their religious habitus.

The Metropolitan Community Churches

Vignette: Paul

Coming to an awareness of my sexuality as I grew up was a gradual thing. I was very lucky that I grew up in a supportive family. My dad was a minister – which made it even luckier to grow up with a supportive family. But mum and dad were very, very supportive and encouraged me to be who I was. From their point of view, there was never any disappointment. All they ever wanted was for their sons to be happy, and that, in the 1950s and 1960s, was very, very progressive. So much so that within the church that my dad was pastoring, it became a real issue. It actually led to him leaving the church. He was given a choice of basically his son or the church – and he decided that would not be the way he wanted to go.

[The church's negative attitude towards homosexuality] got worse I think in the 1970s. Once the gay liberation movement started, the churches become quite active in their opposition to homosexuals. Many of our older members here have gone through an attempt to de-gay them. All with totally no results other than some of them with their brains fried and being totally scarred for life from the experience. So I was lucky that my mum and dad were really supportive and then I left the church and then I left school.

Probably [at] ten or eleven [I became aware of my sexuality]. I was never aware of anything else. It's different depending on your environment. If you're growing up in an environment when you are being pushed into a heterosexual mould, well, then you are so confused for so many years you don't know when you become aware. You are constantly conflicting and there will probably be a day when the penny drops. I was very lucky that I never went through that.

Dad and mum weren't particularly intellectually progressive people, just good people. They've been dead over thirty years now. I still have aunts and uncles alive and it's never been an issue and I think that's pretty unique. I think what it's given me is a balance. I don't have to fight my own battles. I can sit down with other people and journey with them on theirs, comfortable with who I am.

I joined the [military and] and served for six years. [In the 1970s I knew lots of people in the military who] got caught out and got a dishonourable discharge [for being gay]. It was tough, and, in retrospect, I regret it was like that because I would have loved to have had a twenty-year career in the armed forces. It was a fabulous time – I really, really enjoyed it. Then from there I went into industry.

I drifted away [from the church]. Part of it was how the church treated my dad, that really was a key thing. But the other thing was the time – you've got to remember this was sex, drugs and rock and roll! Sydney was a party town – the gay community was exploding, we were exploring ourselves in ways that now seem quite frightening, and I wonder at times why I am still alive! So church became really, really irrelevant. We looked for our spiritual enlightenment in other places, in other ways. The way of our parents, as supportive as they may have been, were very old fashioned. [It was] a time of great freedom.

Then I found myself at MCC in the early 1980s. I walked into that church that night, and I remember one thing and it was the communion. The pastor at the time was preaching on John 3:16, 'For God so loved the world that God gave his only begotten son, that whosoever believes shall have everlasting life' and that connected me back to my Sunday school, because on top of the arch in the Sunday school hall, was: 'For God so loved the world.' Something that night just created a link. From that night to this, I have not missed an MCC worship service except when I've been in a place where there's no MCC.

It sounds corny, [but it was] like coming home. I suddenly realized what I was looking for was that spiritual thing. We might be emotionally stable and we may physically have all our needs met but without that third spiritual component [we are missing something]. I think for so many of our people today, that's what they're looking for. They're looking for it in drugs, alcohol, in sexual addiction, in addictive behaviours at all levels and they're looking in all the wrong places. I'm not saying that Christianity is the answer, but it is one of the answers.

MCC [was] founded in 1968 so that's even before the Stonewall riots. We were really the first of those organizations and our role still is to be a thorn in the side of mainline Christianity, to make them stand up and look at themselves.

During the AIDS epidemic we were the first people to do anything. The pastor of the church in Sydney at the time helped put the first HIV victim in his coffin because no one else would touch him. We were involved right from that day one and there was a stage in the mid-1980s and the late 1980s when I was doing three, four funerals a week. We were one of the major HIV AIDS care organizations, particularly here in Sydney.

[At the back of the church there is a large banner with names of] all the people from, or associated with, the church, who've died. It's a lot of people and worldwide our churches lost about 15,000 members and many clergy. [It] really pulled us together. One of the struggles we have at the moment is, now that epidemic phase is passed, where is the church's role? Back then it was really clearly defined. There was no argument about what the church's role was. When there were hearses pulling up at the front every second day of the week. We used to have lunches on Sundays in our place in Darlinghurst for people with AIDS; we ran a pantry service for people with AIDS. Lots and lots of things were really clear cut and defined.

Now of course things have changed and the church has to try and redefine itself. What does it mean now to be a church in this community, in this day and age, and who do we reach out to? But it still provides a place for people who don't feel comfortable in other places, doesn't it?

There are big differences in practice [between the MCCs]. But there's the same message, there is a common thread. We have our statement of faith that ties us together in what we believe. The sacrament is always celebrated in all of our churches. At every worship service of every MCC in the world, the sacrament must be celebrated. It is a physical manifestation of an expression of faith that is a common part of all MCC. Another practice [of all MCC congregations worldwide] is inclusive behaviour, and that stems from our language, the way we make people feel welcome, the way people try do things within the worship services so there are no feelings of exclusion. You could go to, say, MCC in Texas where you have one MCC which will have 500 people in worship with a full orchestra and a full choir and full traditional robes and processions, and all that stuff, and you go around the corner to another one which will be charismatic with the healing of the spirit happening at the same time. But the practice that ties them together is [that] both of them will celebrate the sacrament and it will be inclusive and open to all people.

Ritual is very important. I think all of us need ritual in our lives. Coming to church is part of the ritual, the continuity. [For example] for our morning traditional service, they know when they come to church what is going to happen. They know they are going to walk in the door, they're going to be greeted, they are going to sit down, we are going to sing a hymn, we're going to have a prayer, we are going to have a reading, we're going to have scripture, we are going to have the sacrament, we are going to have a hymn. The familiarity is important. To be in a place where the familiar can happen around you.

For some of our people this is the only time of the week that they have contact with others, particularly some of the older people who come to the morning service. They will also come to some of our [other events]. For them it's the friendship thing, the connectedness, that's more important. The spiritual component is a bonus. Yet there are others who come and who don't even stay after the worship services. For them it's the worship. [They have] been fed that way, [and they] don't need the rest. I think most people fall somewhere in the middle.

[Back in the time of] the AIDS epidemic, I'd often do a funeral for a young man, and his friends and partner would be at the funeral and then they would come to church for about four or five weeks afterwards and then they wouldn't come any more. It used to worry me. What are we doing wrong, you know, that they are not staying. I was talking to one young man about a year after his partner died; he came back to church on the anniversary. I said why haven't we seen you? He said, it was wonderful that you were here when I needed it. While I needed that safe place to be spiritually connected with my partner and with God, you guys were here. He said, you know, I've always known that. Another time I was doing a funeral plan with a young man whose partner died and he was there and the partner's mother was there. There was a bit of conflict about where the funeral was going to be held. I'd never seen the young man before – ever. Not part of the church and all that. The mother said to him, why do we have to have it in this church? She had wanted it in the local Catholic Church somewhere. He just looked at her and said, because this is our church. Suddenly it dawned on me then, that we meet a need for our community by just being here. In our community, people know that when all else stuffs up there is one place they can come and even if they only come for a couple of weeks just for an hour on Sunday, there is a place where they don't have to explain who they are, where they can be with God however they want that to be, because we don't say you that have to be Christian to come here. For many people, this is just the safest place when life gets tough. I think that's what church should be about.

Introduction

There are three notions embodied in MCC ritual. First, God's grace is radically inclusive and without conditions. Second, no one is turned away, for the table is open. Hospitality supersedes all denominational politics of the table. Finally open invitation expresses a central practice of Jesus' ministry that every person is loved equally by God. Combined this ritual invitation would become the core mission of MCC: God's radical inclusive love. (Shore-Goss 2013: 3)

We held hands and we took communion together in front of a minister of God who said: 'You are accepted, you are forgiven, and you are loved.' I had tears running down my face, a lump in my throat and I just felt, 'I'm home.' This is where I want to be. This is what I've been searching for. This is what has been missing in my life as a good person (Laura).

The above quote from Laura illustrates how the Universal Fellowship of Metropolitan Community Churches (UFMCC)[1] core mission of 'radical inclusive love' is experienced by one congregant. Laura expresses unequivocally the central importance of her congregation. She describes the empowering nature of ritual and its contribution to her sense of self, through belonging and acceptance. In this study, the majority of the interviewees (n=26) attended Metropolitan Community Church (MCC) congregations. Bronwyn also conducted participant observation at three MCC churches. The experience of participants varied but the majority overwhelmingly describe its value and importance to them. The practices within the safe spaces of the MCC congregations enable the creation of new understandings and emotions that endow legitimacy to participants' sexuality, gender and religiosity. This in turn transforms their religious habitus, further encouraging individuals to live as authentic Christians.

The UFMCC as an institution is multifaceted and complex. It varies from country to country and in Australia from state to state. For example, within Sydney there are three MCCs that offer quite different experiences to the congregants. This chapter provides a descriptive account of some of these diverse yet fundamentally connected spaces. They are the backdrop that both informs and is informed by the individuals who actively participated in the study through formal interviews. This chapter first provides some historical background to and information about the MCC, both worldwide and in Australia, including a description of the MCC's response to diverse sexualities and gender. We then briefly discuss the ecumenical nature of the church, and the role of the church in the lives of mostly lesbian and gay Christians and the two transgendered interviewees, touching on the diversity and tensions that exist within the denomination in Australia. Finally the chapter describes the subjective experience of the MCC, and the meaning that MCC has for congregants.

Universal fellowship of Metropolitan Community Churches

A year before the Stonewall Riot (1969), the Pentecostal minister Troy Perry received a revelation to begin a ministry to provide lesbian and gay Christians a safe space within which to worship. Perry, who had been defrocked as a Pentecostal minister on revealing his same-sex attraction, conducted the first service in a small room in Los Angeles on 6 October 1968 (Shore-Goss 2013). From these humble beginnings emerged the largest inclusive (embracing of alternate sexualities and genders) denomination in the world, where upwards of 200,000 people attend 222 congregations in thirty-seven countries each year (MCC North London, n.d.).

The UFMCC is an ecumenical, postmodern, eclectic mix of different worship traditions, due to the need to provide a safe space to worship for Christians of all backgrounds. It maintains a flexibility in its expression of religious practice, tailored to suit each congregation, which vary considerably due to a wide range of congregants' religious upbringing and religious worldviews (Wilcox 2003). Behind this flexibility, the UFMCC is united by theological principles based upon the Apostolic and Nicene creeds,[2] and four core values: inclusion, community, spiritual transformation and social action. According to the founder, it is committed to 'the three-pronged Gospel of Christian Salvation, Christian Community, and Christian Social Action' (MCC North London, n.d.).

The denomination was initially formed, led and populated largely by homosexual men. In 1972 the first woman, Freda Smith, was ordained as an MCC minister, and since then the number of women involved in the MCC has steadily increased. Initially Smith fought for recognition of women and for the institutional use of gender-inclusive language. Currently the UFMCC moderator is a woman, Reverend Nancy Wilson, and at the time of writing women actually outnumber men in the ministry (51.5 per cent women clergy), a fact bemoaned by one male member in the present study who maintains that the UFMCC is 'feminized'. This percentage is in part due to the AIDS epidemic in which many male UFMCC ministers and potential leaders died (Perry and Swicegood 1990; Warner 2005). Membership is more difficult to assess. According to some sources, the gender proportion of membership is fairly even, whereas others maintain there is a high proportion of men (Wilcox 2003). In Australia, according to our observation and reports from members, men outnumbered women, both within congregations and the ministry.

Photo 3.1 MCC Melbourne. Photo by Douglas Ezzy

As an organization that is committed to equality and diversity, the MCC uses gender-inclusive language in all hymns and other documents. Despite this, there is significant variation in understandings of gender and the implementation of gendered understandings in roles and relations within each congregation, which at times indicates deep-seated tensions between the sexes. Research by Edward Sumerau (2012: 461) indicated that within the US MCC congregation he was studying, men felt inherent privilege in relationships to God and Jesus, maintaining 'paternal stewardship' and valuing highly what they understood as masculine characteristics of emotional control and rationality. While our observations and interviews revealed no such extreme tendencies, there were some overt practices and covert attitudes that reproduced traditional patriarchal understandings of gender. Occasionally tensions were expressed in the interviews. This is discussed more fully in later chapters.

The ecumenical MCC in Australia – the place and the people

There are presently five MCC churches in Australia: three in Sydney, one in Brisbane and one in Melbourne. Due to the ecumenical nature of the UFMCC, and the eclectic mix of congregation members, each has developed its own characteristics. This became evident during Bronwyn's visits to each of the three churches that are the focus of our research. The congregational and religious practices are co-constructed between the minister and congregation, which enables a dynamic development and the possibility of experimental change to the format of the services, theological emphasis and expression of worship. This dynamism is accompanied by tension and a state of flux, which at times creates instability. As one interviewee mentions: 'So yes, it is a complex sort of place. You can understand why there is this fair bit of political things. I mean it happens everywhere you go but in MCC perhaps even more so possibly because of the complex backgrounds of everybody.'

The diverse congregational backgrounds of members results in tensions that centre on theology and/or corresponding ritual practices. Bronwyn often heard criticisms of the congregations, which partly met the needs of participants and partly caused irritation or even disenfranchisement. The most common criticisms focus on worship style, with one participant noting of one congregation: '[It's] more about rituals and liturgy than … about Christianity.' Others comment on the fundamental purpose of the MCCs existence, 'that some MCCs were more about being gay than being Christian'; and others focus on age and gender: 'That they were mainly the domain of older gay men waving rainbow flags.'

Many lesbian, gay and transgender Christians who participated in this study experimented with more than one congregation, moving around until they found a congregation that suited them. As Luke says of his experience in the first MCC congregation he attended: 'It's an awful thing to say, but the truth for me, I felt that having to be part of MCC was really part of my punishment for being gay.' Upon finding a congregation that suited his form of worship, his experience was transformed: 'I think I rediscovered my Pentecostal spirituality … and worship for the first time in six or seven years ... [I] was absolutely flattened by it. It was like I had come home!'

Luke's vivid depiction of the MCC from a place of 'punishment' to 'coming home' indicates four main issues. First, it illustrates the intensity of the struggle some individuals experience. Second, connected to this, he illustrates the power of the individual religious habitus in both imparting fear and judgement, as well as instilling the importance of worship practices, in this case Pentecostalism. Third, he expresses the importance of a safe space to live an authentic spirituality. These issues are dealt with in Chapters 2, 3, and 4. Finally it demonstrates the substantial diversity within this denomination, and its strength in adapting to those from diverse religious backgrounds.

Paradoxically, from this strength emerges vulnerability. The denomination, precisely as a consequence of being open to diversity with the resultant flexibility and fluidity of practice, is vulnerable to criticism and the ensuing development of factions. Congregants described various tensions, in particular when there was the perception that the needs of minority subgroups were not adequately met. We only describe such political tensions in skeletal form as these are not our focus of interest. However, some tensions pertaining to gender and patriarchy within the institutions of Christianity are discussed more fully in Chapter 5.

Those involved with the MCC in this study are mostly people with an intensely religious upbringing, where their religious habitus is deeply embedded in their identity. Religious practice is important to them. Of the interview participants, twenty-six of the twenty-eight were brought up in a strongly religious environment. In addition, individuals remained deeply connected to their specific congregational upbringing – in particular to worship practices. As illustrated by Luke, those who were brought up Pentecostal sought an MCC congregation that expressed a Pentecostal-like form of worship, and those who were brought up Catholic gravitated towards congregations with other disenfranchised Catholics. For this reason, the three MCC congregations varied according to the background of the congregants. While transformation of religious habitus did occur, it was quite specific – dealing with same-sex attraction and gender identity.

Experiencing the MCC

Bronwyn attended three MCC churches. We provide a broad comparative account in terms of space, people, governance, and congregational and worship practices. In addition, we provide a comparative overview of hierarchal arrangements, religious practices and gendered interactions in the three churches. One church had two services with distinct congregations attending each service. We therefore refer to three churches and four congregations. In order to protect the privacy of the participants we are sometimes vague about the congregation we are discussing.

In sketching this account of MCC, we draw upon data from various sources including interviews with the pastors and congregants, data Bronwyn obtained through participant observation at the churches, public data from church websites, and pre-existing academic accounts. As an observer, Bronwyn describes the use and arrangement of space, interaction patterns and religious performances such as communion. As a participant, Bronwyn draws on experiential data and subjective emotions and feelings as she engaged in the services and interacted with congregants. The MCC as a denomination is broader and more complex than we can describe here, but we can provide a brief introduction.

Participants invariably describe the MCC as a *safe haven*. This feature is strikingly consistent across the interviews. For Luke, finding the MCC 'was like coming home'! The participants consistently describe the MCC space as 'home' and the fellow congregants as 'family'. Natalie reports: 'The first thing I really felt when I walked in there was this place is just like a really big family'. Anthea also explains: 'I wanted to be in a church environment but I never really fitted in ... here I can be myself, I feel extremely comfortable; this is my community ... I thought I'm home'. Of the twenty-six participants in this study who attended the MCC, the overwhelming majority describe the feeling of comfort and safety at finding 'home' and 'family'. A safe space 'like home' is critical in transformation of habitus. It provides a space within which emotional responses towards same-sex attraction can be transformed and relationships legitimized, as well as a space where doctrine can be discussed. The sense of coming home is complex (Sixsmith 1986: 287) but here it refers to the experience of 'belonging', of 'self-expression', and the 'quality of relationship'.

Belonging is a central aspect of participants' experience. The MCC policy of inclusivity is central to both the theological basis and the everyday practices of the MCC. Each individual is welcomed upon arrival at the services, fostering the sense of belonging. William speaks for the majority of the participants who attended all three MCC congregations: 'We felt welcomed as soon as [we] walked in the door, people come to you, welcome you ... I felt comfort in knowing we were all possibly of the same beliefs ... the welcoming and the fact you were in a safe group'. In most cases, the welcome generates a sense of belonging, which is a dimension of habitus (Wise, Harris and Watts 2005). Individuals meet others who are struggling through a very similar journey. As Luke explains: 'I mean almost everyone who comes to [MCC] has the same story ... we are united in our narratives.' While the practice of welcoming congregants is not unique to the MCC, it is of particular importance in that it legitimates LGBT sexualities and enables LGBT people to practise their Christianity safely and to feel affirmed in regard to both their religious, sexual and gendered identities.

The feeling of being able to 'be me', to express the authentic self, is connected to the sense of coming home and being with 'family'. As Angela says: 'It always felt like home, like there are real relationships, not just the talk of real relationships.' Judith also explains: 'You can be who you are.' Others explain that the safety within the MCC spaces enables the resolution of conflicts of doctrine through non-threatening discussion. According to Emma: 'I think [the MCC] is a safe space where you can ask questions, and people are very happy to sit down with you and talk about those things and share their journey.' She adds that it is also 'a place where you can worship freely and articulate what is meaningful for you'.

Queer religious worship is made possible and meaningful because the MCC is experienced as a safe place. Participants voice the need to 'do' their religion as a group, to perform the rituals repeatedly and to be recognized in front of God and in front of others. Luke, for example, describes this need to worship together as invaluable to experience God's presence: '[For] me ... that experience of God's presence is happening all the time but when you come together and you cele-brate it, it's intensified and it's shared.' The queering of worship spaces and ritual practices is essential to the transformation of habitus.

The importance of this affirmation is illustrated by Nathan, who belongs to the Uniting Church – a liberal denomination which officially offers welcome to all, regardless of sexual orientation (The Uniting Church in Australia 2015). Nathan explains that the feeling of safety he experiences in his congregation is tempered by its fragility: 'I mean first of all, we [he and his partner] were just accepted as a couple like anyone else ... the group was really good.' While the chaplain and congregation of mostly young university students always welcome him, 'there are some really conservative people [that have] kind of taken an issue with the whole gender inclusive thing ... so we're in this situation that's kind of whoa ... if you have a problem with talking about God in gender neutral lan-guage, how are you going to feel about gay people'? Nathan also describes that when talking to Uniting Church members outside of his congregation, he some-times has to 'go back being on guard and being careful, being wary about what you talk about'.

Diverse Congregational Expressions

Each congregation exhibited a fascinating and unique combination of institutional structures and religious practices, negotiated between the minister, the governing board and the congregants. These negotiations produced significant differences both between and within congregations. Each congregation differed according to the average age, congregational and worship practices, and hierarchical positioning of the minister. Most congregants were 'older', being baby-boomers over fifty years old, or 'younger' Gen X aged 30–50 with a small number of Gen Y in their twenties. There is considerable variation in the extent to which gendered characteristics are understood and enacted traditionally or queered, and whether gender-inclusive language is used. Worship practices, including the service liturgies, the music and communion practices, also vary. While these observations are broad and generalized, they give some insight into the complexity of the MCC.

The largest of the three congregations was the only congregation in Australia to have purchased its own premises. The octagonal-shaped building, a former Church of Christ Scientist building, was bought in 1999/2000 and has the

Photo 3.2 MCC Sydney. Photo courtesy of MCC Sydney

potential to seat upwards of 100 people. In contrast, other MCC congregations rent space. For example, two congregations rent space in old Uniting Churches. One rents space for the Sunday afternoon, with a 3.00 pm service, the other congregation has an evening service. The halls in both rented buildings seat up to forty people. Renting makes sense for some of the MCC congregations that are relatively small and/or recently formed. For one congregation, the choice to have an evening service was for the explicit purpose of allowing its members to visit other denominational services during the day. Some congregations arrange their worship space in a traditional way, with the seating facing the altar, various musical instruments to one side and a pulpit on the other. In these churches, the altar is covered with a white cloth, upon which are two white candles, a covered silver communion plate and two silver chalices containing grape juice. In contrast, another congregation places the altar behind the seats, at the *back* of the hall. As in the other congregations, this is covered by a white cloth, and placed upon it are two white candles, two glasses of red grape juice and a covered loaf of bread.

The average age of the interviewees from each of the four congregations is indicative of the average age of all members of each congregation. The average ages for the interviewees from the four congregations are: 56, 40, 32 and 60 years. Dress codes of both the congregants and the ministers tended to parallel the age of the congregations, with the two older congregations adhering to more formal dress codes in contrast to the more informal dress of the younger congregations.

Decoration in all the three MCC buildings is simple. Two congregations use the rainbow to symbolize inclusivity of sexuality and gender. The rainbow is combined with the Christian symbol of the cross by various means. One congregation has rainbow-coloured crosses embroidered into long, white, full-length, ceiling-to-floor white banners either side of the stage. Coloured lights are used to illuminate the altar and cross at different times in the services. Another congregation has brightly decorated, long ceiling-to-floor rainbow curtains in front of the altar upon which a simple white cross is secured. Similarly, the pulpit is also decorated with a rainbow banner. The emphasis on rainbow symbolism is more common in the older congregations. Bronwyn was informed in the interviews that many young LGBT people find rainbows 'old-school'. Another congregation with a younger demographic has little external decoration, and no rainbow banners. The only clue to their presence on Sunday is an unobtrusive sandwich board outside with the words *MCC Dynamic, Inclusive, Progressive* in blue-and-white lettering. In both space and symbolism, this congregation distinguishes itself from the more traditional of the MCCs.

Photo 3.3 MCC Melbourne banner with rainbow colours behind the cross. Photo by Douglas Ezzy

Two congregations display clear signs of political action indicative of the social justice agenda of the UFMCC. Political action is institutionally and formally encompassed as part of the founding principle of the UFMCC (Perry and Swicegood 1990). The back wall of one congregation is dominated by three ceiling-to-floor memorial tapestries, brightly coloured, and embroidered with the names of those who died of AIDS. Underneath is a rainbow banner with the words *Born This Way*. On the side wall of the hall are political statements indicating commitment to marriage equality. For example, one banner states, *MCC will not have fulfilled its purpose till marriage is available for all.* A few other banners stressed the inclusivity of the MCC to all.

The church with two congregations (morning and evening services) was the largest of all MCC congregations Bronwyn visited. This church has been served by a part-time pastor intermittently for over twenty years. This has resulted in greater continuity than in other congregations. The pastor says that this continuity has contributed to a 'solid' and stable congregational base. Although the congregational base, according to the pastor, would number 'about 300 – a very revolving group of people (with a) strong core', each service is attended by approximately thirty to fifty people each week. Services at other MCC churches are smaller, attracting approximately fifteen to thirty congregants each week.

During the time of Bronwyn's visits, men outnumbered women consistently at all congregations, approximately two or three to one. The predominance of males is not an unusual phenomenon in the MCC (Enroth and Jamieson 1974; Primiano 1993; Yip 1999; Kirkman 2001; Morrow 2003; Wilcox 2003; Wilcox 2009). In contrast, women outnumber men three to two within most other Christian churches in Australia (Bouma 2006; ABC 2012). The congregation with a traditional morning service is strongly male dominated, consisting mostly of older men with a few core older women members, while the 'charismatic' evening service attracts a fairly even mix of younger men and women from a

Photo 3.4 Banner at the rear of MCC Sydney. Photo courtesy of MCC Sydney

broader age spectrum. The other two congregations are also male dominated. In all congregations there are a small minority of heterosexual congregants who are either relatives of other members or are impressed with the MCC message of inclusivity for all.

At the time of the study, congregants were on the whole Anglo-Australasian, with some of southern European ethnicity. There was also a significant minority of younger men of Asian background. The majority were middle-class and well-educated. While this description sounds typical of a mainstream church congregation, this would be misleading. The 'gender-bending' of many of the members of MCC congregations contrasts starkly with mainstream churches. Clothing and bodily expression are in many cases 'queer', that is, individual congregants are 'doing gender' in ways that transgress the sex/gender norms of mainstream society. Some men, for example, wear flamboyant clothing that is reminiscent of Judith Butler's (1990: 137) subversion of gender through drag. Similarly, some women wear fatigues and 'do' masculinity through gestures and bodily posture. The tendency to queer gender through clothing is more manifest among the older members. The younger congregants seem generally comfortable in clothing, such as jeans and t-shirts, that is informal but, in most cases, gender neutral. The choice of 'queered' clothing contrasts strongly with the traditional format of the services, the conventional nature of some aspects of the space, and the traditional dress of the pastor.

In all four congregations, interviewees expressed a strong sense of 'belonging through difference'. According to one interviewee, 'it's a wonderful mish-mash of people. It's such an eclectic group and everyone is kind of a misfit somewhere in their little worlds but everyone is incredibly open.' This beautifully sums up MCC congregations. Interviewees described the MCC as a 'motley crew', or 'the dregs of society', and according to Michael, they come 'not because their family deem it the right thing to do, as often with the Uniting Church … here it's more they come in because of either their experience with God, the reaction of other Christians or a general longing for something'. Michael highlights not only the predicament of LGBT Christians who are often rejected by mainstream Christianity, and the sense of belonging that worshipping together engenders, but also the necessity to question their Christianity. This connected to the desire to live an authentic existence expressed by a large majority of the interviewees and is discussed more fully in Chapter 4.

The governance of each MCC varies considerably. The UFMCC church model stipulates that a size-appropriate and culturally appropriate administration be set up (MCC 2013a: para. 373). Some of the congregations had a more formal structure with leadership roles clearly defined. Others had a more fluid structure, with a variety of people taking on leadership roles as required.

All MCC churches encourage congregants to participate in the services in some form, as an expression of the inclusive MCC policy. Congregants may, for example, not only serve through congregational and community activities, but also through doing readings such as the 'calling to service', by singing or playing instruments (music ministry), Bible readings, prayer, collecting offerings or aiding the pastor with communion (as an acolyte). In this respect MCC is fairly traditional; however, two congregations also invite lay members to give sermons and to preside over communion, an expression of their egalitarian agenda. Several of the interviewees mentioned how empowering this was. For example, Emma, who had been unable to participate in any way in her previous church, exclaims: 'And the preaching, I think the preaching is really great and it's given me opportunities to serve that I wouldn't get in other churches. And I love that!' One MCC was particularly community-based, with approximately one-third of the congregants taking part in the service in some capacity. Participation in the services was mentioned consistently by the study participants as essential to the development of their faith and well-being and is discussed further in Chapter 4.

All three MCC churches encourage fellowship as an integral part of their inclusive policy and congregational practice, providing safe, dynamic spaces to LGBT and heterosexual Christians alike. After each service, refreshments are offered in either an adjacent community room or in the service hall. Congregants in all churches are encouraged to bring savoury or sweet dishes, and to help serving coffee and tea on a rostered basis. Most attend this gathering and find it affirming. Fellowship is extended into time after the formal gathering. After one morning service, some congregants meet for lunch at a nearby cafe (usually once a month). Similarly, the younger people attending the evening service socialize after the service. As one young congregant explains:

> The youth usually go out to dinner afterwards which is an awesome time to keep talking about things that are a bit more personal to us – it's really uplifting afterwards to go home and that's just what I need to end my week or start my new week.

At one evening service, depending upon the group on the day, congregants meet informally nearby in a pub for a drink and snacks. Church members also meet at each other's houses or for meals regularly during the week, and many holidays are celebrated together. One woman, for example, always arrives with a male member of the congregation after sharing lunch together – 'the couple who aren't a couple'. It was clear from the interviews how valuable the friendships are. As one congregant explains: 'Just speaking to people who had been through similar experiences and hearing amazing teaching … and hearing, just exploring those ideas with people like that, that were well thought through.' One explains that until her not-very-religious partner attended the MCC, she had 'never realised how important it is to have gay friends till now. You need to have friends to support you; that just sort of know what you are and what you're going through'. The affirmation of being accepted 'just as you are' and forming bonds of friendship aids in transforming habitus. This is discussed further in later chapters in relation to its importance to the process of transformation, and integration of seemingly incompatible parts of the self.

Socializing or 'fellowship' was reported by most interviewees as extremely important to their life of faith. While some congregations had mid-week prayer and study groups in the past, these have either been discontinued due to lack of interest or difficulty in organization. One female congregant expresses disappointment at this, explaining that while it was a safe place to go, 'I was disappointed at first that there was no follow up care or anything. I would have personally have liked to ask questions about being gay and Christianity'. Some congregants expressed that this could be due to the small and widely scattered congregations, making mid-week activities impractical. Time is also a factor in some congregations, as many members are employed full time and/or studying, and others are actively involved in other churches. In addition, none of the pastors are employed full-time.

Despite criticism aimed at its members based on interpretation of specific Bible passages, the churches did not dedicate formal time to Bible study. It is perhaps indicative that some individuals had already resolved theological issues before they become involved in the MCC, as concluded by Wilcox (2003) in her study of two MCC denominations. It could also be that rather than emphasizing doctrine, MCC emphasizes welcoming and providing a safe place, as well as enabling the religious experience of God as a healing strategy. This is in line with the understanding of the religious experience as fundamentally emotional and relational (Riis and Woodhead 2010). Of the twenty-eight interviewees, eleven experience no internal conflict with their sexuality within the context of their religious worldview. This suggests that doctrinal conflicts do not necessarily lead to the internal disruption of self, and when they do these are resolved in conjunction with relational and emotional experiences, and religious iterative practice. This is discussed in more detail in Chapters 5 and 6.

With the exception of one congregation, outreach is limited, a fact that for some causes concern and disappointment. One young congregant expresses the desire to improve this, saying:

> That's one thing the MCC should do more of ... doing more outreach because that's a really important core element of churches, is getting out into the community and helping people out ... I think there should be something for people to find out about churches that are accepting and stuff. I don't think there's enough information out there. I would love to work with the MCC to reach out to people who were like me and thought there was nothing left out there ... I'd like to make it known that you can still be loved and build your-self back up after being hurt by not-so-loving churches.

One MCC has organized outreach to local poorer residents who live on a nearby housing estate. Members of this congregation meet every Wednesday in the community, provide afternoon tea and, through talking to people in this community, gain an understanding of their needs.

Worship practices

The UFMCC, while being flexible in styles of worship and religious practices, is underpinned and united by foundational mainstream doctrinal creeds and practices. Beyond these, each denomination has the freedom of emphasis and practice. Consequently, each MCC congregation differs in their interpretation of worship and ritual. Each is described briefly according to the inclusive and transformative practices of liturgy and music, the spoken word and communion.

Interestingly, the older congregations were more likely to use gender-inclusive language, with the youngest congregation taking a more relaxed approach to gendered language. This relaxed approach to gendered language contrasted with a distinctively queer understanding of gender roles in this congregation. The older congregations tended to retain more traditional understandings of gender roles, with some variations. Two of the congregations have a formal communion ritual, where wafers are placed on congregants' tongues. Two have a more informal approach to communion, where each individual breaks bread and dips it in grape juice. Three practice the laying on of hands and one does not. Two congregations sing traditional hymns, and two have a more charismatic style of singing and worship.

One of the congregations has a more traditional worship service that mixes Protestant and other worship practices. It is tailored to the needs of the largely older congregants from a variety of traditional Christian backgrounds. The pastor describes the service format: 'Our morning service is a typical Methodist worship service', which is not surprising as the minister identifies as a 'Wesleyan Methodist'. Following the traditional approach, the minister dresses in a white cassock or robe and a clergy collar with a purple-coloured stole. The service is structured and intentionally predictable. The minister explains the importance of ritual and predictability as another central strategy for building an inclusive and welcoming atmosphere:

> I think all of us need ritual, and we might call it something else, maybe continuity, in our lives. So, yes, coming to church is part of the ritual … they know when they come here what is going to happen … they are going to be greeted, they are going to sit down, we are going to sing a hymn, we are going to have a prayer, we are going to have a reading, we are going to have scripture, we are going to have the sacrament, we are going to have a hymn. So the ritual is maybe much more the familiarity, to be in a place where the familiar can happen around you.

The order of service is rarely altered, or if a new practice is introduced it is arranged experimentally in mutual agreement with the congregation, as explained by the pastor: 'We have an unwritten agreement, the congregation and me, that they will give me permission to try new things, but the deal is that if they are uncomfortable with that after six weeks, it will stop.' As he goes on to explain: 'So with ritual there has to be a dialogue. It's not my ritual and not yours. Let's find ritual that will work for all of us that will enlighten us, empower us, strengthen and comfort us.' The importance of ritual and predictability is validated by Anthea, an older member of this congregation, who explains:

> I just feel so good. The traditional, even the hymns are pretty traditional; I know them from the Anglican Church. And the structure, it's always the same, you know there's not going to be any surprises; it's laid out in certain ways. Yes, I like that. I do like it and it goes by the gospel and the readings and I know are from what other churches do.

Tradition is important to enable LGBT church-goers continuity in their religious life. Anthea continued to outline that it was important to her that the MCC services be similar to 'other churches', as she explains:

That lectionary thing, they are not like out there and running their own thing. They follow a set pattern that other churches do. I think that's been important to me too, they're not radical in any way. Like I say, if you went in blindfolded, you would just think you were in another church.

It is important for Anthea not to feel different, in any way devalued because of her sexuality. The traditional format offers her continuity, familiarity and inclusivity.

Another congregation is also influenced by the Uniting Church background of the pastor. In this second congregation, the service is also predictable and structured. Between songs, for which the congregation stands, formulaic prayers are spoken by a congregational member with set responses intoned in unison by the congregation. Other prayers are prepared by congregational members and given at certain times in the service. Continuity is stressed.

In contrast, the other two congregations have services tailored to meet the needs of a very different demographic. In these services, the minister is typically dressed informally, perhaps in shirt and jeans, one with a clerical collar and one without. The service begins with songs, each seamlessly melding into the next. There is no set liturgy as in the traditional services, where the congregation

Photo 3.5 MCC Sydney. Photo courtesy of MCC Sydney

responds in a set way to words of prayer. Rather, the sermon and sacrament of communion are both preceded and followed by contemporary songs of praise and worship in charismatic style, accompanied by a small number of instruments. As is often the case with charismatic music, each song is drawn out with long repeated choruses. The singing of contemporary songs of praise might be led by female singers backed up by guitar and bongo drums. The music is intended to be a form of worship and a sacrament in itself, drawing the participant into communion with the Holy Spirit (Veith 2013). Some, but by no means all, hold their palms upwards, either with their arms raised or at their sides.

Music is central to all MCC services as an inclusive worship practice. All the congregations visited had small choirs with assorted musical instruments. At one traditional service, music is mainly hymns that many participants would have sung as children. Many interview participants describe the value of the singing for them, the power of the memory of childhood practices. May, an occasional congregant explains: 'The singing, I really like the old songs – it evokes my past. My mother used to sing a lot and often she'd sing hymns. So sometimes I hear my mother singing the hymns.' In general, singing is an important element of praise and worship, whether traditional or charismatic. Vickie describes the meaning of singing for her as: 'It is the most powerful thing in my life. I remember whenever I sing. I can just sing for God and that makes it okay.' This emotional response to music or 'embodied memory' is indicative of a shared religious habitus that drew individual congregants to worship together.

A second core practice of the MCC churches is the sermon. The spoken word is a powerful performative tool. The MCC is committed to inclusivity and to preach God's love for all people, regardless of age, race, sexuality or gender. This message flows through all sermons – regardless of congregation. There are, however, differences of emphasis. One sermon Bronwyn heard emphasized the message that 'faith will set you free if you just believe in Jesus'. The sermon was based upon the writings of Paul. The pastor pointed out that while Paul didn't necessarily 'get it right' regarding sexuality, women, slavery and relationships in general, he was clear on the importance of the relationship with Jesus. This could be understood as subversive, a queering of Christianity, taking ownership of words that 'damaged' and reworking them as affirmations. The sermon did not concentrate upon same-sex attraction or what some would understand as justification of this. The message was simple: 'We are Christian and we are inclusive as Jesus would be.'

A second sermon Bronwyn heard concentrated on practical strategies and ways one could become like Jesus. The pastor reportedly delivers powerful and

challenging sermons and according to one congregant: 'We are sometimes challenged by some views ... but I do like the way it does create a discussion afterwards. It's not a lecture, it's often to stimulate discussion which I think is great.'
Gary Comstock's (1993) gay theology also understands Jesus in a non-hierarch-
ical light – as a brother or friend.

In one congregation there was an emphasis on sin, which seemed contradictory to the progressive nature of the services. The pastor explains that this is a
reaction to the inclusive ecumenical nature of the UFMCC:

> For so long we've been afraid of the word sin. I mean we never in Australia take
> out the word Jesus ... but we definitely take the word sin out, we wouldn't even
> talk about it, and so we weren't aware of our need for growth. And that's why
> I think we got stuck in the place of healing, but never healed because we didn't
> have a sense of repentance and needing to change. If I thought that I was already
> whole and complete I wouldn't need God. I come to God because I want to be
> transformed and that is what we want at [this church].

This helps to explain the apparent contradiction between, on one hand, the
inclusive contemporary fluidity of the organization and relationships, and on the
other the exclusive nature of the message.

The spoken word extends to the use of gender-inclusive language as a means
of breaking down inequality and divisions, a fundamental tenet of the UFMCC.
It is practised in varying degrees in the congregations we visited. Gender-inclusive language is used in all MCC hymns, which are sung with words such as 'kin-
dom' replacing 'kingdom', or the use of 'God' or 'God's' rather than the pronoun
'He', or 'His'. Some pastors articulate strong support for the use of gender-inclusive language. Another pastor, however, does not support its use.

People were ambivalent about the use of gender-inclusive language. This
ambivalence was present in all four congregations. It was surprising to note
that despite gender-inclusive language in hymns or prayers projected on the
overheads, congregants sang or spoke using traditional masculine Christian
wordings or pronouns. These institutional and individual responses to gender-
inclusive language are discussed in more detail in Chapter 7.

The Eucharist, or communion, is arguably the most powerful of the ritual
practices at the MCC. MCC communion is 'open table' – open to any person
who wishes to partake. In each of the MCC services attended, the open table was
stressed. A clear majority of interviewees mention the open table as being central to their religious experience at MCC, central to their being accepted 'just as
I am'. Eucharist is also unique in that congregants come forward for communion

either as a couple, with family members or with a group of friends. This relational element was stressed at all the MCC services attended and, from the accounts of interviewees, it had a powerful impact on them. The effect of the repetitive act of communion incorporating same-sex relationships is a critical element, a queering of Christianity, leading to the acceptance of self and transformation of habitus, and is discussed further in Chapter 6.

The majority of the MCC congregations practice the laying on of hands after communion. Each individual, couple or group of individuals (including the occasional canine family member), are given the opportunity to be prayed over by the minister or acolyte. After communion or the laying on of hands, it is not unusual for couples to embrace and/or kiss, a practice that made a strong impression upon Bronwyn, and many newcomers, according to the interviewees.

Communion at the more conventional services involves the pastor, or a respected elder consecrating the communion. In these congregations, those who wish to receive communion are asked to come down each of the two aisles where the minister and acolytes receive them. A wafer is placed on each congregant's tongue and they are given a drink of grape juice. In another service, a loaf of bread replaces the wafers of the traditional service. Congregants are prayed over mostly in groups, at times for many minutes. At the end of communion, each of those helping then serve each other and pray over each other. This gives the appearance of a quiet harmony and warmth between the central worship team.

A unique feature of one of the churches was that after communion each congregant took a candle to a table on the side and lit it for a loved one in need of prayer. This is reminiscent of the High Church of England or Catholic practice. However, its use in connection with communion is a unique and eclectic development which appears to be valued by the members of the congregation. One congregant from a Protestant background reported: 'Probably the most Catholic thing for me is something that I've actually really enjoyed at this church was the little candle table on the side … I've actually embraced that little thing.'

One congregation is unusual in that the communion table is placed at the back of the room. After the sermon, communion is held, during which the congregation all stand up and walk towards the back of the room, gathering in a horseshoe formation around the altar. The pastor explains that although his intention is to form a circle, the congregation has always placed him at the head, especially during the blessing prayer. The pastor presides over the communion, consecrating it, welcoming all to the table. As in the other congregations, the pastor stresses a totally open table, invoking the spirit of Jesus to be there. He then breaks the bread, a large soft white loaf. Each congregant moves forward, taking some bread and dipping it in the grape juice, eating it, some 'hanging around' in the circle while they do so and some returning to their seats. During communion, guitar music is played. Many approach the table in small groups or with their partner, taking communion together, holding hands or arm in arm. Distinctively, however, there is no laying-on of hands after communion.

Conclusion

This description of the spaces, people, governance and worship practices of three MCCs serves to illustrate both the similarities that characterize the institution and the diversity of experience within it. No institution is homogenous, although structures are put into place to encourage homogeneity. In the case of the MCC, the basic tenets of belief and practice are structured into each congregation through regulations, documentation and the MCC-ordained ministerial obligations. While practices vary, they are centred on inclusivity: open communion at each service, the use of inclusive language, and welcome to all, irrespective of background (Shore-Goss 2013).

Inclusive ritual practices enable congregants to experience the love of God and Jesus and to transform their individual religious habitus to come to a point where they can recognize their same-sex attraction as legitimate. The spaces and the people make possible the expression of individual agency within the constraining heteronormative order of broader society. The following chapters concentrate on the process that individuals go through to resolve the tension between the religious worldviews of their upbringing and their growing awareness of their same-sex attraction.

Chapter 4 centres on the desire articulated by a large number of the participants in this study to live meaningful lives through being true to themselves. Their actions are driven by the moral imperatives based upon their 'horizons of significance' and include living as an authentic Christian and living an authentic life according to their 'true sexuality' and/or gender.

4

Seeking an Authentic Self

Vignette: Lynne

I was born into a [church going] family, so being Christian was just a natural path for me. I made a commitment in late primary school. We used to go to Sunday school and church on a Sunday. We were always taught and encouraged and there was always the call to come forward and accept Jesus Christ as your saviour at quite a lot of the Sunday evening services. Some of my friends had gone up and I thought, I think God's really calling me to go up too. So I went up and you were counselled by the minister for a couple of weeks and then you were baptized and then you were welcomed into the church and I think that was just part of being Christian for me, being in a Christian family. My two brothers were baptized as well, so, I think it was just a natural progression.

I was ecstatic at the time. Absolutely ecstatic! It's just like a bit of utopia. I didn't have to be alone I suppose. I was always bullied at school. I had a friend and we read devotion books and Christian story books. We read the Bible at home. It just seemed like the right thing to do.

Right through my teens I went to church because they had a lot of youth activities and they were my friends from school. When I went into nursing I drifted out of church for a while, probably for a few years. I always believed it was me that wandered from God, not God from me. I wanted to move flats to a house and then I asked my girlfriend to help. [She said] "You can only have my help if you come to church tonight with me." [I said] "Alright." So I did and then I met my future husband and we started going out together and he was a Christian and so there was the expectation of the church thing and being committed! Getting married and bringing up the kids. [My children] were brought up to go to church and to Sunday school. My two boys now don't go to church. The girls are both still going.

When I was around about twenty-two, I did have a brief female relation-ship with a friend who I shared a flat with. [Growing up, lesbianism] was never accepted. You had to have a family and be married and live happily ever after. When I was divorced, I lived on my own for twelve years. I'd known Liz for a long period of time and her husband died. I said to her at the funeral, "I'm not here for the short term; I'm here for the long term so when you're ready we can do things together." Over a period of time, Liz and I started bike riding, camping and going away together. I always spent a lot of time in female company. I really didn't like the company of males. I felt quite uncomfortable. So it just evolved through the friendship with Liz. I was reading the paper, looking at the ads, same sex, mix and match. I said, oh, same sex; I might look for a woman! Well, what's wrong with me? It evolved like that!

It was a bit of a shock for the family. I had a lot of confrontation with [some family members]. They didn't accept it. Liz and I probably kept it quiet for quite a while. Once my [children] knew, the church knew. The female leaders within the church turned a lot of people against us. We were basically rejected. The minister never did and he talks to me, But the friends that I thought I had within the church just abandoned me. So I didn't feel comfortable there. The conflict really hurt Liz, and me as well.

I challenged [one family member]. I said, "Look, we can't keep going on like this, the way we are. We are just hurting each other. We might as well go our separate ways. Do you want that?" [They said] "No, I'd actually like us to go to mediation." [They] said, "I've got the number, here's the number, I've rung them up." I thought, "Okay." So [we] both had to go to mediation, so [they] went off independently, I went off independently and then we met together with the mediator. I think it actually bought out a lot of who we were, where we were going, what we wanted and how we could get around the problems. From then on [they have] slowly come round. Liz's [family] have always accepted us.

Liz and I made a commitment that we were going to be together and, regard-less, we were going to stay together. Liz and I were living together in the same house. We knew we hadn't abandoned God but we just hadn't found our niche where we belonged in a church. We tried a local home church. We were fine there for a while but there was nothing that we could really do in service because we were lesbians in a relationship.

[For] the first part of our relationship we didn't go to church. [Then] Liz [and I] wanted to go to church and have fellowship with people of similar interests, people of similar beliefs. We are not night clubbers, we are not drinkers. [We] don't want to mix with the wild and loud. I think our spirituality needed to be fed as well, needed to be nurtured for a little while, and that's what we did.

We soon knew about MCC, and just put it off, and put it off for a while, and we started a new year, and we started to go to MCC. Then we were very accepted and I think that first twelve months I just battled through a lot of the [doctrinal] issues and sorted out who I was and where I was really going and where I sat with God and did a lot of reading.

[The MCC] service was wow! It was different! It wasn't conservative, but it wasn't Hillsong either. It was a bit behind the times! But you grow to love it as you sit there. There were courses that they ran at the church that helped you just unravel your burdens. [The people there] were always very supportive of us. They'd give you any time of day or night to talk. If I wanted to talk to them, I found them very supportive. We found [a couple of people who are] very solid friends. We're really good mates. Out of church. We were welcomed and could do things within the church.

There was the rainbow colours. You think, what are the rainbow colours? [Then you realize] oh yes, look at that man over there in a dress! You think, OMG! Is this really for us? This fear was, I hope no transgender talks to me! And after the service it was a transgender that came up and spoke to [us and they became] best friends. The people cared. You could see they were genuine. There was a genuine love of God. The preaching was good. The songs were different. You had to get used to the language. Not God as he, but God of your understanding, or God as her or him. I'm thinking, "How could God be her or him?" [Now] I like the inclusive language.

Communion is always special to me. Having that every week, yes. It reinforces that, yes, Christ died on a cross for our sins, that he shed his blood for us. We have communion, the wine, the bread, as his body and blood, but I think it also reinforces to me as well that it's not just the fact that he died for our sins, it's the fact also that we are going to be reunited with him in the future.

At first it took me a long time to get used to going up the front, and having your bread given to you. Once you realize it stops the potential cross-infection. The praying after communion – I found that really hard. We used to have congregational prayers. We didn't have individual prayers. The lighting candles! That was really hard too! Now, over the years I find that really an essential part, almost essential, because anything can change,

[Going to the church] is almost the highlight [of my week]. It's very important to me. It's just part of the way of my upbringing, and my culture. It's just part of you and it gives you food for thought for the week as well, like the sermon, and the songs and things like that.

Introduction

I was searching for the truth – I wanted to be truthful to myself. I was coming to terms with my sexuality as being gay but I wasn't hundred per cent sure because I thought maybe I'm right, maybe I'm wrong. But I wanted to be truthful to myself and to God, to God. 'Seek first the Kingdom of God and all his righteousness. And all these things shall be added unto you.' I thought oh, I won't lose because I will be in the right … I had … a sudden connection with my sexuality by the age of twenty-four. And I remember, after going out and having a lovely time, I went to my room. And I was down on the floor in tears crying as the whole world is just revolving. And within me, a voice started from the ground and just … the grace to be myself, to start to be myself … That helped me a lot just to come back again. It was really restructuring myself. And I'm following my inner voice through all this time (Nova).

Once I realized that that is who I am, I just ran with it … I knew that there was no alternative. I could not deal with this by burying it. And to be honest, I didn't want to. So again, everything I do is underpinned by my spirituality. It's underpinned by my relationship with God. I'm going: 'God, what is it that you want me to do? What's going to make you happy?' And that underpins my motives for transitioning. It's what told me that it was the right thing for me to do. Not that I really had the choice not to do it, but it's what told me that was going to work for me. And going into something knowing it's going to work, you sort of, you go in knowing you just can't fail. And that's a huge bonus when you're tearing your life apart and rebuilding it. (Sylvia)

Nova and Sylvia are two transgender women whose stories express unequivocally their desire to live Christian moral and authentic lives. Nova says she is seeking 'the grace to be myself' and Sylvia to discover and live 'who I am'. Their desire is to seek, as Taylor (1991: 28) articulates, their 'original way of being human … called upon to live in this way and not in imitation of anyone else's [life]'. Nova experiences tension and self-doubt as she seeks to 'be truthful to [herself] and God', saying, 'Maybe I'm right, maybe I'm wrong'. This initial questioning is commonly experienced by the majority of the lesbian, gay, bisexual and transgender Christians in this study. Sylvia, too, questions what would make God happy and concludes that the right thing to do is to transition 'to be who I am'. Both Nova and Sylvia illustrate the dialogical nature of self-identity: as they search for the 'true self', they seek answers through a dialogue with God. Finally, they illustrate the profound and deeply transformative nature of the moral and identity challenges they face as they grapple with same-sex attraction and gender identity: Nova describes her experience as 'really re-structuring myself' and Sylvia as 'tearing her life apart and rebuilding it'. They challenge and transform the religious habitus of their upbringing.

This chapter introduces the lived experience of the lesbian, gay and transgender Christians who took part in this study. As exemplified by Nova and Sylvia, a key theme that arises consistently throughout the interviews is the desire to live an authentic life, across the dimensions of sexuality, gender, relationships and faith. The lesbian and gay individuals express the desire to be 'be true to themselves' (Taylor 1991: 26), true to their sexuality and true to their faith. All, however, were cognizant of the tension created by the desire to merge their sexual and religious selves. The moral values of the participants were based upon the heteronormative Christian habitus of their upbringing. For the majority, the morality of their sexuality was therefore brought into question as they deviated from the normative cultural moral order, causing deep internal conflict. Others experienced tension derived from extrinsic factors, such as relationships with family members, church leaders, peer groups and other social interactions.

Charles Taylor's (1991: 15) concept of the 'ethic of authenticity' helps to explain the aspiration of the participants to be 'true to themselves' to express their authentic individuality. Saving authenticity from accounts of narcissism (Hookway 2013), Taylor proposes that the subjective and individualistic project of the self is constrained within external standards beyond the control of the individual. He names these common moral precepts 'horizons of significance' (1991: 38), shared understandings of what constitutes a moral life. They are necessarily relational, dialogic and provide meaning beyond the self.

Each individual's horizons of significance are dependent upon contextual factors and therefore not immutable. They are sites of contested moral values open to transformation through relationships, emotions, cognitions and practices. Drawing upon Taylor (1991: 38), we suggest that those who experienced *intrinsic conflict* were themselves the site of contested 'horizons of significance' where the external standards of their upbringing were at odds with the expression of their 'true' sexuality. This conflict is associated with a prolonged negotiation of their religious habitus and religious worldview.

The problem of sexuality for Christians

Sexuality is a profound moral dilemma for LGBT Christians. Arthur, a candidate for ministry in the Uniting Church, explains that in order to deal with the 'problem of sexuality', the idea of a body/spirit dichotomy has been promulgated in many Christian churches. He expands:

> He [the Baptist minister] didn't see himself as a sexual being. I thought: 'You are a married man with children, what's going on there?' He was just so ultra conservative that it was the old body/spirit dichotomy stuff … the body was evil, the spirit wasn't, so what the body did was evil … Well, for him celibacy was the only right and proper thing [for me as a gay Christian] but that was not possible for everyone … you don't expect [celibacy] from everyone, but if you are in any way different you've got to be [celibate].

According to this thinking, those in heterosexual relationships are given the option of marrying, which is deemed the only expression of sexuality acceptable for conservative Christians. However, LGBT Christians are denied this and are expected to live a life of celibacy. Very few LGBT Christians embrace celibacy and instead question their sexual and religious identity, including relationships with God and others. Many face deep shame.

The dominant conservative Christian understanding of sexuality as hidden, private and shameful is underlined by Emma, a young woman, as she recalls her experience in a fundamentalist group. The greatest of all sins was seen as sexual:

> You had to confess your sexual sins in front of the ministers. And they would yell at you in the service, that was sometimes how they preached, or preaching with their eyes closed because they couldn't look at us because we were so sinful. And so people had to stand up and confess their sins. (Emma)

May also explains her Christian upbringing and the silence around sexuality:

> And then as far as my sexuality, you know in fundamentalist religion there's no such thing as sexuality or it's hidden behind marital doors, kind of. So, no preparation for that really, just the assumptions that you know at a certain age I'd meet somebody and get married and have children. (May)

Within conservative Christian theologies, the expression of acceptable sexualities is extremely restricted. The boundaries are also strongly enforced. The Christian moral dilemma of the uncertain place of sexuality in a 'good sexual life' is deeply embedded in the religious habitus.

Several of the LGBT participants distinguish between 'healthy' monogamous relationships as opposed to a promiscuous lifestyle. This distinction is made consistently as individuals negotiate their sexuality within the bounds of their faith. For example, Anthea is single and living a celibate life. When asked about how she feels regarding same-sex attraction within the context of her faith, Anthea says: 'I don't think I would feel any different if I was in a relationship. If I was promiscuous I might. But that would be more about, even if I was heterosexually promiscuous, you know what I mean?'

Anthea's position illustrates the complexity of the contested morality of LGBT Christian sexuality. For Anthea, the problem was not same-sex-attraction per se, but rather how a person expresses their sexuality. This overlaps with Christian teaching that promotes monogamous relationships. Monogamy is deeply embedded in the Christian religious habitus, and this contributes to how individuals feel and act. On the one hand, Anthea's commitment to monogamy exemplifies a normative Christian view of sexuality. A commitment to monogamy was common among the majority of the participants and is discussed further in Chapter 7. On the other, Christian heteronormativity, as a horizon of significance, is challenged by all participants. As previously indicated, most LGBT individuals with a Christian upbringing enter a state of moral questioning, with the majority abandoning their faith. In contrast, a minority remain Christian. For the active Christians in this study, their faith is entrenched and deeply important to them. As a consequence, their life of faith becomes a place of discomfort and, at times, distress, as they negotiate the profound tensions between their sexuality and religiosity.

The uncomfortable experience of an LGBT life of faith

The individuals in our study often experience conflicting desires – to live according to an authentic sexuality, to express their authentic gender, as well as to remain true to their religious worldview. The questioning of their own faith leads to a reflexive negotiation of their faith. This, in turn, implies struggle against social conformity, in this case the implied or enforced rules governed by a heteronormative institution (Taylor 1991: 63). For example, Liz explains that for LGBT Christians there seems little possibility of remaining in a comfortable stage of faith:

> Well, I think for all gay (LGBT) Christians you have to be absolutely committed to your Christian life because it is just so hard. It is so hard because you are

rejected by the Christians in community; you are rejected by the gay community. Unless you are totally dedicated you won't last.

She articulates the irony that those who were most sceptical, distrusting and occasionally hostile to LGBT Christians are fellow Christians who espouse 'loving thy neighbour'. In addition to this, many of the wider LGBT community shun Christians. They understand Christianity to be a patriarchal and heteronormative institution. Luke Gahan (2013: 51) also describes the life of faith for LGBT people as one of deep questioning:

> A common misconception of LGBTIQ people is that we lose our spirituality as a result of being ostracized and marginalized by our societies' faiths. Instead it is within this space that we are forced to question our religion and the existential questions that others can take for granted … it is in this place we are forced to discover the one thing that can sustain us on our tumultuous journey – our spirituality.

An authentic life is a questioned, reflexive life. Taylor (1991: 27) explains: 'The powerful moral ideal … accords crucial moral importance to a kind of contact with myself, with my own inner nature, which is in danger of being lost, partly through pressures toward outward conformity.' The LGBT Christians in this study engage in a struggle against 'outward pressures to conformity' to be true to their sexual and religious identity. Through this, they pursue the possibility to experience a deeply meaningful religious/spiritual life. The 'abject' (Butler 1990) alternative position they struggle with can heighten their religious experience, a finding shared consistently by a variety of studies (Gorman 1980; Wilcox 2003; Yip 2005). O'Brien (2004) describes this reflexive experience as providing a deeply meaningful purpose for existence, or a 'raison d'être', rather than as a compromise or an apology.

Nicky struggled for over forty years to accept her same-sex attraction. She says that: 'I now believe God saved my life for a reason and that reason was to help other people and to understand them.' At the time of the interview, Rebecca had a quiet calm about her same-sex attraction. She explains: 'I think coming to terms with my sexuality has made my faith stronger in a way: 'cause you realize how much he loves you, what a plan he must – like he throws these curved balls at you but it's always, obviously for a reason.' The sense that they are part of a bigger design is central to the self-acceptance and self-understanding of LGBT Christians.

The participants consistently indicate that their religious lives are not only shaped but also enhanced by their sexuality, in particular by the difficulties they face through this. For example, Andrew feels 'privileged in being gay and being Christian and being happy, and having that creates a different journey'. Like Rebecca, he explains: 'I think adversity makes you a stronger person ... to have a stronger spiritual life', adding: 'You don't take things for granted. You don't feel a sense of sort of coasting through life.'

The difficulties Nicky, Rebecca and Andrew experience as LGBT Christians become meaningful and their religious identity more authentic through the struggle. The struggle facilitates a deeper appreciation for God, Jesus and his purpose for their lives. The so-called dichotomy between their sexuality and their faith collapses when their faith calls for living 'true to themselves', encompassing authentic sexuality. Being authentic to one's sexuality, one's gender and religion can be conceptualized as queer – a place where multiple aspects of identity are fused, where borders dissolve (Epstein 1994). Becoming an authentic lesbian, gay and transgender Christian was aspired to, and achieved by, most of the LGBT individuals in this study, a place of negotiated tension and reflexive questioning of moral values.

Contested moral imperatives

The above diagram (Figure 4.1) illustrates the conceptualization of the authentic self. While the sexual and gendered self is distinguished from the spiritual self, these are interrelated and overlapping. Necessarily the spiritual self informs the desire of participants to accept their same-sex attraction. The authentic self is a fusion of the two, as conceptualized by Abes and Kasch (2007: 628) as 'intrasections'. This analysis based on personal accounts is broken down into two parts: the moral imperatives attached to being authentic to sexuality and the

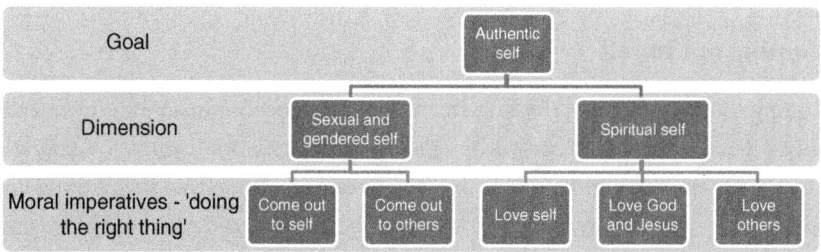

Figure 4.1 Model of the authentic self

moral imperatives attached to being an authentic Christian. Both are understood as the right thing to do in front of God and following Jesus's example.

Coming out as a moral imperative

'Coming out' is the popular term used to refer to a stage of identity development that many lesbian and gay individuals experience as they recognize their sexuality, then integrate this into their self-image. They then relay that to others (Cass 1979; Shallenberger 1998). Coming out is a difficult process that is intensified by religious belonging. Scholars analysing the process of 'coming out' for religious people suggest that coming out is an act of love – understood as a morally right choice and responsibility to others far beyond the private sphere (Eichberg 1991). Glaser (1998) describes coming out as a sacrament, emphasizing the act of coming out as a sacrificial act. The individual offers their vulnerable self on the altar in order to experience God's grace, the unconditional love of God (Glaser 1998). Coming out for religious people often involves a profound sense of loss in order to gain the grace of God. As a result of pursuing an authentic religious self, LGBT Christians take the risk of losing the love of others in order to gain the love of God, of Jesus, and of the self. Both Eichberg's act of love and Glaser's sacrament highlight an understanding coming out as a moral imperative.

Coming out is a performative act that contributes to the transformation of habitus. Coming out is a process that first involves coming out to the self, and then to others. It is a site of confrontation – confrontation of moral values and confrontation between loved ones and significant others. The findings of this study corroborate a large number of studies (Shallenberger 1998; Wilcox 2002; Drumm 2005 among others) that demonstrate 'coming out' as critical to a resolution of conflict between sexual and religious identities.

Coming out to self

Coming out to the self is the first step to living according to a God-given sexuality when life is understood within a religious framework. Lynne, for example, explains: 'You are taught to love your neighbour as yourself, so if you don't love yourself for who you are, you can't love your neighbour, you can't really love anybody else. So you really have to come to terms with who you are to love yourself completely.' To love the self becomes a moral imperative and enables many of the participants to seek and live according to their authentic sexuality.

After struggling to embrace her same-sex attraction, Lynne eventually reaches a stage of acceptance, saying: 'I feel at peace. Yeah. I'm still me, I haven't changed, I am who I am.' Participants frequently use the words 'I am who I am' to both express the essentialist sentiment that God made them as they are, and that their goal was to be comfortable and open about that. As Natalie expresses: 'It was a slow coming to terms type of thing. I'm not one to argue how I feel if I know how I feel. I know that I feel like I have God in my heart and if I know that I'm attracted to women, then that's who I am. And so it was just a matter of me coming to terms with being able to say that out loud.' Such sentiments resonate with Taylor's (1991: 29) self-discovery based upon 'moral feelings deep within us'. The authentic self, the 'true self', articulates this 'out loud' and defines the self in relation to others. Natalie also describes the meeting of sexual and religious identity and being at peace with that as part of loving the self.

The process of coming out to the self was for many a painful process where the body became a key site of struggle. It became clear to Nova, for example, that being in a heterosexual relationship was inauthentic. As she explains, initially as a [male] teenager she 'really wanted to be in the norm, to have a heterosexual relationship with a woman'. However, after a year of being in a relationship she realized that 'I am in the wrong position. I mean the wrong place, this is not right.' Her religious upbringing continues to haunt her:

> I still feel guilt, there's a sediment of guilt. In a bottle of wine you will find at the bottom the sediment. That's the nature of it – which has been brought about by religion and society as well. Facing my sexuality, [it] was best to kill, destroy myself . . . because I'm bad for society.

At this dark moment, she finds solace in nature and her religious understanding:

> The next day the day was still the same, like a lovely day. I thought with the positiveness of Christianity came 'love your neighbour as yourself'. I was taught how to love your neighbour but I haven't really loved myself because I don't know who's me. And now that I'm beginning to know who's me, I'm freer.

Here Nova clearly articulates the ethical ideal of being 'true to herself' (Taylor 1991) and connects that to her faith. She states emphatically: 'Religion, coming back to religion saved me!' Rather than deny her faith, Nova finds refuge in her faith. She stresses both the importance of and the strengthening of her faith. The moral imperative of being true to herself that springs from her faith enables her to have the strength to live according to what she perceives to be her authentic sexual self, to know 'who's me'. She describes the eventual integration of living an authentic sexuality and living according to what she understands as God's higher purpose.

Like Nova, many (but not all) participants initially felt a profound tension between their same-sex attraction and religious worldview and struggled with the seemingly irreconcilable contradiction. Anthony, when faced with this dilemma, articulates the importance of being honest about his sexuality in order to be authentic as a Christian. He had previously lived a fragmented life, at times outside Australia, where he lived openly as a gay man, while passing for straight back in Australia. When asked whether he feels internal conflict between his same-sex attraction and his Christian beliefs he explains:

> Well, I did because ... the thing is God is seeing everything I'm doing and probably the hardest thing as a gay man as a Christian ... I wasn't living an authentic life, I was living a closeted life and for a single gay man that's not often a healthy thing.

As he says: 'God is seeing everything'. His desire was to be true to the authentic sexual self, in front of God and others. The relationship with God propelled him to resolve his 'inauthentic lifestyle'. For religious individuals, coming out as same-sex attracted is framed as part of a religious journey. This is a religious journey that encompasses all their relationships with others and the relationship with God. Coming out as same-sex attracted is an expression of authenticity, and a fusion of two negotiated dimensions of authenticity – the religious and the sexual. Belinda Rives (2005) also notes that the resolution of internal conflict among lesbian Christians in her study leads to 'an authentic state'.

The majority of participants express the desire to 'do the right thing' and are mindful of living according to what God wants. This desire is characterized by self-questioning and prayer. Natalie describes the conflict she felt when questioning her own sexuality: 'I argued it in my head a lot ... I always put on a confident front. But in my head I was kind of like: "Oh, I don't know." Like I just didn't know exactly what should be right and stuff.' Liz appealed to God in prayer:

> So I spent a few months praying about it, and basically saying to God, well if this is wrong, you know, take these feelings away because I don't want to do anything that is against doing what you would have me do. So I guess first and foremost always was my relationship with God, and not doing the wrong thing by him.

Liz entreats God to help her resolve her conflict, praying to find what God would have her do. Emma formed her first same-sex relationship at the age of twenty-five. She explains how she felt during this time: 'Six years of struggling, just thinking, I don't know if I should be really doing this. Am I jeopardizing my faith in order to have this? But I really love this person and for the first time I feel complete. And whole – but not free.'

Emma says that she feels complete and whole when in touch with her authentic sexual self. In her early twenties, she is unable to integrate this dimension of her identity fully with her religious self. She struggles, as she puts it, to feel 'free'. Many participants struggled initially with this dilemma, understanding their same-sex attraction as sinful, a violation of their upbringing. Andrew, for example, when confronted with the awareness of his same-sex attraction, says:

> Well, either you hope and you pray and you pray hard enough that it will go away and live a good Christian life, get married to a woman, have kids and live happily ever after. Well, no, that's not happening. But the disappointment to God and my parents and family and friends and everything, how do I [reconcile it]? Or, I remember I had it all worked out, well, the one obvious one was to live a gay lifestyle, coming to terms with everything but that would mean turning away from God. And the third one would be the worst to my mind, living a double life and feeling incredibly inauthentic and incredibly guilty the whole time.

Remaining in his church as a Christian and simultaneously living as a closeted gay man seemed inauthentic. He could not initially find a way to live according to what seemed conflicting moral imperatives. On the one hand he was driven to express his true sexual self, on the other, he understood this as turning away from God, according to his religious upbringing, his religious habitus.

Angela, who also could not initially accept her same-sex attraction, dealt with the conflict strategically, choosing celibacy to manage her conflict. This response was made with the desire to do the right thing, so as not to violate her deeply embedded commitment to Christianity. She made a commitment to God, saying: 'I needed to figure myself out or I was going to hurt people, so I made a commitment to being celibate for a year.' At the same time she felt closer to God because of her struggle:

> When I committed to the year of celibacy I felt so close to God in a way – it was my time of purity and coming back, so to speak. I felt I had done such a terrible thing in committing this sin – I didn't really rate many other sins like it – like I'm not very greedy for example, I don't really struggle with giving etc.... but this sin was so intense and so shameful in both mine and the church's eyes that

for me to let it go I felt a depth of his grace and I felt so close because of that. It's almost like because I felt I was 'the worst of sinners' I felt that God was the most amazingly gracious of all beings – I just couldn't get my head around how much I was forgiven and the reality of that.

Angela, through grappling with a moral dilemma which was causing her deep shame, paradoxically feels closer to her God. In order to find and express the authentic self, Angela denied herself sexual relationships in her desire to do the right thing, to live authentically, which at this time was according to the religious worldview of her upbringing. Angela's experience clearly illustrates the profound moral questioning in which participants engaged, and the sincere desire to be authentic to both their sexual self and religious self.

There were six participants who chose celibacy as a means of managing the tension between their conflicting aspects of identity. Most realized it was a temporary stage and was not an ideal way of living. Patricia, for example, a woman who continually struggles to serve God and simultaneously be in a relationship, expresses that:

> In the past when I've been in a relationship I've lost my focus on God. I have people around me who successfully seem to manage to do both. Yeah, but I find it hard. I've had a friend of mine saying that that's really the only way us humans get to experience God is to love someone and be loved and I understand that.

She expresses the aspiration of many to live a religious life, where sexuality and the love of God are fused and cannot be separated. The individual is the site of the fusion of love of God, self and others. This can be described as a queer Christian life that the participants sought, one in which they could express their authentic sexuality as a reflection of God's unbounded love.

Coming out to others

For some participants, their internal conflicts were not an issue; the problem was learning to live with the responses of others towards their sexuality. Several articulated the importance of being honest with others regarding their sexuality and that without honesty they were not being authentic. Anthony, for example, explains that 'you can't be authentic if you're not being honest to the people around you. And I couldn't feel I could be honest so therefore I wasn't being authentic.' When asked what has the MCC has given him, he emphatically responds: 'Authenticity again. I know I'm now not hiding anything about myself.

But at the same time, I'm probably living a much purer life and that's because I'm comfortable in my relationship with [my partner].' As a consequence, he is now able to live a healthier emotional relational life, which he interprets as 'purer'. For Anthony, like Andrew, being authentic is being honest with himself as well as with others.

Being honest was important because individuals were committed to living according to higher principles, in a meaningful way, despite the often difficult consequences. Angela, a musician, also describes the importance of honesty in regards to her sexuality, explaining:

> Honesty has always been really important to me, it's been really important that as [my partner] and I committed to being together I was honest with those that approached me to do gigs or for church or whatever, I would always say that I was in a relationship with a woman, that we're Christian and committed and it didn't change my relationship with God, but that I'd understand if they didn't want me to play or lead. Nine times out of ten I was given a polite no thank you, though you could tell it troubled people to say it. I could have just accepted the gigs but I just wouldn't have felt honest, like I had any integrity before God.

Angela, through living by her principle of coming out to others regarding her sexuality, lost many opportunities to perform and was also ostracized by others. She describes being authentic as being honest with others and having integrity before God. This led to a breakdown of relationships with previous significant others. When her partner, for example, was not invited to her previous best friend's wedding, she turned down the invitation, explaining:

> It's really tough, that was a really hard decision for me because I am a people pleaser and her wedding is really not about me, but it's also a stand I thought I had to take, for my sake, and for [my partner].

Her desire to be authentic was also for her own sake, to be true to herself 'despite being a people pleaser'. She was willing to lose friendships for the sake of living according to a higher principle, a broader horizon that made her life more meaningful, of greater significance. Similarly, Arthur was stymied in his desire to become a minister with the Uniting Church due to his sexuality:

> The selection process within the Uniting Church didn't become stressful until I was not deemed ready ... they didn't think that ordained ministry was a good place for me ... they just made the decision on the basis is if we proceed to ordain will we be unable to place him because within the Uniting Church unless you have an appointment you can't be ordained. There was no way

I could hide [my same-sex attraction], but I didn't want to either. As the professor at theological hall [who] was responsible for pastoral care issues said, 'You've maintained your integrity throughout, no matter what', and that made me feel good.

In all these cases, the desire to be authentic, to be true in their relationships with others, challenged normative expectations, causing personal discomfort and occasionally significant loss. Despite the rejection they experience, both Arthur and Angela articulate how they feel 'good' and find meaning by maintaining their integrity in front of others and God. The requirement of being authentic in their relationship with God is to be authentic with others, often leading to loss and discomfort. Anthony, Arthur and Angela all exhibit the qualities of being 'uncompromising' and 'genuine'. In her study of lesbian Christians Cynthia Speakman (2009), ascribes these qualities to 'authenticity'.

Coming out as liberation

Coming out was also a journey of release. Ruth, a retired minister, describes how the experience of coming out publicly was liberating and deeply entwined with the spiritual and religious life. For Ruth, this is an authentic life, and a life worth living.

I must own my sexuality, for the sake of other people of homosexual orientation but also so I'd be honest about myself and not be hiding it in any sense … I went to the microphone and said that I believed that I needed to now advise the assembly that I was a lesbian. And here is me standing there with tears running down my face … I got a standing ovation when I finished … Because my life was so uplifted the creativity just flowed. It's sort of coming from me – not my head as much as my being … But a lot of this was coming from me because of the lifting of my heart. It really was, I mean, I wrote this poem, called '*the unutterable experience of the grace of God*'. I wrote it just after I came out. I felt as [if] I was flying. I just felt for the first time I felt whole and free and alive. I'm going to risk everything when I come out: my occupation, my reputation, everything that I value, I am going to put at stake here. I'm going to risk because I don't know how people will respond. And it felt like stepping off a cliff. And it was. I was – I was just lifted up, as though I was flying into the universe and I remember feeling alive and whole and free for the first time in my whole life. And that was, I just thought if I lose everything, I don't mind, I am alive. I'll grieve it. Of course I would mind, I did mind, but it was nothing compared to my sense of fullness and alive – being alive. So I never regretted it for a minute, not a minute.

Ruth's experience of 'feeling alive, and whole and free' is an indication of the performative power of 'coming out', of 'stepping off a cliff', as she articulates it. The freedom and creativity she experiences as a result is a powerful and emotional catalytic moment, a moment that turns the direction of her life. Ruth was willing to risk all in order to be authentic to what she understood as her 'true self'. She also articulates the moral responsibility of a very public position: 'for the sake of other people of homosexual orientation'.

Coming out is a site of profound tension between the desire to express a God-given authentic sexuality and the desire to live an authentic life according to the Christian principles. As illustrated above, these two supposedly conflicting aspects of self speak to each other and inform each other. Individuals are empowered through their faith to live according to their authentic sexuality. The following section concentrates on being a true Christian by loving God, following or becoming like Jesus and loving your neighbour as yourself. The moral imperative is to be an authentic Christian.

Being an authentic Christian

A second dimension of 'doing the right thing' and living an authentic life is to live according to basic Christian principles, as articulated by Lynne, of 'loving the Lord as your God, and loving your neighbour as yourself'. The individualized faith of the LGBT Christians involves a tension between living according to their authentic sexuality and living as an authentic Christian. The participants negotiate this tension and aspire to both, in the most part successfully. The Christian tradition is a shared 'horizon of significance' and creates a meaningful life for the participants. The ethic of authenticity is lived through the relationships with God, with Jesus and with neighbours.

Relationship with God

For LGBT Christians, a relationship with God is pivotal in seeking and remaining true to the authentic self. By living a 'good life', they embody the authentic self. This relationship also works as an anchor when conflict occurs with Christian institutions. God provides a meaningful moral benchmark that remains stable despite struggle and conflict. In their youth in particular, the LGBT Christians often felt confused and rejected, turning to God as their salvation and stalwart, a significant Other that did not change. As Vicky expresses: 'God was always there … a comfort … that never changed.' The relationship with God was also one that was grappled with and questioned. Sylvia encapsulates the intense questioning of self, faith and God:

> I guess that conversion experience [took place] somewhere around eight or nine [years old], I began to take more seriously this relationship with God. But for me, it was something I took almost literally. Because of the challenges of listening to a spiritual being that you can't just sit down and have this sort of conversation with, it's very easy to hear what you want things to be and as a result, you are looking very closely at the theology that you're hearing from the pulpit. And checking that how I'm understanding the relationship, because a sense of presence is tangible to what that means in terms of the way I live, that's where I let the theology inform.

Sylvia, who was brought up in a conservative Protestant church, slowly 'chipped away at the heteronormative theology' through a complex process of reflective prayer and researching theology. For her, theology was powerful and influential. Her relationship to God was informed by her grappling with theological issues. God was very also real to her, experientially significant and a powerful emotional support:

> I didn't take this as an exercise in faith or theology. The word was relationship so I treated it as a relationship … it's a sense of awareness in your heart internally … for me it has been a very strong sense of presence … My relationship with God is something very tangible, as tangible as my relationship with [my partner].

Sylvia relates to God on a very personal level, and it is through this relationship that she slowly reassembles her understanding of same-sex attraction within her religious worldview. 'I focused on my relationship with God. God, I need help here. I'm really struggling. He was helping … I began questioning the theology, twenty years of conservative theology that said relationships are always opposite sex.'

God represents a higher moral standard, one that does not change. In a study of four rural lesbians in the United States, Jennifer Hansen and Serena Lambert (2011) concentrate on grief and loss associated with religion. Similar to many participants in this study, they report that despite this loss these individuals conceptualize God as loving and accepting, and find their own way of being Christian. The relationship with God, whether personal or more distant, is significant to the LGBT Christian participants. To love God and to love as God does is the aspiration, the horizon of significance, which sustains the individuals in their search for authenticity. A second theme that emerged was the desire to follow the path of Jesus and/or become like Jesus.

Relationship with Jesus

The desire to get back to what participants believe to be basic principles of Christianity, to follow the footsteps of Jesus, and to become a 'true' Christian, is expressed by many despite, and in many cases in response to, being rejected from mainstream churches. There are two distinct patterns in the way individuals understand loving Jesus: following in Jesus's footsteps, with Jesus as a leader, and walking on the same level, with Jesus as a friend.

Arthur explained his commitment to following Jesus. From his childhood, he was moved by the story of *Pilgrim's Progress*, and from that time determined to walk the 'right' path out of gratitude to Jesus:

> The awareness that because of what Christ had done for me I needed to repay that in committing my life to that. And that story of the Pilgrim's Progress of the right thing and the following of the message, the following of the story of Christ and the leading of God. It all made sense at that point that that was the only appropriate thing to do. I believe that that was where God had led me to that point and that was what was right for me and I haven't changed that in all of that time, yeah.

Rebecca, on the other hand, understands Jesus as a friend. She describes how her relationship to Jesus was basic and integral to her Christian life. She compares Jesus and Paul in a short but revealing statement:

> It's like Jesus was the hippy that told everybody to love everybody, then Paul came along and he was the harder act, kind of thing ... I just love the way he taught, like, what a friend I have in Jesus ... keep Jesus Christ in your heart and you will see his face in everybody you meet.

Rebecca explains further: 'Jesus says there is no law except to love the lord as your God, and to love your neighbour as yourself. And really, I mean, the rest of it is just rules that Paul made to guide the people that he was trying to help.' Rebecca understands Jesus as a friend, a move away from the predominantly patriarchal and legalistic conceptions of the mainstream institutions of Christianity. This Jesus is the *existential Jesus* (Carroll 2007), an 'anti-institutional Jesus who raged against the temple cult, the huge religious industry linking religion and state in a profit-seeking, order-enforcing and grace-denying institution' (Bouma 2007: 1). This distinction between the basic teaching of Jesus and that of the institution of the 'church' was voiced by many of the LGBT Christians involved in this study. The 'church', as many experienced it, represented the exclusive patriarchal and heteronormative institution, while Jesus represents inclusivity and love. Inclusivity and love of Jesus are the moral guidelines upon which some of the LGBT Christians seek to live their lives.

Rebecca, among others, also expresses that besides having a friend in Jesus, she could become like Jesus. This is again a move away from a hierarchical Christianity where one legalistically follows Jesus to a Christianity where one embodies Jesus, or at least walks with Jesus. To be Christian for Rebecca was to be like Jesus: 'I am very rarely a perfect Christian but I think life is about – the term Christian means Christ-like and I want to try and be like that.' She elaborates what this means to her:

> You look at what Jesus did, he sat down and communed and ate with the dregs of society. As such, I'm not saying that we commune with the dregs of society, but it's, but they would be welcome if they were there! [Laughing] I don't consider myself to be any better than the dregs of society because I have done terrible things, [I have] made mistakes and just because I happen to have a job, and I'm not a drug addict, you know, but I mean, life could have been different for me in any way, in any path. Why are we better than anybody else? We're not, because we grew up maybe more blessed.

Anthony explains that whenever confronted with a decision he asks himself: 'What would Jesus say, [I] walk with Jesus too … think God wants us to live like his Son did and that would make this world an amazing place.' He further expresses that to be Christian is not simply about a self-centred concern with whether you are going to heaven or hell:

> Something has happened in the translation of the Bible I'm sure because I think a lot of people turn to the church because they think it's a ticket to another life. The one you've lost, I don't see that. To me that means you are doing your faith for selfish reasons and that doesn't make sense to me.

For him, to be Christ-like is to be honest with others, to love as Jesus loves and to live in healthy monogamous relationships.

Similarly Laura and her partner aspire to be more like Jesus:

> So we went to this Buddhist meditation class and … Buddhists were teaching how to be a better person every week – any person of religion or non-religion could come to the Buddhist meditation class and learn to be peaceful. And we did that for years. But what that taught me was [they didn't intend this] but it taught me to be more like Jesus.

A clue to the importance of the lived experience of following the path of Jesus is given by Ruth, as she explains in a little more depth what that means for her, and its effect upon her life. Ruth distinguishes between Jesus (God who has lived on earth) and God (the Father), in that Jesus has been on earth and can therefore understand the journey as she (and humans in general) have experienced it. She described an embodied being who empathized with the earthly struggles and temptations of humans:

> I wanted to believe in a God that has literally walked my path, you know, that has trodden the ground with us human beings, a God who is not separated into some distant heaven, sort of watching us from above, but someone who's walked our way, knows the temptations we have, the struggles we have, the pains we have and also demonstrates what life is about. As far as I'm concerned it's about walking towards life and if you do that – fullness of life, that's justice, integrity and truth.

For Ruth, the fact that Jesus understood the struggle of living an earthly and bodily existence has enabled her to live a life of goodness and integrity. Her horizon of significance is the embodied Jesus, whose example she follows in her life. She understands that her goal of living a life of goodness to the full is enabled through this relationship.

Anthony, Arthur, Rebecca, Ruth and Laura, in common with many of the participants, all aspire to live like Jesus, become like Jesus. This principle guided their life, gave hope and a vision to sustain them. In particular, they stress the desire to be inclusive, to love others, to find inner peace and to live a life of integrity and honesty. The way Jesus lived is the benchmark for their existence, providing a horizon of significance for moral choices. The relationship with Jesus enables these individuals to live a good life of integrity, one that is articulated as 'authentic', and one where they can be true to themselves, fulfilling the parameters of an ethic of authenticity.

This horizon of significance in Jesus's example is empowering precisely when participants experience rejection. Angela, for example, upon being rejected by a friend on account of her same-sex attraction, explains:

> I tried to explain and thought she might change her mind but she didn't – I emailed her and just explained how that made me feel, and that I didn't think that would be what Jesus would do – in terms of equal treatment and discrimination on that basis.

Rejection and loss experienced by these individuals in the course of maintenance of their integrity are often understood as an integral part of the Christian journey of faith (Ritter and O'Neill 1996; O'Brien 2004; Yip 2005). Andrew describes how he can relate to the journey of Jesus: 'Well, there's a whole theology of the down-trodden so that's what Jesus really [preached] … He ate meals with prostitutes and tax collectors.' Jesus epitomizes values he aspires to, treating people with equality and justice. This is the crucial point in the lives of many of the LGBT Christians in this study, who, in their desire to live authentic lives, encountered rejection, often from mainstream Christians, that could be endured when relating this to the life of Jesus, who was rejected and misunderstood. Ruth also relates not just loss, but new life – a new reason to be – to Jesus:

> As far as I'm concerned it's about walking towards life – fullness of life, that's justice, integrity and truth, if you do that you will be a threat to somebody and they'll try to stop you as they did Jesus. And yet this Jesus walks through that and life is restored. Not just restored but appears again because it's lived, you see.

The fullness of life, the new life offered by Jesus, provides deep satisfaction to the individuals in this study. The reflexive religious practice of identifying with Jesus gives meaning precisely because of being outside of the norm, it provides a 'raison d'être' (O'Brien 2004). The individuals' moral goal of living like Jesus, their horizon of significance, is the benchmark for living a meaningful and authentic life. This resonates with Carroll's (2007) existential Jesus, and is a decidedly non-institutional form of religious expression.

Relationship with self and others

Not all the participants articulate a desire to live like Jesus in terms of struggle or rejection. Many simply express the desire to 'do the right thing', most particularly seeking, as Rebecca expresses: 'to love the Lord as your God, and to love your neighbour as yourself'. Participants understand their lives as meaningful and authentic through 'loving your neighbour'.

Anthea, for example, has always felt she was 'able to do good' despite, as she expressed, 'being gay'. Anthea experiences liberation in her new congregation through service. Through the simple act of baking cakes each week for the congregation, and doing the 'call to worship' each month, she feels able to live a meaningful life. She also 'prays for friends at that [MCC] church everyday', and works on becoming a better person at work through prayer. As she explains:

> If I focus and I pray on [issues], I have a much better day because I put my mindset that, okay, God help me today to shut my mouth and not get involved in something … I am starting to get unsettled here, I'm getting angry … I hand it

over as they say, let God deal with it. I'll be surprised when it will work out okay, the unexpected and you're asking God to help you and it will be amazing what happens ... God jobs, I call them.

For Anthea, doing the right thing is living with God in a relationship to the betterment of not only her own, but also others' lives around her. Michael describes how being involved in church services and the community is far more important 'than just being a body on a seat ... I think it's the interaction and the ability to express something of how I see life and how I see Christian experience through what I do'. William reiterates throughout his interview that his life is only meaningful if he contributes beneficially to the lives of others:

> We [he and his partner] are sort of disciples; I'm helping people with their prob-
> lems – just the feeling of listening to them and talking to them is so great. I mean
> we had a customer in her nineties – and she was depressed ... she used to ring
> up for her grocery order and we'd take it on Friday and bring up some fish and
> chips there and have tea there. Every week. We adopted her.

As William sums up: 'So that's life. You help other people.' Doing the right thing, loving your neighbour, based upon his Christian horizon of significance, makes his life meaningful. Being 'a sort of disciple' is a moral guideline that allows him to live according to a higher purpose. The culture of authenticity articulated here through 'being an authentic Christian' is morally productive (Hookway 2013).

Individuals also engage in outreach as a way to 'love your neighbour'. This was practised in various ways, some within an institution and others informally. For example, a long-term member of one MCC explains: 'During the AIDS epidemic here, we were the first people to do anything. We ran a pantry service for people with AIDS ... You know, the pastor at the time put the first HIV victim in his coffin because no-one else would touch him.' Others involved themselves in 'intentional ministry work' at some point in their lives. Luke, for example, describes working at a Catholic-run homeless centre for double-diagnosed individuals with substance abuse and mental illness:

> People with [multiple problems] get rejected from everywhere. It was just a
> surreal experience and we would help these people. And I was twenty-two
> and we were cooking meals for them ... we had to dispense medication to
> them and they would refuse their medication. We were there for about six
> months.

Angela also worked at times in serving doing 'beach mission' with a Christian organization:

> There were a small group of twelve of us from all different churches and we'd go to the beach over Christmas and run a drop in centre for youth over New Year's, basically giving kids a place to hang out and feel loved; if they were drunk we'd feed them and give them a couch. If they wanted to chat about spiritual things we'd be there to chat.

While most participants have at some time involved themselves in outreach, there is debate as to whether this type of service is necessarily authentic. According to Andrew, for example: 'if you're not going out and starting a soup kitchen or going out to convert the world and be very evangelical, being a missionary in that sense, not everybody's born to do that, so [you] don't need to feel guilty in that sense'. To be authentic, for Andrew, is about finding what is right for each individual, the original self, and acting upon that. The key to being an authentic Christian is finding the 'inner truth' for the original self. This 'inner truth' is itself of moral significance. Further, Andrew aims to live according to moral guidelines that are sourced beyond the self, from the Christian God and Jesus.

The horizons of significance which form the backdrop of the moral decisions that participants make are external to themselves. They are a product of the religious habitus and based upon relationships with significant others. These horizons of significance are also contested. In order to make moral judgements that are in accordance with these horizons of significance, the participants often moved away from the teaching of the church as an institution and reverted back to basic church teachings which entail doing the right thing according to God and Jesus. These moral principles involved being honest and showing integrity in relationships, whether sexual, between friends and peers, within congregations and churches or within the wider community. This they see as an authentic way of being Christian. According to Taylor (1991), authenticity makes sense as a moral value when it is constituted in the context of horizons of significance. It is not just an unfettered celebration of self and freedom.

Conclusion

This chapter demonstrates that LGBT Christians seek to live authentic lives through integrating their sexual, religious and gendered selves. All the participants are cognizant of tension between, on the one hand, the religious worldview or habitus of their upbringing, and, on the other hand, their same-sex attraction or gender identity. A small majority experience this tension as internal moral conflict. Through deep reflection and the exercise of individual agency, their religious worldview is questioned and reworked. This is not an arbitrary or hedonistic reworking. Rather, the reworking is a carefully considered and painful process, often accompanied by a deep sense of loss. The participants act according to an ethic of authenticity as they seek an alternative way of being Christian, exercising their faith, remaining within 'socially constructed and communally constrained' horizons of significance (Berger and Ezzy 2007: 121).

LGBT Christians are forced into a reflexive faith as a consequence of being alienated from the heteronormative institution of mainstream Christianity. They respond by developing an individualized faith that is reminiscent of Grace Davie's (1994) 'believing without belonging' and consistent with Melissa Wilcox's (2002) argument that individualism is used to express agency when other options are denied. However, the participants indicate strongly the necessity of a shared faith experience. The shared faith experience contributes fundamentally to the transformation of religious habitus.

The transformation of religious habitus and reworking of moral guidelines is a process that requires time and effort. This process is fundamentally relational and emotional. The following chapters follow the path of the participants as they grapple with their faith and identity and work at integrating their religious worldviews, their same-sex attraction and their gender. Chapters 5 and 6 examine the process of becoming aware of the tension and at times conflict, the initial response to this, and the catalytic stage where relational and emotional factors enable a freedom to discover a new way of being. This is followed by a stage of transformation facilitated by embodied practices, leading to a state of fusion between sexual and religious identities.

Chapter 7 discusses the tension between the queering of religious practices and the resistance of the Christian habitus, especially in terms of gender. Through the desire to be authentic to their sexuality, to their gender and to the Christian faith, the participants queer Christianity and spaces in order to accommodate the seemingly disparate horizons of significance. This queering, however, is restricted and remains to a large degree within the bounds of the institution of Christianity.

Shaken Worlds

Vignette: Matt

I grew up in a Christian home. Both my parents are Christian and [I] have always gone to Sunday school from as young as I can remember. From the time I was around about eight years old, I noticed that what other [boys] in the school playground were feeling for girls, I was feeling for boys. [I thought] it's just a phase; I'll grow out of it (Laughing). I'll just continue on with life and not tell anyone, it's not that important. [It was] not so much an issue until puberty hit. Around the age of twelve or thirteen, my sexual attractions started to become stronger and more pervasive, so became harder and harder to ignore.

I went through a stage where I was trying to force myself to objectify women and to deny my sexuality. I have since found out that what I was doing is one of the most common methods anti-gay psychologists use to try to change the sexuality of their clients. Whenever I would climax, I'd force myself to think of women. I did that for probably about eight years. I found that while I was awake I could control my thoughts but when I fell asleep, same-sex erotic dreams just became stronger and stronger. I was dragging myself around all day because I was absolutely exhausted from erotic dreams all night, and then forcing myself to objectify women whenever I was conscious.

I hadn't told my parents at this stage. When you've been in a church family for so long you do pick up on the sentiments towards gay people. Because it was about me, and something I was struggling with, I was very highly attuned to any talks on same-sex attraction. You certainly pick up on any subtle things that the pastor may say or that your parents may say. It seemed most people had a repulsion towards anyone who was same-sex attracted.

I'd cry myself to sleep every single night. If you could pray the gay away, I would have been straight long ago. There was a huge amount of internal conflict going on. The conflict between what my parents' expectations were, what the church expectations were and me not living up to that internally. I wasn't out to anyone at that stage but I knew I wasn't what I had to be, to be accepted by the church. [I was struggling with this by myself.] I thought I was the only gay in the village.

I knew I couldn't continue on like this so I decided to look at what scripture has to say about being gay. Regardless of what the conclusion was, I had to follow scripture at any cost. I went through my Bible and had a look at all of the, what they call gotcha passages. I looked them all up, found every other translation I could throughout the house, and had a look at those passages.

I found that some of the passages were clearly talking about inappropriate behaviours and others varied greatly on how these gotcha passages were translated. None of them described my situation, having a heart for God, being in close relationship with him, yet finding myself attracted to the same gender. So I put it to one side. I couldn't see how people could come to such firm conclusions and dictate someone's life based on something that didn't fit the situation or that even the Bible translators don't agree on.

Eventually I came into in contact with someone from a small church group that I knew from school. [I was] around about twenty. One of the people that went to that youth group who I developed a close friendship with, ended up telling me he was gay. When he came out to me, I didn't respond terribly favourably. I thought this was something I could deny or change. We had numerous conversations and I could see that even though he was someone who is really weighed down and finds life really hard, there was just this ease about him as far as being gay and being comfortable with it. Whereas I still had this internal turmoil and conflict going on. Some people are particularly mean and get very nasty when they have that internal conflict going on. I don't think I was like that, but I knew it was happening inside – it's just that I wasn't letting it out.

Through this guy I eventually met other people and I was invited along to a youth group for young gay people. It wasn't a Christian group. At this stage I was twenty-three and that's where I met [my partner].

This part of the process involved understanding that scripture is not clear on this topic, meeting other people and seeing perfectly normal gay people, then being comfortable enough to actually go to a meeting and decide this is where I can meet other people struggling with the same thing I was.

I think [there are some people who have a] really, really adverse reaction [to homosexuality] who are using [scripture] as a weapon. [But it] is not as clear as they make it out to be. [It is] almost a reactive response, overcompensating for what they want to be true. People are using this adamantly as a black-and-white condemnation of loving same-gender relationships but this is clearly not evident. It is a misuse of scripture. They are dictating people's lives based on passages that are vague or don't apply to the situation in question. I have since reconciled those scriptures and it is clear they are not referring to relationships such as I have with my partner. I'm now at a point where people cannot use scripture as a weapon against me. I will not tolerate that.

[At that point] I felt really frustrated that this had had such an impact on my life, and it was not a positive impact at all. On the contrary it was quite a negative impact.

I never told dad. My dad died about twelve years ago so I never actually told my dad. Because my dad was my best friend, I wasn't willing to risk that relationship on something that he may be prejudiced about.

From the age of about twenty, I had decided that if someone asked me directly, I would tell them. Mum asked me directly so I came out to my Mum when I was twenty-two. Her response was not at all positive.

Mum said, this house was dedicated to the Lord and I will not have this in my house. But somewhat more impassioned than what I stated (laughing). [She eventually calmed down and] we were both in the house for about another four years. She brought it up quite a bit, only to convince me that what she thought was correct, but I wasn't going to be bullied. Mum did eventually come to accept me as her gay son but that process would take her another fourteen years.

Through work, I connected with some Christian friends of Mum's that I respected very much, who were remarried after both of them having been divorced. Looking at their lives, I could see that their faith was vibrant, their relationship with Christ was of utmost importance in their lives, yet they were still remarried. I looked at a book that one of them gave me concerning divorce and remarriage. This book contained many principles which also applied to my situation. These people really have a solid relationship with Christ, yet they don't take the passages about divorce and remarriage on face value and blindly apply them. So, using that same principle, [I changed how I looked] at scriptures concerning same-sex relationships.

I was still going to the church I grew up in. I had been teaching Sunday school in that church for probably ten years. I moved away from that church when I moved [cities] and moved in [with my partner].

After we moved in together, I started to go to a small church. It amalgamated with another church that was not at all affirming. I had built up relationships in the amalgamated church, so I was prepared not to make this an issue. I don't know everything about these other peoples' lives, and they don't know everything about my life. Whenever they would talk negatively about homosexuality, I was willing to disagree on that point. I just kept quiet. I was the good little minion! Doing what needed to be done.

I had been going to that church for probably about sixteen years, so I was part of the furniture there. Over that period of time, a new pastor was appointed. He had been there for probably ten years. He had a gay brother and was reasonably respectful towards gay people, but a little controlling.

[In the last few years] it became more and more controlling in the church. Whatever the head pastor said, that was law! In conversations I have had where we disagreed, I was certainly put down very quickly.

Among other things happening in the church, there was one occasion where I thought, wow, that's a lot more than being passively anti-gay. That's just downright destructive. At this point, I was vehemently opposed to what they call reparative therapy. Another thing which started me thinking about my future in the church was when the church suddenly decided that they couldn't have any females in leadership over a male. There had been godly women faithfully serving on the leadership team for over ten years. They had been leading Bible Studies, being very positive influences in many people's lives and mentoring others.

I think that was probably the straw that broke the camel's back for me. I guess it was at that point that I knew my days in that church would likely come to an end. After a while I saw the pastor and said, I believe it's time for me to move on.

I had numerous conversations with Mum. She had read a lot of books – both pros and – probably more cons actually (laughing). I had given her a little bit of affirming theological material. The point at which I knew she had come to accept me was when [my partner] and I were up at her place [one] Sunday having dinner. Both Mum and I were in the kitchen and [my partner] was sitting in view over on the lounge. Mum looked across at me, having observed us interacting for the last fourteen years, and said, you really love him, don't you? I said, yes, of course I do. She said, I'm pleased you have him. That was the moment at which I thought, yep, she's okay with us. She's actually okay with us being together. Sigh.

Mum ended up becoming one of my stronger advocates. She'd tell me "It's interesting, you'd be amazed at how many people I speak to that start off saying, oh what about these gay people, then say something negative." Mum would say, "Well, I'm not so sure about that." Mum would start to stick up for gay people and said, "You wouldn't believe the number of people who would eventually say, you know I think gay people have been treated poorly by the church."

My standpoint is, I am primarily a Christian, I am a child of God who just happens to be gay. Not the other way around.

I had been looking for gay-friendly churches for quite some time and couldn't find anything. There was an MCC church which we attended once but it felt like we didn't really fit in. It seemed to be more about rituals and liturgy than it was about Christianity and a relationship with God. That was my experience of it. I had just come out of a strongly evangelical church and so I still had a strong evangelical bent. I was after something more evangelical. After a little bit of searching we found [an MCC] which was very Christ centric. That was what I was after. My partner liked it. So here we are.

The worship is good [at this MCC]. I would see the leaders sitting around in a circle praying before service. It just felt like home. It's a four-hour round trip for us to go so we only make it about once a month or sometimes a little more often. It's quite a commitment for us to attend.

When I was first going to [this MCC] some of the leaders arranged to come up and have lunch with us. We made connections and met someone who had just moved into the area. It wasn't long before we had a Bible study group running which has now grown to about ten people. It's obviously an affirming Bible study.

I think the point at which I had totally reconciled my faith and sexuality was when I wrote Bible studies on the 'gotcha' passages. On top of all the reading and research I had done previously, I spent about thirty hours researching every single passage, delving into the original language and putting studies together. It was through that research that at the end of it I thought, this is it, I'm certain of my relationship with Christ and I don't need to research this any longer.

I have reached that tipping point where I'm not going back. I have totally reconciled this and nothing can send me back to that place of self-loathing. I'm okay with me and I'm a lot more out to people now. The vast majority of my friends know that I'm gay and know of my relationship with [my partner]. Some people have had considerable difficulty with that, others have been perfectly okay with it. For me it's just not an issue any more. I know there are a lot of people in the [Bible study] home group that still need that regular affirmation. I am just at a point where it has been resolved and is now laid to rest for me.

My heart is for people who believe the lie that they can't be gay and Christian and as a result discard their faith. Mum eventually came to the point where she believed that God allowed me to be gay so I could be an example to show that you can be gay and Christian, and to support other gay people in their faith.

Introduction

> I'm still going through the process. I'm still struggling with (the concept of sin) ... still wrestling with it. I am still going through the process ... It's hard when you've had all of these set concepts of things built up over a long time, I was at my old church for fourteen years, and then suddenly everything's shaken. It's taken a long time to trust again, and to learn how to trust God again, and I still struggle with that sometimes. I've gone back to the beginning, I'm trying to figure out sin, do I agree with it, what is it, what does the Bible say and how do I trust that ... it's a long slow process. (Angela)

The previous chapter demonstrated that the LGBT Christians seek to find ways to live authentic lives, both authentic to their sexuality and gender and authentic to their religious worldview. In the quote above, Angela describes how she 'wrestles with the concept of sin'. LGBT Christians negotiate ways to be Christian within the context of the growing awareness of the tension between their sexuality and their religious worldview. Angela's world has been shaken, and she is entering a self-conscious 'long slow process' to rebuild this world. Chapters 5 and 6 look in detail at the processes that LGBT Christians follow when seeking to integrate their religious worldviews and same-sex attraction, and to reach a state where they feel they are being authentic.

In order to describe the process of integrating Christianity and same-sex attraction, we rework a conceptual map of a process developed by Denise Levy and Patricia Reeves (2011), which is based upon their qualitative study of the experience of lesbian, gay and queer Christians in the United States. Levy and Reeves describe a five-stage process of internal conflict resolution, with each stage influenced by contextual and personal factors. The stages are: awareness of conflict; initial response; catalyst; working through the conflict; and resolution. Chapters 6 and 7 critique and enhance this conceptual map to reflect the findings from our interviews with twenty-eight LGBT Christians. Chapter 5 covers the first two stages of awareness of tension, and initial response. Chapter 6 discusses the latter stages: the catalyst and working though the conflict. The final stage, integration, is the fusion of the sexual and religious self, the authentic self, and is discussed in Chapter 7.

Internally experienced conflict between sexual and religious identities does not always exist. In the present study, eleven of the twenty-eight interviewees report no internal conflict despite being aware of tension between Christian normative beliefs and same-sex attraction. While the awareness of tension is universal to all participants, internal conflict is not necessarily engendered by this. This in itself is noteworthy, as most studies report conflict as if it were inevitable (Rodriguez 2009). Wilcox (2003) and Yip (1997b), however, note that Catholics in their studies had less difficulty in recognizing dogma as outdated and irrelevant.

In our revision of Levy and Reeve's process, the first stage is renamed, 'awareness of tension'. We also question the emphasis on 'religious beliefs' as the source of tension or conflict. For our participants, the source of tension or conflict is based upon a more holistic conceptual understanding or the 'religious worldview'. The religious worldview is built upon religious habitus, which includes but is not limited to cultural understandings, dispositions and emotional responses. This is not to discount the cognitive and theological understandings but to suggest that cognitive factors are integrally linked to emotional and relational factors. Emotional factors are primary in distinguishing those who were conflicted from those who were not. Sara Ahmed's (2004) conception of emotionality provides an excellent framework to analyse the emotional factors central to the experience of the LGBT Christians.

Two categories also need to be added to Levy and Reeve's second stage of conflicted individuals: one, a denial of same-sex attraction, which among participants in our study was a temporary experience, and second, a decrease in religious involvement, which was also temporary.[1] Denial of same-sex attraction was common to six participants and a decrease in religious involvement was an initial response shared by fourteen individuals. This chapter focuses on these two initial stages of this process: the awareness of the tension and the initial response to this, as illustrated in Figure 5.1 below.

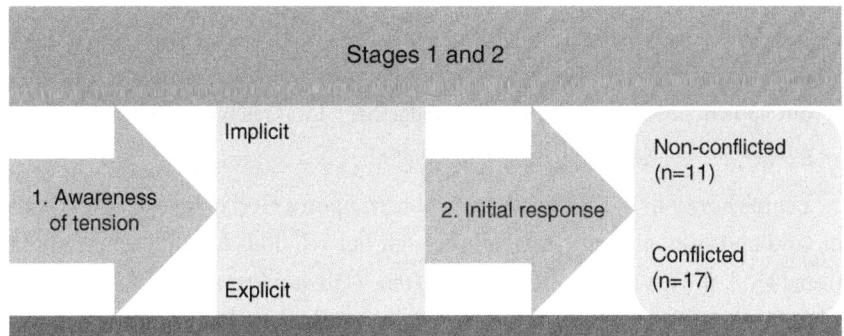

Figure 5.1 Process of resolution of tension – stages 1 and 2 (adapted from Levy and Reeves 2011)

Non-conflicted individuals

> As far as God, I don't think God has a problem because no disasters have hap-
> pened to me because I'm gay; I can still do good no matter what I am. So I don't
> really have that conflict. (Anthea)

In common with eleven participants, Anthea feels no moral conflict between her
same-sex attraction and her religious worldview. Some of these eleven participants did experience other forms of conflict with churches, families or significant others. However, they did not feel internally conflicted. Interestingly, this
lack of conflict is a product of their deep confidence in their religious worldview
that successfully enables them to negotiate their same-sex attraction. Anthea, for
example, feels she is an authentic Christian by 'doing good', and that her sexuality
is not 'a problem for God'. Her moral imperatives – 'doing good' and 'embracing
the love of God' – lead to a love of self. She experiences God's love, a love which
translates into a love for her own authentic identity, including her sexuality. Put
another way, Christianity provides relationships with significant others, a horizon of significance and a deeply embedded habitus that enables these individuals
to confidently negotiate the tensions generated by their same-sex attraction.

Only one participant was brought up with explicit acceptance of his sexuality and was so emotionally supported by his minister father that he cannot
recall ever feeling conflicted due to his same-sex attraction. The others recall
events or relationships with significant others that equipped them to deal with
any tension they experienced. These relationships, which could be with family
or God and Jesus, elicit feelings of love and acceptance. Laura, for example,
explains:

> Well, I think Sunday school gave me a very very good relationship with Jesus so
> I felt very happy, very friendly with having Jesus in my life. When I joined the
> fellowship it was more God; so as a teenager it was more God as a protector and
> omnipotent power but no fear and no judgement. I was really fortunate; I had no
> guilt, shame, fear associated with my religion.

Laura's horizons of significance were based upon a God of love, an experience
of God and Jesus that was formed through her religious habitus. At a foundational level, those who felt little conflict *knew God as a loving God*. The emotions
of guilt, shame and fear were not associated with their God or their religion.
Their religious worldview encompassed these positive emotions, and resultant
horizons of significance were based upon a God of love where loving the self –
the whole self – becomes a moral mandate.

Awareness of tension – explicit and implicit messages

Despite being non-conflicted, all of these individuals were explicitly or implicitly made aware of normative Christian attitudes to same-sex attraction. For example, Rebecca was brought up in a conservative Protestant church where she received the explicit teaching that homosexuality was wrong: 'I was homophobic in the [church], I disagreed with homosexuality, because that was what I was taught, that people that were gay were wrong.'

The majority also reported implicit messages that same-sex attraction was unacceptable. William, for example, an elderly male who reports no internal conflict, explains that he had never come out as same-sex attracted in any mainstream church (or to his family), remarking: 'I was very well known and if I'd made a move [to come out as gay] I'd be in trouble because I was involved in the Anglican church and the Methodists, the Baptists.' William knew his boundaries and, in order to maintain his non-conflicted position, remained within them (and still does). He is clearly aware of the tension between his sexuality and the church doctrine and chooses not to challenge it. He also explains that as he respected his father a lot, 'I didn't want to let them down. I kept it to myself … it was hush-hush.' Although William expresses no internal conflict, he remains aware of the attitude his religious father may have had towards him.

There are two major responses to these perceived tensions: negotiation of church doctrine and disregard of doctrine (see Figure 5.2). The negotiation of church doctrine, often described by the participants as 'wrestling', is a filtering of the information based upon relationships, upbringing and worldview. These non-conflicted individuals were able to wrestle with doctrine in ways

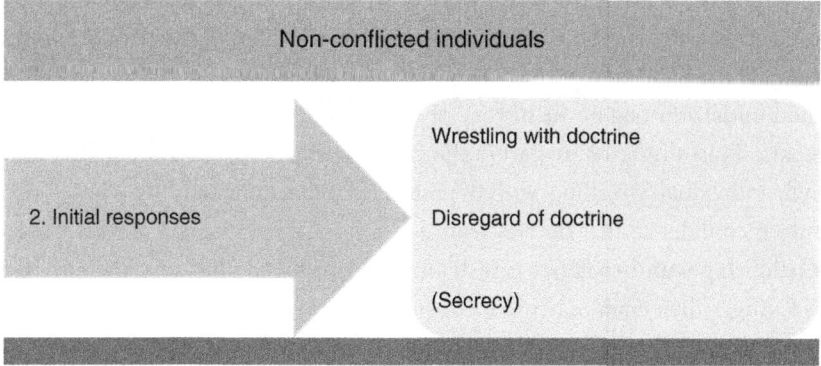

Figure 5.2 Initial responses – non-conflicted individuals (adapted from Levy and Reeves 2011)

that enabled acceptance of their sexuality. Many viewed church doctrine as flawed, or contextual and historical, and were able to reinterpret it. This ability is documented by Yip (2005: 49) who terms this 'theological capital'. The second response of non-conflicted individuals is to disregard church doctrine.

Initial responses – wrestling with church doctrine

Despite reporting little or no conflict, for many participants theology is important. Their religious worldview, habitus and personal relationships equip them with tools to 'wrestle' with Christian doctrine. Ruth, for example, now in her eightees, explains that at the age of fourteen she asked her minister father about why hell should be so cruel:

> And he said, so if there is a hell like that, what sort of God does it make your God? Would you like that God as your Father? Would you like to be a parent like this God, sending people to hell and burning? Well, think again because if that is what you believe transforms your God into someone who is cruel, and whom you couldn't possibly respect or like, then think again.

Ruth's religious worldview contains a God who primarily loves and cares, rather than judges and condemns. Her religious habitus upon which her horizons of significance are based is influenced by the relationship with her devoutly religious father, who instilled in her an understanding of God as loving. She was also empowered to question 'the Bible and "wrestle with it" and find the great themes in there about who God is'. Her religious worldview is such that she can wrestle with theology, even while her fundamental horizon of significance remains unchanged. As she says: 'There is an evolving of theology.' When faced with those who argue biblical 'truths' (that homosexuality is an abomination), she points out that the Bible also says slaves should obey their masters, and that Solomon had many wives. In addition to this view of scripture, Ruth has a good understanding of the history of same-sex attracted individuals, and comments: 'I just think we are part of the great diversity of God.' Despite this seemingly individual 'wrestling' with the Bible, her self-understanding is based upon a deep confidence that derives from her religious habitus and worldview. Her relationship with her father is instrumental in allowing her to experience God as loving, which enables her to be open to the scripture and seek her own truth.

Another participant, Paul, also experienced no internal conflict. From his earliest memories, his religious environment was embracing of his sexuality. He consciously connects his lack of conflicting feelings with his upbringing. Paul, now in his sixtees, was raised in a family where both parents were strongly religious (his father was also a minister) and who loved and supported him and never condemned him for his sexuality. He explains: 'My Mum and Dad were very, very supportive and encouraging me to be who I was and there was never, from their point of view, there was never any disappointment.' They supported him in 'finding his true self', his authentic self. The emotional bind of disappointment or the threat of hell was not an aspect of his life. This enables him to understand and appraise theology without fearful emotions. As he expresses it:

> Because I had a real connectedness with scripture I was guided by those who had done studies in this area, and say, yeah, I can agree with that. So I never had a conflict with scripture. As many people who don't have a real touch, a connectedness with scripture they can't get out their minds, what they call Bible truths ... it's not a Bible truth, it's a truth of man!

Paul describes how his 'connectedness' with scripture allows him to remain open to what he understands as higher truth. Both Ruth and Paul were brought up within a liberal religious environment, where their relationships with their fathers, both ministers, provided them with confidence to approach the scriptures free from negative emotions. This enables them to search for new meanings in the scriptures and to concentrate on the loving nature of God.

Others brought up in more conservative churches, too, recognize church doctrine as contextually interpreted, unimportant in relation to the love of God and Jesus. As Victoria says, 'the theology is good and solid and sound and strong but people's interpretation of that is the bit that's flawed'. Interpretation is also the issue for Rebecca, as she explains:

> You see I don't have an issue with being gay, in regards to the fact God loves me. I know that. And I know he loves me. And I believe he loves everybody and I believe that – I have an unshakeable faith – that it is not wrong.... To be honest with you, I just knew [that the Bible could be interpreted in different ways] ... I'd grown up my whole life with a set of rules that the [church] laid down; you have to wear skirts to church – it doesn't say anywhere in the Bible you have to wear skirts ... women can't talk, and we're [her denomination] one tiny per cent of the Christian community. Does that mean everybody else is wrong? So the whole Bible is really up to interpretation, isn't it?

As far as Rebecca is concerned, 'the most important thing ... in the Bible is that Jesus says: "There is no law except to love the lord as your God and to love your neighbour as yourself."' Rebecca provides a good example of a person who easily sidesteps conservative biblical understandings, saying that 'the whole Bible is really up to interpretation'. In common with other non-conflicted individuals, biblical passages condemning homosexuality held no emotional power for Rebecca.

Bible verses focusing on the love of God and Jesus were a guiding mantra for many who reported no conflict. Similar to Ruth, Rebecca and Paul, others who were non-conflicted were able to sift through church doctrine and seek a core message of the Bible. As Lynne, a member of MCC in her fiftees expresses: 'You know, God created us in His own image and you love your neighbour as yourself.' She continues: 'I can't be doing wrong here, he loves me whether I'm gay, lesbian, whether I've got, you know, half a leg or whether I've got four eyes – it doesn't really matter. He's still going to love me because he created me that way.' Her emphasis is on the essential understanding of her sexuality that reconfirms her identity as an authentic being, one created by God.

Peter, also a member of MCC in his seventies, takes a more aggressive stance: he recalls that when he was a young man, he heard a pastor in his conservative Protestant church say that 'homosexuality is an abomination'. At the time he thought: 'He obviously doesn't understand it. Obviously ... you don't understand what you fear.' Although aware of the tension, he explains: 'I was able to rationalize ... I probably was a strong person both emotionally and intellectually, I was strong enough to just able to look at this as nonsense.' For Peter the words 'homosexuality is an abomination' were not, as described by Ahmed (2004: 10), emotionally 'sticky'. He could understand that fear was the basis for such a proclamation.

All of the non-conflicted individuals for whom doctrine was relatively important, yet easily rationalized, demonstrate the possession of Yip's (2005: 49) concept of 'theological capital'. They exhibit the ability to individualize their faith as documented by Kirkman (2001), Wilcox (2003) and Bates (2005) among others.

Initial responses – disregarding church doctrine

Other non-conflicted individuals were not really interested in doctrine per se, and emphasize that they know God's love and that they would never be rejected. The loving God is also an unchanging element in a changing and unstable life. Victoria, for example, says:

> God didn't influence it, God didn't make it better, God didn't make it worse ... but God was always in my life and always fully accepting, fully loving ... God was real to me in the sense of – a comforting sense ... nothing could break the link.

Victoria continues: 'The part I struggled in terms of sexuality was always about people. So God was never an issue but the people behind God had always been an issue ... God was greater than my sexuality.' Victoria felt emotionally confident throughout the process of coming to terms with her sexuality. Victoria's partner Laura also says: 'I had no problem with my sexuality at all. I felt that I was really glad I'd carried God, a little flame of God, in my heart.' God was always there, and formed an unchanging horizon of significance. She also adds that she 'knew they [her and her partner] hadn't abandoned God'.

Mary also had no interest in theology and took her own experience as her guide. After coming out of a violent marriage, anti-gay sentiment had no impact on her. When asked if she experienced conflict regarding her sexual identity and religious beliefs, she answered simply: 'Not to myself, no! I only had to answer to myself.' This confidence in her inner voice, that she was okay with her God indicates the power of this relationship, the internal connection to her authentic self.

Others also felt they were able to remain true to their God through doing the right thing, and that God didn't judge them for their sexuality. William explains, when talking of himself and his partner: 'We are sort of disciples; I'm helping people here at the moment with problems ... So that's life. You help people. And that's what life's about, I'm sure.'

Ruth, Rebecca, Paul, Lynne and Peter all wrestle with church doctrine confidently because they are able to confidently engage in contextualizing biblical interpretation. This confidence often has its sources in historical relationships that shaped deeply embedded emotional understandings of their relationship with God. They therefore find ways of encompassing their sexuality within their religious worldview. In contrast, Victoria, Laura, Mary and William disregard church doctrine. They concentrate on their own individualized and personal religious experience of a deinstitutionalized experiential God and Jesus, who is real to them (Carroll 2007).

Conflicted individuals

My mum was Church of England, yeah, [we] went to a church where he [the minster] was real hell-fire and brimstone – they were really, really harsh. So gay and lesbian was just out! Gays are not normal! ... Really strong views in my family! (Annie)

Annie typifies the experience of the seventeen participants who were conflicted. She was thrown into moral conflict, a conflict she processed over years. She was convinced that her sexuality was wrong to the extent that she remained unable to form any intimate relationships with either sex until her mid-forties. The power of this conflict is starkly documented by Sandi Dubowski (2001) in his film *Trembling before G–D*, and in studies such as those by Barton (2010) and Hansen and Lambert (2011).

Those who were conflicted describe an experience of seemingly irreconcilable difference between their religious worldview and their same-sex attraction. This conflict caused deep emotional discomfort and moral questioning. Some people, such as Annie, were explicitly informed of this conflict, while others 'picked it up' as implicit messages. The feelings and thoughts that drove this conflict were part of their religious worldview and habitus.

The transgendered participants also describe internal conflict upon becoming aware of their same-sex attraction. Gender transitioning in both cases was a larger hurdle which came at a later stage. The most common conflict was a product of their sexuality being understood as morally wrong according to their religious worldview. Angela, a woman in her twenties, reported that as soon as she initially acted upon her same-sex attraction with a fellow Christian, she felt immediate conflict:

> One night she kissed me, it felt really right and natural, but at the same time I had a Christian hymn going on in my head 'Because the sinless saviour died, my sinful soul is counted free, for God, the just is satisfied to look on him and pardon me.'

Angela continues on saying: 'We both went and read the Bible and we both found we couldn't do it, homosexuality was wrong.' She could not initially resolve this conflict between her same-sex attraction and her religious worldview. Angela and others frame this conflict in terms of sin. Emma, for example, questioned for years whether she was doing the right thing, whether her faith was being jeopardized, whether she was guilty of this sin. When Liz and her partner met, both struggled: 'We were both in this dilemma, well, is it right, or is it wrong, and if we're not supposed to feel this way, why isn't God taking the feelings away?'

For some this was an emotionally traumatic and a fearful awakening, as Matt describes:

> There was an awful lot of conflict there. There was a conflict between who I am as a child of God, and who I am sexually attracted to, which I have tried – I am trying desperately to change but it's not happening and I'd pray myself to sleep, I'd cry myself to sleep every single night.

The majority held a deeply embedded religious worldview within which same-sex attraction was evil, sinful, immoral and/or unnatural. For conflicted individuals, this understanding of same-sex attraction engendered an intense emotional and/or cognitive conflict when confronted by their growing awareness of their same-sex attraction. Words from scripture and church, and responses from significant others towards same-sex attraction, provoke powerful emotions. Through continual repetition, the words that describe same-sex attraction as sinful become sticky with negative emotion (Ahmed 2004: 12).

'Bible truths' were often central to the religious worldview of conflicted individuals. Bible truths were understood as the seven 'gotcha' (as named by one participant) passages that are commonly used to condemn homosexuality. One such passage from the Old Testament uses the word 'abomination', a powerful, emotionally sticky word: 'You shall not lie with a male as with a woman. It is an abomination' (Lev. 18:22 RSV). As one participant explains, it was not until he could detach from the emotional hold of this word 'abomination' that he could begin to face his dilemma as a same-sex attracted Christian.

Heteronormative attitudes which describe the 'natural heteronormative order', based on Bible verses such as Gen. 1:18–25[2] are another problem they experience. Some participants were informed explicitly by significant others of the 'sin' of homosexuality. Others discerned implicit messages from society, church, peers and family. The words had a powerful hold upon conflicted individuals. They reinforced distinctions, separating the 'other' from the normal. These words were used to divide the legitimate from the illegitimate, imparting the message that same-sex attraction is evil and wrong.

Awareness of tension – explicit messages

Of the seventeen conflicted participants, nine reported that the pastor, other church members, friends or religious parents explicitly maintained that homosexuality was against church doctrine, or expressed hostility towards it. Luke, a pastor in his thirties, who was brought up in an evangelical, conservative denomination, describes:

> We used to have prayer meetings against Mardi Gras, and we believed that the Sydney Mardi Gras was like Sodom and Gomorrah happening again. And that led to God's judgement – the world was about to end … it's now not just the fact that there are lots of people who are gay – they're actually celebrating in public. We've now come to the point where our culture is beyond redemption.

Luke adds: 'So when I came out obviously I had a pretty big shadow side to deal with', indicating his clear awareness of this conflict.

The issue for Andrew, in his twenties, was the heteronormative assumptions of Christianity (and the wider society). He was not concerned about the 'Bible truths' the 'gotcha' passages that condemned homosexuality as 'immoral'. These were little problem for him. He explains that as he discussed his same-sex attraction with church counsellors: 'It was a case of immediately, well, going back to theology and Genesis. Adam and Eve [male and female] and that's the rightful way.' Rather, the heteronormative ideal stressing that homosexuality was 'unnatural' held more power over him: 'I think the hardest theological thing ... is questioning the heteronormative approach in the Bible, about a man and a woman.'

A small number of the participants were informed of religious doctrine explicitly condemning homosexuality through the church, a message that was passed on through religious family members. The ensuing conflict was powerful. Nickie, in her fifties, was always and continues to be informed by her mother that 'your sexuality is going to send you to hell because it's evil'. This experience is similar to that described in Bernadette Barton's (2010) study of gay and lesbian individuals in 'Bible Belt' of the United States. Religion-based homophobia permeated through all social institutions and general attitudes causing internalized homophobia. The individuals she interviewed expressed feelings of 'self-loathing' and fears of hell and damnation.

More commonly, messages from churches and families were subtle, although explicit, and, for individuals, deeply emotionally disturbing. Matt, for example, describes a growing awareness of his position, not restricted to doctrinal rights and wrongs:

> So, when you've been in church, been in a church family for so long, you do pick up on little bits a pieces and of course, because it was about me, and something I was struggling with, I was very highly attuned to any talks on same sex attraction ... and you do pick up on – in your church community, you pick up on ... repulsion for same-sex attraction. You certainly pick up on any subtle things your pastor may say, or that your parents may say.

Matt describes how, for him, the church and his religious family portrayed homosexuality as 'repulsive'. The word 'repulsive' was sticky and powerfully emotive, as is the shame it generated. Matt also realized that he was a disappointment to his parents: 'The conflict was also between what my parent's expectations were, what the church expectations were, and not living up to that internally.'

This is described in a similar way by Anthony, when asked why he experienced such internal conflict at his own recognition of being gay: 'It was more about an attitude thing – like my father's reaction to people on telly. I don't hear my father say spiteful things about anything but you could just see the distaste and disgust.' He further describes his feelings:

> When anything to do with gay came on I heard these really negative things. My dad is a mild man really but the vehemence that came with those comments; I'd sit up and suddenly feel like a two-year-old and shrink.

Anthony articulates how he felt shame as a product of his father's 'distaste and disgust'. Similar to Matt, Anthony responds to the attitude of his father with shame, an emotion deeply embedded in embodied experience that initially made dealing with the conflict an impossibility. Luke, Andrew, Annie and Nickie understood same-sex attraction as associated with 'hellfire and brimstone', 'hell', 'Sodom and Gomorrah' and as 'unnatural' – extremely powerful words, also sticky with emotion. The negativity of these responses to same-sex attraction 'stick' to a person's self-understanding. The deeply embedded nature of their religious habitus also deeply embeds the emotions of repulsion, distaste, disgust and shame in relation to their same-sex attraction.

Awareness of tension – implicit messages

Unspoken messages were no less powerful in shaping self-evaluations. Shame was also an emotion felt, for example, by Arthur, who remained within his mainstream church for many years while not being open about his sexuality. He made no mention of theological truths, yet expressed simply that each time he walked into a church, he would be saying to himself: 'But God, you know [that I am gay].' He was responding to the implicit heteronormative Christian worldview that he was violating, a violation that evoked emotional discomfort and shame.

Churches and families also sent implicit but very clear messages of their attitudes towards same sex attraction. Liz, for example, who married into a conservative protestant denomination, reports: 'I'd grown up [in the church] thinking that homosexuality was just wrong but which was never discussed.' Paul, a pastor who was brought up in the Methodist church, explains that homosexuality in the 1950s and 1960s 'was either not spoken of at all, or was accepted in as much as, Fred or George is one of those and looked after the flowers or played the organ ... that was okay as long as you never pushed your boundaries further ... and if you did, then very, very clearly it was made evidenced to you, it was just not welcome'. The implicit message was strongly reinforced through invisible boundaries. He further explains that he had experienced a change in attitudes in the 1970s in that the church had become more extreme after the gay liberation movement arose, saying:

> It got worse [in the 1970s] – then you saw the churches actually become quite active in their opposition to homosexuals and actually condoning behaviour such as shock therapy ... many of our older members have gone through that in an attempt to de-gay them.

Once these implicit and invisible boundaries were challenged, the church responded by explicitly enforcing the boundaries.

The moral dilemma individuals faced was a product of a religious worldview and habitus that did not encompass their same-sex attraction. Their horizons of significance and shared common moral precepts excluded same-sex attraction as a choice. This generated a profound conflict between religiously generated emotional responses to same-sex attraction, and the growing recognition of the reality of their own same-sex attraction. For some, this was encapsulated in words such as 'abomination', 'disgust', 'distaste' and 'disappointment', causing feelings of shame and repulsion. These individuals experienced distressing internal conflict. Many could not love God, could not feel loved by God and could not love the self. They were also not able to be honest to themselves or others regarding their sexuality.

The conflicted participants experienced the second stage differently from those who were non-conflicted. There are four main initial responses to the perceived tension. These are: (1) denial of same-sex attraction often accompanied by an increased religious involvement; (2) secrecy; (3) a decrease in religious involvement with or without relocation and (4) depression and self-harm (see Figure 5.3 below).

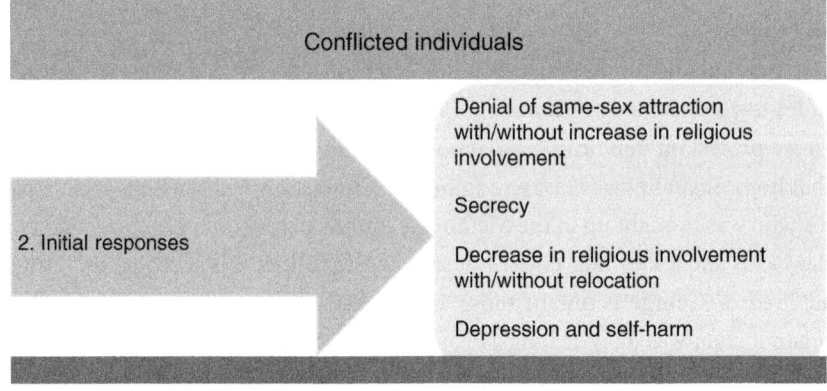

Figure 5.3 Initial responses – conflicted individuals (adapted from Levy and Reeves 2011)

Initial response – denial of same-sex attraction with/without increased involvement with religion (adapted from Levy and Reeves 2011)

In the initial stages of the growing awareness of same-sex attraction, the religious worldview of the LGBT Christians' upbringing remained powerful. The denial of same-sex attraction was a way for the deeply religious individuals to avoid confrontation and to continue living according to their religious horizons of significance. Significant others – in particular, parents – were extremely important, and denying same-sex attraction was an attempt to 'be in the norm', as Nova describes it. The religious worldview of their upbringing retained its dominance over the LGBT Christians, as they sought to come to terms with their sexuality. This response is typical of the cohort, all of whom came from strongly religious families or for whom religion was deeply important. Often relationships with significant others such as church and family were all-encompassing.

Angela, for example, tried to deny her same-sex attraction by dating men, saying: 'I was committed to the church and being straight ... I wanted to feel "normal". Similarly Natalie, in her early twenties, tried to deny her attraction to women: 'I always said to myself, oh no, you're not. You just think you are. And so I have boyfriends and stuff – but it never really means anything.' Sylvia also initially lived a normative life, marrying, but soon realized she was not being true to herself, that this was inauthentic. She describes her wedding:

> Can you imagine what it's like to be an actor at your own wedding? You're happy you're getting married. You're quite wanting to be there but you feel like you're playing a role. That's what I was doing. I was playing the heterosexual role. I wasn't being me.

Many reported feeling 'different' at a very young age and that they quickly learnt to 'forget' this. When Luke told his parents at the age of five that he was going to marry a man, he 'had it drummed out pretty quickly' and he soon 'forgot' about it. Victoria, who also realized very young she was same-sex attracted, explains:

> So as I grew up I'm one of those gay women that from the moment I can remember have always sensed that I was gay ... I guess it was a bit compartmentalized so that sexuality bit I put that into a box and tried to deal with it as best I could but it was really just in a box that I really pushed away.

While not forgetting, she set that aspect of herself to the side to deal with later. Emma, now in her thirties, was brought up in a fundamentalist Anglican church and remembers watching Sy Rogers[3] videos as a teenager. She says: 'I completely internalized that [that homosexuality is against God's wishes] and also just thought it was a no-go zone [her being attracted to women].' She initially responded to her same-sex attraction by denying it, and, rather than dating men, remained celibate for many years.

Denial of same-sex attraction was often accompanied by an increase in involvement with church/religion. By becoming more involved with religion, individuals were trying to 'be right with God'. Emma, while remaining celibate, was 'just single-mindedly involved in Christian activity'. Angela, who recommitted to God after her first experience in a same-sex relationship, focused on her relationship to God, as well as church activity:

> I felt so close to God in a way – it was a time of purity and coming back, so to speak … I didn't rate many sins like it. This sin was so intense and so shameful in both mine and the church's eyes that for me to let it go I felt the depth of his grace and I felt so close because of that … I think that really motivated me to throw myself in to service and giving and being in Christian community.

Luke also recalls his increased engagement with his religion. Although he actually decreased his activity with the church he was brought up in, he became intensely involved with theological reflection, trying to reach, as he describes it, the state of 'moral perfection':

> My religion became more intense. It was like that struggle that I was going through, the stronger the need to recognize who I was, the stronger I would fight against it.

Emma, Angela and Luke were all brought up in intensely religious families, and could not and did not want to walk away from religion. Their intense moral searching and struggle to find 'purity' and 'perfection' indicates the power of their religious habitus and the connected heteronormative horizons of significance. At this point, they felt they were violating these and in response worked harder to prove their worth to God.

Prayer was a form of religious devotion that often increased as an initial response to the internal conflict that individuals were thrown into. Judy and Annie, a couple, spent many weekends away in order to pray to ask God to help them solve their dilemma, as related by Judy: 'You know, we are praying and waiting for something to come down.' Liz, a minister who became involved with a woman after a family tragedy, prayed constantly for the first three or four months, thinking that 'homosexuality was just wrong'.

Matt realised he was gay after reaching puberty. For the following eight years he tried to deny that he was gay and initially attempted to resolve his dilemma through prayer. In his words: 'I'd pray myself to sleep, I'd cry myself to sleep every single night. You know if you could pray the gay away, I would have been straight long ago.' In addition to trying to 'pray the gay away', he remained celibate for this period of time. Luke, Emma, Angela, Judy and Annie, Liz and Matt all intensified their relationship with religion, some through religious activity, and some through prayer.

For some, their same-sex attraction was undeniable. These individuals kept their same-sex attraction a secret as a safe way to continue living with significant others and to continue living according to the religious worldview of their upbringing. In fact, all participants, whether conflicted or not, used this strategy at some point as they grappled with the relational and/or moral consequences of their same-sex attraction.

Initial response – secrecy

Secrecy was an initial response often used as a positive management strategy by both non-conflicted and conflicted individuals. It was maintained selectively and for differing reasons. Some kept their same-sex attraction secret for years, and a few still remain not yet 'out' to family members and/or other individuals at churches or in workplaces. Secrecy often gave space to reflect upon the growing awareness of their same-sex attraction. Liz and her partner, for example, who didn't disclose a newly formed relationship to their families, report that 'it took three or four months to work it through'. In this time they wanted space to question their feelings and how they stood 'with God'. Secrecy was also utilized to avoid possible ensuing conflict with family, church and friends, and to protect both themselves and significant others from emotional harm.

In their churches, most participants initially remained quiet about their same-sex attraction. Anthea, who felt the need to be in a church environment, says that 'I just kept going to the Anglican Church and hiding'. Similarly Michael, who recognized his same-sex attraction while being married to a minister's daughter, attended church each Sunday morning and then secretly attended MCC each Sunday evening once he had 'quietly' located it. Arthur also articulates this management strategy clearly when he describes that when he kept attending church because of his mother, 'it was very much a big secret and it stayed a secret. It stayed a secret till I left there and went to [another city]'.

For most people the risk of being open was too great. Emma belonged to an extremely conservative church that required young people to confess their sexual sins. She explains: 'When I was ... confessing sexuality [my same-sex attraction] was one thing I would never, ever have let out, even though it was something I knew was in me.' In this church there was the threat of excommunication should anyone 'confess' to same-sex attraction. Judy, who continued with church attendance, explains: 'I was like, I'm uncomfortable there ... I'm going to get busted, they're going to come to me and say, what are you doing to Annie [her partner] to corrupt her?'

One participant, Peter, didn't bother to talk about his same-sex attraction, as he had little respect for the discriminatory attitude of the church he was brought up in. When asked by a minister why he attended his church very little, he responded: 'Because I find the church very discriminatory. You treat single people like second-class citizens.' His secrecy was based more upon his disregard for the principles of the church he had been brought up in.

When participants were open about their same-sex attraction, the response of the church and family varied. Some churches remained adamantly and openly opposed to homosexuality. Most churches were tolerant but not accepting. Many participants were unable to take part in any activities or were treated as if they had an illness. Emma, for example, was unable to lead youth group, even for one session, when she was open about her same-sex attraction. Natalie, in her twenties, remembers being called aside during her youth group with a Protestant church: 'and they're like, we need to pray for you. You can be cured of this.'

The greatest risk for most of the participants was the loss of family. They were afraid of hurting or causing disappointment for them, or the experience of withdrawal of love from them. William, for example, never disclosed his same-sex attraction to his family:

> I was very proud of my parents. My father had a good position. He was head waiter ... He used to go off at night-time or during the day in his red striped pants and tails and he used to have a motor bike. He used to tuck his tails up in his coat ... and I respected them a lot and I didn't want to let them down.

He did not want to disappoint them and remained quiet about his sexuality until his father's death. Similarly Andrew, Rebecca and Annie are still not out to family. This is particularly painful for Rebecca, who reports: 'I love them and I've got a very close family and that's the thing – they are so up in my life that – wouldn't it be so much easier to be straight, because why not live the easy life!'

Arthur, who also never revealed his same-sex attraction to his father, expresses: 'I won't push issues like that. I don't think it's wise for me – I don't have the strength to deal with that sort of rejection.' Anthony spent most of his life compartmentalizing and keeping his sexuality secret. He describes that: 'I'd go overseas; I'd go on with a gay life and have a great old time. And a few of my close friends I've told but I've lived quite a closeted life.' At the age of fifty, he eventually revealed his same-sex attraction to his dad, who was deeply shocked and whose reaction was 'worse than I was expecting'.

The majority of parents, though often shocked or disappointed, did not withdraw their love. For example, Laura describes her mother's response when Laura told her of her sexuality: '[her mother said] "Well, I know!" and I said, "Well, why didn't you say?" and she said, "I've just been waiting for you to be ready to tell me."' Although her parents 'went through a long struggle of trying to work out what went wrong', they remained caring and loving.

This risk of losing loved ones was evident and real for some participants. Natalie who was sixteen at the time, moved out of home after her mum told her that she'd 'been brought up better ... she was really disappointed, and she didn't want to see my face because it was too much for her'.

In general, secrecy was a useful and positive strategy that enabled participants to reflect on both their sexuality and their faith. Individuals selectively maintain secrecy, choosing carefully when and if the time was right for them to inform others of their same-sex attraction. Accepting the same-sex attracted self, and challenging the secrecy about it were also major steps in becoming authentic. For those whose attempts at secrecy were thwarted, the ensuing confrontation with significant others was extremely painful and at times destructive.

In the period of secrecy, some individuals increased their involvement with religion. Some, however, when confronted with their same-sex attraction, decreased their involvement with their church and/or religion. This was often in conjunction with relocation, moving away from previous religious and family attachments.

Initial response – relocation and/or less involvement in church

Relocation and/or not attending church for periods of time were initially common, but temporary, responses to the predicament of participants. Movement from place to place was a strategy used in resolving not only internal conflict but interpersonal conflict as well. Some left the church after being rejected from the church of their upbringing. Liz and Lynne both felt unwelcome after their same-sex relationship was exposed by family members. They remained away from church for some time, even though Liz had been the minister of her previous church. Luke, though not rejecting church altogether, wandered from church to church, remaining anonymously in the background, after being ejected from his conservative family congregation. This liminal space enabled him to reflect upon his relationship with God and his religion. It was a transitional space where previous norms were temporarily set aside to allow transformation of his identity (van Gennep 1909/1960). Often liminal space is associated with physical movement, emphasizing the embodied nature of transformation (Yang 2000; Beckstead 2010).

Others left due to the painful internal conflict they experienced. Anthony felt 'fearful of what he was inside and a shame to the world' as he attended Bible study group, and 'just let the church drift away' from him. To deal with the division between his sexual identity and his religious worldview, he left the church and would spend times away from Australia as an openly gay man. He was not able to remain both a church-goer and same-sex attracted. Nathan similarly articulated that he didn't think he could be same-sex attracted and remain in his church. His choice was to leave the church, to pursue the desire to find his authentic self.

This is similar to Patricia, who remains internally conflicted. Her initial response to actively living in a same-sex relationship was to move away from the church, explaining: 'I didn't get into a relationship until I was twenty-three or twenty-four and at that point I stopped going to church for quite a number of years.' She continues to compartmentalize her life, recognizing that 'there are two halves to life, personality and beliefs ... at one time I focus on my relationships and at the other times on God'. Victoria, although not strongly conflicted, also had compartmentalized her life while attending church. In order to explore her sexuality, she both geographically relocated and stopped attending church.

By geographically relocating or becoming less involved in church, individuals were able to reflect upon their conflicting realities away from the influence of their families and churches. Relocating and leaving church meant a break from the continually reinforced religious habitus which, in the majority of cases, was in conflict with their newly developing same-sex attraction. At the same time they could build new relationships, free from restrictions of the past, and explore new aspects of the self. It was a liminal space, a space between their past worldview and a developing transformed worldview. For those who left the church, the majority stressed that, as Anthony says, they 'never left God, never denied God'. Lynne and her partner both had left their church due to being rejected. Lynne 'knew they hadn't abandoned God'. Despite struggling with the Bible and doctrine, they felt no change in their relationship with God. Their relationship with God remained their horizon of significance as they initially struggled to incorporate their sexuality in their religious worldview.

Some, however, did feel abandoned by God, which often led to anger and frustration, depression and/or self-harm. Their fundamental horizon of significance, the relationship with God, was distressingly disrupted by the conflict between their same-sex attraction and their religious habitus.

Initial response – depression/self-harm

Eight interviewees entered a state of depression for varying lengths of time. Anger at God, confusion at their predicament and frustration were elements leading to serious struggles that for some were so intense as to cause physical and emotional illness. Luke recalls:

> I was very, very depressed and I think it was obvious to everyone that I was in trouble emotionally … Yeah [I was] angry [at God] because I didn't feel like God had told me the answers that I needed. And I didn't feel like there was any direction from scripture about what I was supposed to do. I mean the primary motivation for everything you do is meant to be love, and then these rules force you in a direction which in order to obey, you've got to somehow stop loving. And there's absolutely no help in reconciling that contradiction.

He had been brought up with the idea that anything contrary to his church's view of the Bible were 'words of the devil'. For years he couldn't begin to deal with his conflict, the total contradiction between who he 'was' as a gay man, and 'what he believed'. In describing the extent of his conflict, he continues:

> And then … I came to another point which was, I think I'm just going to hell. Yeah. Which was for me very physically real, like it was a literal religion that I'd grown up with. So that was – that meant fire. So, it was terrifying.

'Hell' and 'fire' were powerful emotive words that held Luke in his distressingly conflicted state. He also could not resolve his predicament rationally and experienced deep frustration. Nicky was also brought up in an extremely conservative church. She struggled with suicidal thoughts and self-harm for most of her life, reporting: 'I started cutting myself up with razor blades because I hated myself so much. Oh, I hated myself so much for being gay because I thought God doesn't want me.' She has still not completely reconciled her same-sex attraction and her internalized heteronormative beliefs.

Those who struggled with depression and self-harm were in the minority. These individuals on the whole came from fundamentalist Christian back-grounds, in which their religious habitus had profound consequences for their sense of self-worth. Their extreme response to conflict is indicative of the inten-sity experienced when individuals felt they were violating their own horizons of significance. The emotionality of the conflict – for Luke the fear of burning in hell and for Nicky the self-hatred and fear of losing God's love – is highlighted by the experience of these two individuals.

Conclusion

For the LGBT Christians, becoming authentic is a process. In order to inte-grate the two dimensions of the self – the religious and the sexual – indi-viduals in this study search for ways to reconcile their sexuality with their religious worldview. This requires time and effort. This chapter has outlined two stages of this five-stage process. The first stage of the process, becoming aware of the tension, indicates that individuals respond in two distinct ways when confronted with emerging same-sex attraction and their deeply imbued religious worldview. Some become strongly internally conflicted while others are able to negotiate their sexuality and religious worldview with minimal internal conflict.

Those who are less conflicted but well aware of the tension are equipped with the means to 'wrestle with theology' without the powerful and binding emo-tional attachments to the 'sinful' nature of same-sex attraction. They are guided by horizons of significance centred on the religious self – such as loving and being loved by God and others – that override any negative associations with their sexuality. Although they are aware of tension, the assumption that same-sex attraction is inimical with Christian principles has no power. This confi-dence in a loving God is associated with relationships with significant others that are based upon acceptance and love.

The majority of LGBT Christians in this study are internally conflicted and enter a protracted process of struggle. For these individuals, same-sex attrac-tion is bound up with sticky negative connotations and emotions. Their sexu-ality is understood to violate their horizons of significance. This disrupts their connection with God and others. They feel their morality is compromised, questioning whether their sexuality is right or wrong. The non-conflicted and conflicted individuals initially responded in different ways. The non-conflicted either 'wrestled with scripture' or disregarded scripture, concentrating instead on the relational aspect of their faith. Their emotional well-being was not affected.

One strategy is shared among all LGBT Christians, that of secrecy. Secrecy is a strategy used to gain time for reflection upon faith and sexuality. In many cases, it is a positive management strategy to enable a safe space for self-questioning and reflection before moving forward. For conflicted individuals, the initial response stage was protracted, and characterized, in addition to secrecy, by denial of sexuality, an increase or decrease in religious activity and, for some, depression, disillusionment and self-harm. This was a time of intense struggle where individuals were unable to move forward in integrating the sexual and religious dimensions of identity.

The next stage, the third stage in the process of achieving integration of their sexual and religious identities, is characterized by sudden illumination and empowerment: *the catalyst*. This is a memorable event or a series of events that individuals experience, which they interpret as a catalyst to their transformation. These events are discussed in the next chapter. The catalyst experience is stage 3, resolving conflict between religious beliefs and sexual identity. Stage 4, working through the conflict, is discussed in the second half of the chapter. Once individuals are empowered to move forward, they engage in various strategies to integrate their sexuality and religious worldview and achieve a state of authenticity, where they are true to their sexuality and true to their religious convictions.

Rebuilding Worlds

Vignette: Sylvia

I wasn't able to figure out gender until I broke free of the theology, the very conservative theology I grew up with. My social circle said I'm male. My physiology, anatomy said to me I'm male. I didn't know any different. But pretty much since my puberty, I've got a sense that there was something that was not working for me. My peers were able to form opposite-sex relationships. I got nowhere with that. And even my friendships were difficult to establish.

My first prayer that I recall was: "God, why am I the way I am?" Without knowing what. The answer I got was rather unhelpful. "I made you that way, put up with it." It gave me a sense that at least God had an idea what was going on even if I didn't.

Somewhere around eight or nine [years old] I began to take more seriously this relationship with God. I didn't take this as an exercise in faith or an exercise in theology. The word was relationship, so I treated it as relationship. It's sort of hard to describe because you're relating to someone not through the usual physical senses. It's a sense of awareness in your heart internally, obviously metaphorically, a sense of thoughts coming to mind. For me, it also has been a very strong sense of presence. I have a very strong sense of Jesus literally walking with me. My relationship with God is something very tangible. I don't know where it came from. I took God seriously from day one.

Since I was a teenager, I began questioning the theology. I began asking the basics like, why a de facto relationship is such a no-no apparently? What difference does a marriage ceremony bring to the relationship? And, I said, if a marriage ceremony is so important, why isn't it more strongly described in scripture? They talk about marriage but they don't talk about how it's defined. We've had to work that out ourselves.

It's the same actually to sexual immorality – the phrase is used but it's never fleshed out. Sorry, no pun intended there. I understand something like sexual immorality now as going against the norms of the community. It's more defined community-wise. That will change from culture to culture. For scripture to be universal, that makes a lot of sense. But it also means, people define it very narrowly and super impose their cultural perspective on everyone else. Right-wing fundamentalism.

I read an article on men who cross-dress, and for the first time I read about men that I identified with. That was startling. Words like gentleness were used. And I thought, hang on a minute. That's describing me. By that [time], I'd chipped away the theology enough to open the door to allowing myself to cross-dress. Guess what? That started to feel like something I should be doing.

Even though I didn't realize yet that I was trans, the wanting to cross-dress was escalating. The woman, I guess, inside me was very much increasingly wanting to come out. Again, that's looking back and interpreting. But that was the experience. And that's consistent with other trans stories that I've read about. And so, I've got this intense build-up of something that I'm not understanding, along with a literal isolation, and I mean like I would go weeks literally without even touching a person. Not even a handshake. I was going to a large church [in a regional area]. I hadn't really connected with people.

I found myself visiting brothels. I'd never done this before. It was also very clear it was born from a sense of desperation. It was the touch I was needing. On some occasions, sex didn't happen. But it was at least physical intimacy and touch that did and that's, frankly, what I needed. And what got me curious was, I really didn't have a sense of God frowning upon me. If anything, I had a sense of understanding. The theology of [my upbringing], said this is wrong. I hadn't reached the point of being suicidal. But that was the trajectory.

[The turning point was when] I bought my first wig just up the road here, sat down in the store, and tried out, and went, "Oh shit." It feminized my face. It was a long-haired wig. And the face I saw, there was a recognition there. It was like, that's me. It wasn't an image thing. It was something in here that went, "That's me." And I've read enough by now [about] transgenderism to know what that meant. And so quite literally, yes, seconds, life was not going to be the same again.

I unpacked that awareness over the next few weeks, shedding a lot of tears, and relived memories that now began to make sense. Twenty, thirty years of things that just didn't make sense now began to make sense. Can you imagine how confusing it is? When I was at university, I began buying feminine hygiene products. Something in that process felt like it should be a part of my life experience. But I'm male. You can't ask anybody that question. There was just nothing in the public consciousness. Internet was only in infancy. I was expressing something for me but had no way of understanding what. That's more confusing than cross-dressing.

[I began to think] why am I worrying about what these same people think? And that became a turning point that subsequently enabled me to transition, that enabled me to buy a wig. Once I consciously stopped thinking about what other people thought, and I began to free myself, and began to free me up to make my choices and ironically to become the person I understand God wants us to be. He wants us to make our own choices. He gave us free will. He did that for a purpose. It wasn't just a theological necessity or nicety. That's to be made, whatever we understand of God, that's to be made in God's image. God's got the ultimate in free will. We have free will because we're made in that image. And that is so important that God does not change our will for us. We have to make the choice to change our will. If we harden our hearts, and don't change our will, God's not going to do it for us. However much we pray, it's not going to happen because to circumvent our free will, God's got to circumvent his own character. So, almost ironically, I worked out what I've been trying to figure out since a teenager. I finally began to formulate a theology that made sense that in turn drove my ability to buy dresses and skirts and so on. To actually go to try on in store without worrying about what might be thought of me. It drove that process that finally enabled me to realize I was trans. So, I can't separate the two.

Trans is something that's been with me since birth. [The] best understanding of what I read about what causes transgenderism is, it is something you're born with. It's not something that the awareness might develop later on, but that's why you get, three-, four-, five-year-olds who have a sense of being in the wrong body. And they have that sense because it is something that's present from birth. But conservative theology is incredibly strong and I went along with what I felt people around me wanted me to do. And that's something I'm only just starting to break out of now.

[My relationship with God] has been the driver for my transitioning. Realizing I was trans meant I understood a lot of the confusion I'd been experiencing. That [confusion] resolved itself and I was able to focus much more strongly on my relationship with God that became less focused on just desperation. God I need help here, I'm really struggling. He was helping [over the] twenty years of chipping away at the conservative theology [where] being trans just didn't come into the picture anywhere. Just to be able to break out of that, even when I began cross-dressing, was something. Theology informs the relationship. I knew that I had to work the relationship that way because otherwise it's very easy to hear what you want things to be. As a result, you are looking very closely at the theology that you're hearing from the pulpit. And checking that with how I'm understanding the relationship.

[One of] the scariest moment since transitioning was the eight-week break [at work] when I finished up as Tony to when I started back as Sylvia. I come back eight weeks later with an artificial bosom and this feminine hairstyle as I can manage and earrings. I remember stopping [as I walked in to work]. I just had to stop and breathe because I knew I had to go and walk through the door and sign on. A lot of my colleagues knew, [and some didn't know]. I didn't know how fast through the grapevine the news had got. And it was actually boringly, like just "Yeah okay. You're here to work." That was all they were interested in, which is kind of good. But it was somewhat surreal. I was thinking: "Hey guys, I've just gone and torn up my life as I knew it and rebuilt it." And just life goes on around you as though nothing's changed. Sometimes people who haven't previously known me just identify me as female. Other times I still get identified as male. If somebody's stirring me, I just go, that's what they see. But essentially, work's been no real problem.

I think God's had his fingerprints on my journey. There's things that I'm able to do, I've done my part of it. But there's things that have worked out could've been beyond my control that I put it in God's control. One of them has been the timing. I've had it almost too easy compared to what I've read of other people's experiences.

[In the Protestant church I grew up in] there was no room for gender queer, let alone gay or anything in the LGBTI spectrum, just no footprint in there at all. And the image of the early teenager in the [church] meeting, and the woman I am now, the only way I can sit them together is in the steps that led from one to the other. I cannot sit them together as the same person. They're not the same person. They're both me but they're not the same people.

I understand the idea of ritual being a conduit enabling us to connect with God, because it provides a physical framework through which we can touch base with God. But my relationship with God is tangible without that ritual. The church model that is so centred on ritual, it doesn't speak to me. And yet, I can't throw it out because meeting with other Christians is important to God. That's very clear in at least the New Testament. So I can't throw it out.

Prior to MCC, I was going to a [mainstream] church. They had every intention of being supportive with my transitioning. They just weren't equipped to deal with it at least in part because they tangled transgenderism with sexuality. They're so focused on "Thou shall not be gay" that once they got that tangled with being trans, that was kind of what mattered to them. I remember the minister there just double checking my celibacy. I should have said: "Frankly, it's none of your business." But I'm politer than that. I understood where he was coming from. So I gave him what was at that point a truthful answer. Church was actually the last place I came out at.

I told the minister: "How do we want the congregation to know?" Essentially, he just sat on the problem. He did not move on the problem until I waved my new birth certificate in the front of his nose and said: "Minister, I am no longer Tony." It was very awkward, being (out, as a woman) full time at work and everywhere else but church. We finally got over that public introduction. [But he] really just totally missed the point. Individual people in the congregation got it. [He was] simply not equipped. So, subsequently, I left.

The sheer attitude shown by [conservative Christians] got me worried. I wasn't hearing Jesus in the attitude. I was not seeing God in the attitude. They might be Christians, but at this point, I'm not seeing or hearing Jesus.

Just before I left, I'd actually attended an evening service at MCC because I was aware of MCC's existence. I knew it was the gay church. MCC was the first time I attended church as a woman. MCC has been good.

So, however unconventional some of my understanding is, they're broadly in my scripture as best as I can understand, draw them together there. And that altogether, it convinced me it's from God. I am not going to throw that out even though it causes issues with church. It's church that has to catch up. How to bring them together is what I'm still struggling.

But all of that is quite independent of being inclusive. Inclusive is better than what [the Church I attended earlier] was managing to be. But it's still … Being trans is about identity. Gender is about identity. Gender is not the whole picture. Being gay is not the whole picture. It's a part of this larger picture of identity. And unless LGBTI is put in the bigger picture of identity, the point is ultimately going to be missed.

Introduction

When I met Bernie [Anthony's partner] I already had that information [of an alternative theology] ... I did the search at that point. So it was probably Bernie. Bernie was the big catalyst for me in big ways to take this step, to come back to the church. And we went to MCC together (Anthony).

It was a process ... so the steps in the process were, Scripture is not clear about this, meeting other people and going and seeing perfectly normal other people, and then being comfortable enough to actually go to a meeting and decide this is where, this is where I can actually meet other people struggling with the same thing I was. (Matt)

LGBT Christians search for ways to reconcile their sexuality with their religious identity, to be authentic to both their sexuality and to their faith. Finding authenticity is a process, a process of integrating their religious worldviews with their same-sex attraction and/or gender questioning. The previous chapter details the first two stages of this process, the *awareness* of, and *initial response* to, tensions between LGBT identity and religious worldview. A key finding is that more than one-third of the LGBT participants experience little or no conflict, despite being aware of the tension. Those whose religious worldview is built upon supportive relationships could easily negotiate doctrinal issues or disregard these altogether. Cognitively articulated doctrinal issues had little emotional hold over them. These individuals emphasize a deinstitutionalized form of religious attachment based on God and Jesus's love.

In contrast, those who experience internal conflict described powerful 'sticky' negative emotions that were bound to their same-sex attraction. Relationships with significant others and their own internal sense of self suffered. Their sexuality violated their religious horizons of significance, and many felt their morality was compromised, questioning whether their sexuality was right or wrong.

This chapter examines the rebuilding of previously shaken worlds of faith through two stages: the 'catalyst', and 'working through the conflict' (Figure 6.1). The catalyst is the first stage of rebuilding a new foundation of faith. Catalysts are 'moments of comprehension stimulated by new knowledge that propel the participants forward' (Levy and Reeves 2011: 58) and enable individuals to begin to reinterpret their sexual and religious identities, to break out of the initial responses to the tension. Levy and Reeves emphasize new knowledge as being critical to this stage. Anthony, quoted above, reports that his partner was the catalyst for him to begin integrating his same-sex attraction and his religious conviction. It was through this relationship that he came back to the church and began practising as a Christian once more. Relationships are an integral part of catalyst events.

Catalysts for the LGBT Christians occur through recognition that the religious worldview is questionable and/or the recognition and acknowledgement of their same-sex attraction. This recognition occurs through the breakdown of old and the building of new relationships and enables individuals to receive either new knowledge or to reframe old knowledge, which takes on new meaning, opening alternative ways of being. The catalyst is thus a complex mix of knowledge, emotional and relational factors. Kathleen Ritter and Craig O'Neill (1996) frame this moment as the moment of acknowledging loss, the loss of past expectations and dreams according to an old heteronormative framework. They understand this as a necessary moment before the process of rebuilding a new framework.

The fourth stage, 'working through the conflict', is characterized by individual reflection, information seeking and discussion. As the quote above from Matt articulates, part of the process is meeting people, people who could identify with his own experience, with whom he could share. Working through conflict often revolves around significant relationships in safe places, and shared religious practices (Figure 6.1). Relationships and practices have a fundamental effect on identity, and have the power to change deeply engrained religious habitus and worldviews (Wilcox, in Shore-Goss 2013).

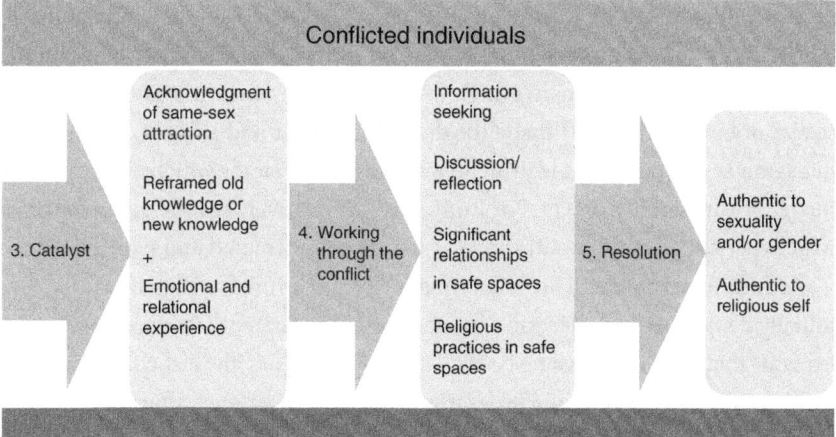

Figure 6.1 Process of resolution of conflict (conflicted individuals) – stages 3, 4 and 5 (adapted from Levy and Reeves 2011)

Stage 3: catalytic moments

Half (n=14) of the participants describe a memorable catalytic moment where they felt able to move forward and deal with conflict between their same-sex attraction and religious beliefs. For the gay, lesbian and bisexual participants, these catalytic moments occurred at the intersection of two aspects of self, the religious and the sexual self. For the transgendered individuals, the catalytic moment could be either a moment of recognition of sexuality or gendered identity. For some the recognition of their same-sex attraction as real and lasting, and/or desirable, was the trigger for questioning the religious worldview. This recognition occurred through intimate relationships, which triggered powerful emotional experiences that dispelled any further questioning of sexuality. For others, the disparity and tension between their feelings and doctrine was no longer tenable, and ensuing conflict was inevitable.

The catalytic moments experienced by the participants in this study enabled them to break out of the initial denial of same-sex attraction, and associated avoidance, secrecy and depression outlined in the previous sections. Catalytic experiences are of two types: those involving acknowledgement of the permanency or desirability of their same-sex attraction, and experiences that led to questioning their religious worldview.

Acknowledgment of same-sex attraction through relationships

Participants who denied their same-sex attraction could not begin to question their previous religious worldview until they acknowledged their sexual orientation. Ruth, for example, who experienced little internal conflict between her sexuality and her religious worldview, remarks that 'once it was resolved [her sexual orientation], once I made the decision, I never had a doubt'. Recognizing her same-sex attraction as legitimate was the pivotal factor which allowed her to move forward as a Christian. For Ruth, this was relatively seamless, but for those who experienced conflict, this process was often protracted and painful.

Arthur, for example, who was brought up in a strongly religious family, had initially denied his sexuality and experienced a high degree of internal conflict. He explains that at a young age he booked a Pacific cruise as 'the last chance to prove that I could be heterosexual'. He describes a pivotal experience after this event:

> That was a disaster in a whole lot of ways, to the point where I was so keyed up when the cruise came back and it had been two weeks of doing nothing

effectively because I shared a cabin with another guy who obviously played up from time to time. And I didn't feel at all interested in any of the people [women] I got to know. Coming home I had an encounter that frightened the life out of me. It was with another man and whoa, that was that. It made it perfectly clear that I was gay and I had to learn to live with that and deal with that. The only place I could see dealing with that was coming to the big city. Yes, it frightened me in that it was so intense and nothing to that point had been that intense. I knew that I had to learn to work with this or deal with this or I had to come to terms with it in one way or another and the only way I could do that was to get away from home.

The 'encounter that frightened the life out of him' with another male was a powerful emotional experience that shocked him into recognizing the nature of his sexuality. This was an intense emotional moment, a moment that propelled him to move away from home, a move that enabled him to break old attachments and build new ones. He could begin dealing with his sexuality and eventually church doctrine. The encounter changed his reality.

Similar moments of recognition of their 'authentic sexuality' allowed others to begin meeting other same-sex attracted people, both Christian and non-Christian. Natalie, the youngest participant who also initially tried to deny her same-sex attraction, reached a point where she realized: 'And when I finally did date a girl, I realized, "Oh, yeah. This is what it means. All of that [dating boys] was just pretend stuff"'. At that point she could meet other lesbians and begin the process of resolving her conflict with church doctrine. Until then, as she explains: 'I kind of explored sexuality in the Bible … it never meant anything to me'. The emotional realization through her same-sex relationship – 'Oh, yeah, this is what it means' – dispelled her doubts regarding her sexuality, and was the catalyst to move forward and meet other lesbians, and begin questioning doctrinal issues that until then had no meaning.

Emma was only able to recognize her same-sex attraction after spending time in therapy as a result of her depression. Through the trusting relationship with her therapist she began to recognize and acknowledge her sexuality: 'We dealt with all this stuff and within that, stuff to do with my sexuality came out. And it put things into perspective. I could see all my journey, little hints of being attracted to women'. This led her to meeting a lesbian from a Catholic background with whom she could 'explore' her sexuality, saying: 'It was an incredible time, a freeing time … but just thinking, am I jeopardizing my faith in order to have this, I really love this person and for the first time I feel complete'. Until Emma had recognized her same-sex attraction, she couldn't begin to deal with the doctrinal issues. After this point, she could begin to approach doctrine, but with a conviction that her sexuality was an authentic aspect of her identity: 'I really love this person and for the first time I feel complete.'

Reframed old knowledge

For other participants, relationships with significant others were catalytic in that individuals were able to reframe old knowledge or receive new knowledge, either through the breakdown of an old significant relationship or the building of a new more important one. Each breakdown or rebuilding of relationships signified a transformation of emotional attachments (Ahmed 2004). In the context of this analysis, 'old knowledge' is awareness of alternative doctrinal interpretations which participants were unable to process as meaningful or to accept as legitimate. 'New knowledge', discussed below, refers to theological interpretations that are immediately processed as either meaningful or other knowledge that leads the individual to question previous doctrinal understandings.

New significant relationships or the breakdown of previously intimate relationships led to the reframing of theological knowledge that participants were already aware of. This was often experienced as a sudden pivotal realization. For example, Luke, who was brought up in a fundamentalist charismatic family and deeply involved with the church, initially recalls how alternate understandings of the Bible had no meaning for him:

> I've known about this gay theology[1] for years, and I've never even allowed myself to see where it is. Because my perception was it would be just people trying to justify sin, and it would be a trap ... if you start listening to the devil then he gets a little finger in and then will slowly take you over and you won't even know you've been deceived.

Luke was previously aware of gay theology but could not detach himself from the emotion surrounding it, saying that 'it would be just people trying to justify sin, be a trap'. He goes on to describe the transformative moment, notably a moment of interaction with a person close to him, where he came to question the validity of his previous worldview:

> And I'm sitting there with all those Greek books around me on the floor. I'm just reading the Bible and researching and my Dad walked into the room, looked at me, and said: 'What are you doing!' And I realized – this was a transforming moment because my dad was saying you're not allowed to research what the truth is. That was like the changing moment.

For Luke this was an intensely personal and profound realization. He says: 'It was so personal to me; it was the realization that the people that I'd been trusting as the "real people" had actually twisted something and caused me all this hurt. And all of a sudden the perception that these are the real guys and those are the liars [the gay theologians] just changed.' The breakdown of a previously trusting relationship, in his case with his father who had prevented him from researching what he perceived as 'the truth' was pivotal. It was a catalytic moment that enabled him to begin to question previous church doctrine. In addition, his trust in his church leaders was broken, and he could open himself to reinterpret the 'old knowledge', the gay theology he had been aware of but distrusted, as legitimate. He could begin to detach from the sticky emotional binds of the biblical words signifying homosexuality as his emotional orientation to the 'Other' changed (Ahmed 2004).

Andrew similarly changed his views on gay theology. He could reinterpret old knowledge (gay theology) through the building of a new trusting relationship. He had despaired at the three options he faced as a same-sex attracted Christian:

Well, either you hope and you pray and you pray hard enough that it will go away and live a good Christian life, get married to a woman, have kids and live happily ever after. Well, no, that's not happening. But the disappointment to God and my parents and family and friends and everything, how do I reconcile it? Or, I remember I had it all worked out – well, the one obvious one was to live a gay lifestyle, coming to terms with everything but that would mean turning away from God. And the third one would be the worst to my mind, living a double life and feeling incredibly inauthentic and incredibly guilty the whole time.

A psychologist he was visiting explained: 'Well actually there is another theology.' Until that point, Andrew says, the 'other theology' had been 'made out to be absurd' in sermons that disparaged gay theologians. In his case, through the new trusting relationship with his psychologist, Andrew could acknowledge the possibility that this knowledge was valid. He eventually was able to reconcile his same-sex attraction and theology.

New knowledge

For a small number of participants, new theological knowledge was catalytic and enabled them to question their previous religious worldview. This new knowledge was discovered in connection with emotions provoked within a relationship. For some the relationship was with an invisible but very real God. In line with other theorists of the religious experience, the encounter with God, whether through prayer or other forms of communion, is a form of relationship (Bouma 2006: 10). A number of participants (n=8) told of the disappointment with, or anger at, their God for putting them in the predicament of being same-sex attracted. Liz, for example, expresses her frustration, saying: 'Well, if we aren't supposed to feel this way, why isn't God taking the feelings away.' This frustration led her to an exploration of the Bible, saying to her partner: 'I'm going to have to go back and study the Bible for myself, and see if I can come to terms with it … And looking at all the passages in the Bible that mention being homosexual and interpreting it a different way.' Her frustration with her God enabled her to release previous attachments to Bible truths, and to begin searching for new knowledge within which she could reinterpret her same-sex attraction.

For others, a rebuilding of the relationship with God was crucial. Judy and Annie, who met while both were active Christians, made three trips away to meditate and pray about whether their relationship was right or wrong. Eventually, as Judy explains, we 'definitely came back with eventually realizing that God isn't saying that we should break up'. From that catalytic moment, Judy began the process of reinterpreting church doctrine.

Angela and Nathan were both introduced to a new way of thinking through a new intimate relationship that became so important to them that it enabled them to question their old worldview. They both began resolving their conflict between same-sex attraction and religious doctrine in conjunction with their partners. Angela, for example, was conflicted for more than four years, trying to deny her sexuality. As she explains: 'I was committed to the church and being straight.' She believed her same-sex attraction to be wrong, that 'this sin was so intense and so shameful in both mine and the church's eyes'. When she eventually became involved with a woman within the church, they decided they had to 'have some space and figure things out', and her partner then travelled overseas. Angela recalls:

> Kari was more questioning than me and more open to other interpretations. I had been set in the Anglican mentality for a long time. She started sending me [from overseas] information from other viewpoints of how to read the Bible that I had never contemplated before. My views started to change and I started to think that maybe there was another way of being Christian; maybe God didn't think homosexual relationships were wrong.

The value of this new relationship with Kari allowed a questioning of her previously held views, enabling her to glimpse the possibility of an alternative understanding of the Bible and reframing her position within her Christianity as same-sex attracted. The sticky emotional attachment to the 'sin' and the associated entanglement with same-sex relationships engendered shame. These were slowly dissolved through the new trusting relationship.

Nathan remembers that as he recognized his same-sex attraction, 'I'd gathered the idea that if I was gay I couldn't be Christian.' Considering a relationship more important than his religious conviction, he stopped attending any church. However, his partner introduced him to a new way of understanding his religious worldview, giving him a book 'dealing with some of this stuff about sexuality in the Bible, so I read that and that was like the first time I'd really read anything that … went through all that stuff and said: "Yes, it is possible to be gay and Christian".'

Several of the older male members of MCC mention that a pivotal moment was meeting Troy Perry, the founder of MCC as a worldwide organization. An ex-Pentecostal minister, Perry not only espouses the essentialist view that same-sex attraction is God-given and thus legitimate, but also emphasizes the God-given nature of human sexuality per se, affirming the union of sexuality and spirituality. Arthur, for example, was very moved by Troy Perry, saying:

> I think something that has become more apparent … is how much Troy Perry meant to my understanding of sexuality and Christianity. Yes, I knew it helped me to become more open and more aware, but now it is obvious that was quite pivotal in my experience of wholeness.

He explains that the minister of his mainstream church didn't see himself as a sexual being, believing that 'the body was evil, the spirit wasn't … so you had to be celibate till you were married, but gays couldn't marry, you had to be celibate, end of story'. For Arthur, this attitude to sexuality led to incredible injustice and hopelessness … It was resolved through hearing and reading about Troy Perry. In Arthur's case, the relationship with Troy Perry, a figure of authority with, as he perceived it, great wisdom, gave him a window of hope which allowed him to begin working through his conflict.

The catalyst is just the beginning of the positive process of achieving fusion of the sexual identity and religious worldview, of living an authentic life. This continued process can be understood as the positive process of rebuilding a new framework of understanding both self and the religious worldview.

Stage 4: working through the conflict

And from that moment on – I was – I just started reading everything I could get my hands on. Like that was the changing point. But very, very quickly going through and changing, you know, you have to kind of rebuild your whole way of looking at the world, from the ground up. (Luke)

The catalyst was the beginning of a positive process of working through internal conflict between a Christian worldview and same-sex attraction, to reach a state where individuals could feel pride in their same-sex attraction, pride that they were living an authentic existence where their moral mandate was to embody their 'God-given' sexuality. Luke, quoted above, describes that after the 'changing point' he needed to 'kind of rebuild [his] whole way of looking at the world, from the ground up'. Once conflicted participants became open to new ways of being, they continued the process of resolving conflict, and employed various strategies for rebuilding their worldview, challenging the heteronormative religious worldview of their upbringing. Levy and Reeves (2011) identify information seeking, reflection, discussion and new behaviours as integral to this stage. Our study supports Levy and Reeve's analysis; however, greater emphasis should be placed on the importance of relationships and practices within safe spaces to the process of resolution of conflict (Figure 6.1).

A safe place is a 'queer' place where the participants find affirmation of their same-sex attraction. A safe space enables and enhances the building of relationships, discussion and information seeking. Sticky, negative emotional attachments to words, acts or relationships can be slowly undone and power dynamics reversed (Ahmed 2004). In the words of one participant, the safe space of the MCC enabled 'healing' and finding 'wholeness'. The safe space promotes the feeling of belonging, identified by Wise, Harris and Watts (2005) as an aspect of habitus. A safe space enables a gradual transformation of the religious habitus.

A safe place is also a place to practise a queer Christianity. For LGBT Christians in our study, living as a Christian is a group process which requires congregational worship practices, and participation with other Christians. Some of these practices can be understood as queered practices that are also integral to life as a queer Christian. The religious practices are healing and transformative, aiding the process of resolving tension and conflict between religious doctrine and same-sex attraction. New behaviours are the crux of identity transformation and the development of new ways of being. A safe place is a spiritually nourishing space.

Queer religious practices conducted in safe spaces are core to the transformation of the identity of the individuals in this study. The importance of changed theological and cognitive understandings was varied. It was dependent upon upbringing, including factors such as the conservatism of their family, the participant's level of education, their age, and individual experiences. Of all conflicted participants, eight report seeking information as a crucial part of the process of working through the conflict. Three began seeking information individually; however, the majority could only realize change after combining this with discussion in a safe place. The following discussion is separated into 'individual wrestling with church doctrine' and 'safe spaces'. Safe spaces enable wrestling with doctrine in connection with others. They also are conducive to the resolution of conflicted feelings towards alternative sexuality through relationships and emotional attachments to others and the fulfilment of spiritual needs through queer religious practices.

Individual wrestling with church doctrine

The previous section described the catalyst stage in which knowledge, in conjunction with relationships, stimulates individuals to question previous worldviews. In the rebuilding stage of working through the conflict, the questioning process for three individuals leads to thorough research as they wrestle with questions of doctrine. For those who are non-conflicted, wrestling with church doctrine was generally a short and uncomplicated process. For those who were conflicted, this was often complex and extended.

For example, Matt, who was deeply conflicted for years and whose catalyst was the recognition of the relativity of church doctrines, began thoroughly researching Bible truths:

> I think the point at which I had totally reconciled my faith and sexuality was where I wrote Bible studies on the 'gotcha' passages. I spent about thirty hours researching every single passage ... And it was through this research that at the end of it, I thought, I've had enough of this. I don't need to research this anymore. I have reached my tipping point where I'm not going back. I had totally reconciled with this. I'm okay with me.

'I am okay with me' expresses quintessentially that as a same-sex attracted Christian he had resolved any tension between his sexual identity and his religious worldview. He believed he was able to express his authentic self, his original self.

Perhaps out of all the participants, Luke stands out as being most active in his individual wrestling with doctrine, independent of others. His search for information was sparked by the emotional transformation of attitude towards his father and church elders, as described in the catalytic moments. When he began questioning his religious worldview, he began 'reading everything he could get his hands on'. As he says: 'You have to kind of rebuild your whole way of looking at the world, from the ground up.' In addition, each Sunday Luke visited churches, both traditional and MCC, explaining: 'It was like I was getting all my information together.' Information seeking was for him both an individual process of reading books and internet sources, and relational and behavioural, in that he began visiting various churches. He understands that his emphasis on doctrine was exceptional, saying:

> That's probably a really unusual way of processing it – [laughing] – but that was
> my way ... my experiences tended to be that people go through the heart stuff
> first. And then they get to the head stuff ... But what strikes me is that, I was,
> I was head first. And I think it was a few years after that, that I actually started
> the process of coming to terms with myself as an actual sexual person.

Luke self-identifies as being unusual, and maintains that most people 'go through heart stuff first'. Matt also researched individually, but this was within a Bible study group he initiated that was affiliated with MCC. Our research demonstrates that the large majority sought a safe place to wrestle with doctrine, to discuss new ways of approaching church doctrine and to question previous understandings of the Bible. The process of wrestling with doctrine is integrally linked to relationships, emotions and practices.

Safe spaces: wrestling with church doctrine

Emma, also deeply conflicted, provides a good example of an individual who passed through various stages of 'wrestling with church doctrine'. The catalyst for her was the acknowledgement of her same-sex attraction. Until this acknowledgement, she could not approach doctrine at all. Being brought up in a conservative Protestant environment and spending some time in an even more conservative church group, doctrine was deeply important to her. She initially 'did a lot of research online' and also made contact with an online forum to discuss issues of sexual orientation and faith. She explains: 'I connected with people online way before I met anybody [from the church].' From the safety of her home (and a relationship), she was able to begin to explore her doctrinal issues. The online community was a place where she could relate to others with less risk to herself. Through this forum, she was led to an affirming congregation.

Emma soon desired 'to speak with lots of people to really work out what I thought'. Here MCC played an important role. Emma explains: 'I think it's a safe place where you can ask questions and people are happy to sit down with you and talk about those things and share their journey. Coming to [MCC] and meeting people and just feeling more at peace about the whole journey has been incredible.' MCC was a safe space for Emma, where she could challenge her deeply held religious worldview and open herself up to question it. It was the place she could sit with others and 'share the journey'.

Similarly, Lynne and Liz are a couple who experienced rejection from their previous church. Lynne explains that when they started attending the MCC: 'We were very accepted and I think that first twelve months we battled through a lot of the [doctrinal] issues.' Being in a safe space allowed these women to question and challenge their preconceived church doctrine. MCC was also a place to legitimize what individuals had already researched. Liz, who had been reading books on theology, says that after meeting the pastor of MCC she felt 'very reassured about what the Bible said was what I thought it said after I'd been through all these different books'.

Interestingly, MCC congregations in this study had almost no formal structures to discuss biblical and theological issues. While all had previously offered Bible study, these were no longer on offer at the time of the research. In fact, some participants rued the lack of support in this area. While acknowledging that belonging to the MCC provides 'some psychological support', Michael explains that 'my one difficulty is that apart from the occasional social thing and Sunday services there's ... no weekly or fortnightly Bible study'. This is endorsed by Anne, who explains: 'It [the MCC] is a safe place to go – it's basically friendship and fellowship ... I was very disappointed when we first started going there quite regular that there was no follow-up care really. I would have personally liked to ask questions about being gay and Christianity.'

Some MCC congregations had leaflets available that offered an alternative viewpoint of the Bible verses concerning homosexuality; however, from the participants' reports, this alone was insufficient. The individuals described how relationships within the safe space of the MCC enabled them to deal with their conflicts. For the majority of the conflicted participants, a new understanding of the Bible came through the lived experience of an alternative viewpoint, manifested through relationships with others facing the same dilemma, and religious practices – all within a safe space. Sharing the journey, as Emma says, implies a sense of belonging, a characteristic identified by Dickson (2012) and Brumbaugh (2007) among others, as critical to the nourishment of the life of faith of LGBT Christians. The gradual reinterpretation of doctrine is one role that a safe space enables. A second benefit of the safe space is the development of emotional attachments that contribute to a reappraisal of self.

Safe spaces: emotional attachments

Laura, a long-time member of MCC, explains: 'Being at MCC it's a little bit like, see I am a good person.' Recognition of her goodness was a fundamental aspect of the transformation of identity. The moral imperatives identified previously include loving the self as a creation of God. Being recognized as good within this safe place was healing for Laura: 'MCC has been such a big part of my healing; healing without counselling.'

This affirmation of being 'a good person', being loved as same-sex attracted, was a continuation from the recognition and acknowledgment of same-sex attraction that often occurred as a catalytic moment. The affirmation was a further step towards embracing an alternative sexuality and living according to the moral imperative of 'being true to the self' and is indicative of transformation of religious habitus.

How the feeling of being safe contributed to finding the authentic self varied according to individual circumstances. Anthony, who initially felt confronted by his own same-sex attraction, explains; 'It was very scary the first time going in. MCC was definitely aimed at our community [LGBTIQ] ... so I knew I was kind of stepping over a threshold.' For Anthony, acknowledging his same-sex attraction as legitimate was a risk and a step into the unknown. He could only do this in a safe space where he could begin to discover his authentic sexual self. He shared this experience with others, particularly those who had come from conservative families or religious traditions. Annie, for example, describes her first visit to an MCC:

> And then I went with Polly at night time, and I'd go, like, I think that guy over there, is he a girl? Is he a boy? I really found that hard to come to terms with. Because, like, gays, they're not normal! ... Really, really strong views in my family – very confronting for me and it was very hard to deal with ... You're looking around feeling really uncomfortable – because you are like them too!

Visiting the MCC meant that they were confronting the 'Other' in themselves and, through face-to-face relationships, were able to transform their emotion from shame and disgust to acceptance and love. Self-acceptance enabled the authentic self to be expressed. Rebecca, for example, explains that meeting other same-sex attracted people was an important step for her in overcoming her own 'homophobia': 'I've completely changed the way I feel ... I disagreed with homosexuality because that was what I was taught ... I think getting to know gay people made me start to think that it wasn't so wrong – but I did think it was wrong.' The relationships and friendships she formed overrode and disabled the emotional stickiness of the doctrinal beliefs she had held previously.

The people she got to know, and now trusted, gradually changed her orientation to the 'Other' (Ahmed 2004). The development of relationships and emotional attachments are the second major role of the safe spaces. The third is the enabling of religious practices.

Safe spaces: religious practices

For a large majority of the participants in this study, all of whom remain within the folds of Christianity, the third critical role of the safe place is to enable the shared practice of queer religious worship. Laura describes this when asked about the most important thing for her in the MCC:

> Worshipping in community. Having people. I feel better when there's more people, so greater sense of community. So worshipping within a community, sharing communion, having a sermon that makes sense. Now in worshipping I include the singing as well.

Religious practices within the safe spaces of MCC empowered participants and enabled them to deal with their conflict and to express the authentic self. Through relationships and embodied practices, the LGBT Christians in this study strengthened their acceptance of their LGBT identity, and in this space found a way to negotiate their religious worldview to encompass their sexuality. According to Robert Shore-Goss (2013: 18):

> Many LGBTQI Christians in churches may not understand the intricacies of queer theology, but they do understand MCC's invitation to open commensality or the practice of radical inclusive love and hospitality.

For many LGBTQI Christians, the lived experience is often not centred on theology but is a practised and emotional experience, as Shore-Goss suggests. The institutional focus on inclusivity is a value prioritized by the MCC and is reflected in the congregational and religious practices. All are welcomed upon entering the church, the use of inclusive language is encouraged and the sermon preaches an inclusive message. Paul explains:

> Another practice [of all MCC congregations worldwide] … is inclusive behaviour, and that stems from our language, the way we make people feel welcome, the way people do things within the worship services so there are no feelings of exclusion.

The congregational and worship practices in this safe place are healing and empowering. Participants report that communion in particular is a powerful ritual practice that emphasizes the inclusive love of God. Ritual practices such as communion are key to the transformation of religious worldviews and feelings towards self. They contribute to the transformation of habitus. Other religious practices, such as participation in services, singing Christian songs and playing music also contribute to this transformation. These practices of inclusivity all play a role in what Shore-Goss (2013: 16) describes as 'radical inclusive love'. The following section focuses on the practices of communion, participation in 'service', and music. Gender-inclusive language is discussed in Chapter 7, as this practice highlights tensions within the MCC. These tensions are between, on the one hand, inclusivity and queer, and on the other hand, traditional Christian normative thought.

The message of inclusivity is embodied in the ritual of communion and, for many, is the most meaningful and powerful of all the inclusive religious practices of the MCC. As already discussed, MCC's practice is quite distinct from other denominations and is noted by religious scholars and researchers for its impact. Shore-Goss (2013), for example, centres on the performance of communion as representative of the radical love of God imparted by MCC, and Brumbaugh (2007) focused exclusively in her master's dissertation on the practice of communion in the MCC.

Communion, service, and music

Communion in the MCC is a powerful ritual performance. Wilcox (in Shore-Goss 2013: 2) says that 'the habitus that conveys second class status to the world and oneself is broken during the MCC ritual'. Shore-Goss (2013: 2) expands on this idea: 'A new symbolic habitus of grace and acceptance is communicated to each participant receiving communion.' Individuals were brought up with a habitus and religious worldview that legitimized and valorized heterosexuality. During communion and other rituals performed in the MCC, individuals are able to feel accepted and loved to the extent that these feelings of inferiority are eroded. Communion is practised weekly and it is through the repetitive reinforcement of the message of love and acceptance that habitus is transformed. As Arthur describes it, the value of communion is: 'When we as people respond to God's gift and the giving of Christ on a regular basis.' Each week the LGBT Christians come up to the altar alone, as a couple, or with friends where their value as a loved child of God is reaffirmed. The repetition of the performance of communion and of group worship each week enables a new way of being Christian.

Almost all the participants who attend the MCC churches mention communion as an important affirmation of their sexuality in front of God. Peter, for example, explains: 'Going along to MCC, I guess, some of the affirming things were the communion and where somebody could go and have communion with their partner.' Vickie also recalls her first visit to MCC where, although she felt a bit strange in that 'it was a church for gay people – being at heart a conservative', she describes her response to the first communion: 'I saw two men kiss each other after their blessing, and I thought, wow, this is true endorsement [of same-sex attraction]!' Anthea also explains that the communion both affirmed her sexuality and helped her feel included and accepted, saying:

> It [communion] makes me feel connected with my people. My gay people because I don't have that connection at home. It makes me feel part of that community and that it's okay to be gay and these are beautiful people and its nice doing this with these people.

The communion ritual consolidates the value of the self as same-sex attracted and unites individuals. Communion as a group ritual legitimizes alternative ways of being. This ritual affirms same-sex attraction in front of a loving and inclusive God. These rituals transform habitus and it is upon the new habitus that renegotiated horizons of significance are based.

The MCC explicitly emphasizes inclusivity at the table, highlighting the open table.[2] The majority of participants also describe the importance of the open table. As Emma says: 'I love the concept that it's an open table[3] ... and that anybody can come because I think that's the heart of the gospel. You know Jesus didn't exclude.' This sentiment is endorsed by Laurel who attends an MCC service irregularly: 'I really like the communion and I really like that I feel embraced by the way the communion is introduced.' Rebecca, who was not brought up with communion in her childhood religious community, describes the values that it conveys for her:

> It's nice to go up there and hold somebody's hand and take communion and be with people and I like it when whoever's in front says, everybody's welcome, nobody's different from anybody else and that wherever you come from, or where you are going – even if you don't feel right with God, you're welcome – can come to Him – that's I think the most important message of MCC – it's okay. No matter where you are on the journey, God will accept you, God loves you and you're welcome. And that's so special because where can you get that in any church? You never get that!

Each individual or group who take communion are physically embraced and prayed over personally by the pastor, deacon or other church member. This personal connection is extremely important for Anthea, a single woman, who says: 'I love the communion … I like the personal communion that you get, the one-on-one!' Anthony, who is now in a long-term relationship, declares that doing communion with his partner is the 'highlight of the service' for him:

> Walking up to the communion and holding hands and just having communion together is just a fantastic thing. It's such a personal thing and a spiritual thing. And a sharing thing with the person that's praying with you – I think it's such a wonderful thing because it brings you as a unit.

Laura similarly describes her first communion in the MCC:

> We held hands, we took communion in front of a minister of God who said: 'You are accepted, you are forgiven and you are loved' … had tears running down and I just felt I am home. This is where I want to be.

Communion symbolizes the meeting of the physical and spiritual, it is the ultimate religious experience for many of the LGBT Christians in this study. The emotions centre on being loved and accepted, in front of God together with partners and friends. The MCC becomes a place of comfort and peace, where the integration of multiple aspects of identity is fused. Laura's relief is palpable: 'I am just home. This is where I want to be.'

The repetitive practice of this ritual enables change and queers Christianity. The heteronormative institution is transgressed, as LGBT couples take communion, holding hands, expressing love by kissing after communion. This is a bold statement, a performative action that not only enables personal liberation and integration of sexuality with religious worldview, but also changes the institution of Christianity, albeit in small ways. Using Browne's (2010) understanding of spaces as dynamic, produced and contested, the spaces of the MCC are recreated, and in effect queered. The heteronormative assumption of Christian practices is transgressed in the MCC congregational spaces.

A large number of the participants allude to service and participation as extremely important for the affirmation of their identity as same-sex attracted Christians. This is precisely the aspect of their religious life that was denied them in mainstream churches and the source of loss and grief. Emma explains the benefits of being involved in the MCC:

> I was also able to do things again. So, going to the Anglican Church I wasn't allowed to do anything [because of being open about same-sex attraction]. It

[MCC] has given me opportunities to serve that I wouldn't get in other churches. And I love that.

Within MCC (and to a lesser degree within the affirming congregations of the Uniting Church), LGBT Christians are not only accepted but their sexuality is legitimized through being valued as active participants in services. Patricia explains the importance of service as distinct from friendship that she felt in her MCC:

> And while I was very warmly welcomed ... I was able to serve and that made a huge difference ... and so rather than just sit there as a member of the church you are actually supposed to get up and do things, so I got involved in a range of things as soon as I could ... service is probably the most meaningful thing. I suppose it's just being who you are and accepted for that.

Anthony also expresses the importance of involvement in the services at MCC:

> I do like the way that a lot of church community do get involved in the services in one way or another, whether it's singing or being acolytes. There's a task for everyone to do. And that's really good, that makes you feel you are contributing more than just being a member of the congregation and put some money in the basket whenever it comes your way.

Similar to communion, music is a religious practice that reaffirms individuals as same-sex attracted Christians. For example, Patricia, who often plays guitar and sings in a band, says that 'really the music is just a way of serving to me, it's not about the music'. For Mary, singing means being included: 'I love to sing! I know God loves me to sing. I knew I didn't have any voice to sing and [MCC] is the only place I've been accepted regards singing.' Music for others was liberating and important to their religious lives in other ways. Victoria reports:

> I think the gift God has given me is in being able to connect with music. I thought what is the most powerful thing in my life? I remember whenever I sing. I can sing for God and that makes things okay.

The expression 'I remember' is suggestive of a deeply embodied religious habitus, accessed through the performative worship practice of singing. Victoria further explains: 'I can just sing for God and that makes things okay.' Singing brings comfort and validates her in front of God.

Others also note that singing linked them to their past: 'I like the old songs; that evokes my past' (May). Singing is a religious practice that connects the past memory with the present form of action that leads to a feeling of comfort. The central role of these embodied memories that are explicitly identified by Victoria and May is consistent with the conceptual argument for the importance of religious habitus, a disposition that is both consciously and unconsciously instilled through relationships, cultural cues and symbols. Their comments are consistent with Warner's (2005: 226) assertion that music enables a 'deep, emotional, elemental' connection to the self. This also explains why LGBT individuals remain attracted to their Christian upbringing despite being repelled and rejected by mainstream Christianity.

Queer transgresses boundaries; in the case of the MCC it challenges the normative view of choice of sexual partner, the 'heteronormative'. It challenges the generally understood dichotomy between Christianity and sexuality. In this way, the MCC is queer. On the other hand, the MCC reinforces binaries (Daniels 2010). The MCC maintains these contradictions in tension; this is the focus of Chapter 7.

Conclusion

The two stages, catalytic moments and working through the conflict, are complex processes characterized by transformations in relationships, emotional attachments and embodied ritual practices. A catalytic moment is triggered by relational experiences where individuals recognize the importance and validity of their sexuality or begin questioning their previous religious worldview. Old knowledge is reinterpreted or new knowledge gives individuals a new way of framing their sexuality within the context of their religious beliefs. For some this occurs through a breakdown in relationships with significant others and a rebuilding of new relationships in conjunction with new doctrinal knowledge. For others, knowledge that previously was illegitimate within their religious worldview becomes legitimate, most often through the building of new significant relationships.

Significant relationships are relationships with 'significant others' (Sullivan 1940), those who matter enough to effect change in self-definition. For the purposes of this study, significant relationships could be with family members, partners and peers, other persons in positions of authority such as church elders and health professionals, as well as spiritual entities such as God or Jesus. These relationships contribute to the rebuilding of religious habitus. Sticky emotions attached to same-sex attraction can be dissolved and individuals begin to recognize the legitimacy of their authentic sexual selves. Previous religious worldviews are questioned.

The stage of working through the conflict was similarly dominated by relational elements and emotional attachments. In the case of the majority of the participants in this study, the safe space of the MCC facilitated transformation of their habitus and deeply held religious worldviews. The safe spaces enabled individuals to exercise agency and renegotiate their religious worldview and habitus in order to make their sexuality acceptable. Emotional self-understandings were transformed through relationships, cognitive questioning and the performance of ritual practices,. The love of God, which affirmed their sexuality, enabled the integration of an authentic sexuality with the religious self. Each friendship, each relationship, each service, each song and each communion disrupted heteronormative constraints. Practices subvert spaces (Gorman-Murray, Waitt and Johnston 2008; Browne 2010: 231) and spaces are queered, as in this case individuals seek to express their authentic selves.

The safe spaces of the MCC are crucial. These findings are supportive of theories of religious experience as primarily relational and emotional rather than predominantly cognitive (Riis and Woodhead 2010). Riis and Woodhead argue that emotion and relationships are far more important than cognitive and rational aspects in shaping the religious experience. In this analysis, new cognitive understandings which bring previously held understandings of church doctrine into question, cannot alone effect change. Relational and emotional aspects are critical to cognitive changes.

The following chapter, 'Untroubled Christianity', delves a little more deeply into the tension between the queering of the church, in particular the MCC, and the reproduction of normative expectations and behaviours. The LGBT Christians in this study negotiated ways of being Christian in their desire to live an authentic life, seeking ways to encompass their sexuality and gender within their religious worldview. The individuals transgressed the heteronormative Christian assumptions, finding ways to marry seemingly contradictory identities. They partook in Christian practices that repeatedly queered spaces. Through the spaces of the MCC, Christianity itself was queered as queer practices recreated these spaces. This process was multidimensional, at times contradictory, and varied from individual to individual and congregation to congregation. In some ways, LGBT Christians remain entrenched in normative Christian ways of being. As an institution, Christianity remains, in some ways, largely untroubled.

Untroubled Christianity

Vignette: Rebecca

I grew up in [a conservative Christian Church]. Women weren't allowed to speak or anything like that. There was no pastor or minister. See the Holy Spirit led everything. The brothers were all equal. Women had to wear hats, have their head covered in church, and it was a little bit brainwashy, I guess. Everybody had to think the same way. Everybody had to be of the same mind.

I was engaged to be married when I was nineteen, with my boyfriend then of about four years. [He was part of the same church]. And then, I had a bit of pre-wedding jitters, and ended the engagement, which was really, really difficult. [It was] probably about six months before we got married. I'd actually met somebody else, a guy, as well. [I thought] if I feel like this about somebody else, it's not right.

I was going along [to church when I lived with] mum and dad. [Then] I moved cities. I managed to escape from it. [I stopped going to church], which was really hard on my parents. They really struggled with that. 'Cause I think they thought I was walking away from what they perceived to be the truth. Although my parents are amazing. I love them and I'm very thankful for the way I was brought up.

I really struggled as well, because, it's very hard to believe that anything else is right, because this is the way you've been taught your whole life. Very fundamental and very conservative. I struggled to find somewhere to go for, basically until now. This is when I was in my early twenties. So I say this is about ten years [ago].

I tried a lot of churches after I first left the [conservative church I was brought up in]. I went to Brethren churches, I went to a Pentecostal church once, I went to community churches. I went to quite a few Baptist churches with some friends. I tried a lot of different churches. They're so big, and I got lost in the crowd. I lived in [a big city] for a year with my girlfriend. I went to an MCC which was a sort of Catholic, sort of uniting churchy thing and they were all really, really sweet, but it was all men. I just didn't feel very comfortable. [The MCC I go to now] is the first church [I've said to myself] like yep, I'm going to go back. It's cool. I'm happy, good place.

I maintained my relationship with God the whole time. I never lost my faith and I've never doubted for a second that God loves me no matter what I've been through. I've had ups and downs.

I had a few relationships, with a few guys, like long-term relationships. I'm not really much of a (short term) short term, I don't date, I tend to have relationships.

I decided I wanted to go overseas. So, I went and worked on cruise ships and that's where I met my first girlfriend. I met her very soon after I started and I had no real inkling of what I was getting into. I had an experience with a woman before, but I didn't want to think about it. So, I met this girl and she was amazing. Great great girl, very understanding and we ended up being together for about three years.

I told my friends I'd met a girl and I was really happy and dating this girl, and gradually after a couple of years I told my sister who was really accepting and I've told my cousin but I haven't told my parents or anybody about it.

I definitely like women, but it's the person. I'm not saying that [I'm lesbian], I mean it's hard to say that 'cause it's hard not to identify as being one or the other. I hate that term bisexual. I went to this talk and they said that bisexuals have the highest suicide rate, the highest depression rate, 'cause they don't really belong in either camp. Even though it's LGBT it's never really.

But wouldn't it be so much easier to be straight – oh my god – but my parents don't know – after all – I haven't told them. I'm struggling with that at the moment. I've got a few things going on – I really need to make a decision – about where I want my life to go at the moment – so I'm trying to sort that out.

I've got to make a decision about how I want to live my life. I need to make a decision about whether I want to be gay and whether I want to identify with this for the rest of my life. The thing is, I'm not going to tell my parents tomorrow and then turn around and start dating a guy. What's the point of ruining their lives if I'm going to change my mind. I don't think it's going to happen, but I just think I need to work it out in my head and I think for me, my Christian journey is whether I was gay or straight or bisexual no matter whether you're a man or a woman, I think that it wouldn't matter in [the MCC]. 'Cause they're cool. It's a safe place. It's a place where it doesn't matter what you are.

It's hard too when you've been with men your whole life – well, beginning, and you know you like men. I mean some women definitely don't like men at all, it's different.

I don't have an issue with being gay, in regards to the fact that God loves me. I know that. I know he loves me. I believe he loves everybody and I have an unshakable faith that it is not wrong. But I struggle with society and being gay more than anything else. I think, for me, Christianity wise, it's always been okay, though I have struggles, [but] not with being gay.

I have struggled to find where I felt comfortable. Even at the MCC yesterday, I'm not used to all the touchy feely stuff 'cause it's so [different to how I was brought up]. I felt so awkward when everyone was going up to pray.

The thing is, what is life except for changing the way you feel about something? Just because I feel uncomfortable about something doesn't mean everyone else should not be able to do it. I think a lot of people need that [touchy feeling stuff] and I think it's really important. It's not all about me. It's good to have something to put you out of your comfort zone. Every day's a challenge and yeah it's good. I think that in order to move forward in your own life you need to go outside your comfort zone, your square.

I don't like the term religion. I identify as being a Christian. I'm not always perfect. I think the term Christian means Christ-like and I think I want to try and be like that and I have a relationship with God. I feel much easier with God, but don't understand Jesus – I don't understand that. So for me, God and Jesus are quite separate. But that's me.

I was homophobic [growing up] because that was what I was taught. If I met somebody that was gay I would treat them like any other person. I think, getting to know gay people made me start to think that it wasn't so wrong. When you are in a society and surroundings where you never really meet gay people, it doesn't really challenge you very much.

Right from when I was a kid, I've had crushes on women and girls, as well as boys, but I didn't really ever acknowledge [it]. I just thought, ah, its normal,

I think, now, through all the years, has strengthened my faith in God more, and it made me see that we put so many limits on God. We make him out to be this narrow minded person. Can you imagine how incredibly frustrating that must be for him. He must be just like, why can't you all just get along. I just think now that my eyes have been opened and I'm so lucky. That God had chosen to show me that there are better things out there.

There is so many people that believe different things. [They] believe that you can be gay, but don't have sex, or that you should be in a committed relationship, there's so many different things. But I think in the end [it is okay] as long as you feel right with God.

We went out to Mardi Gras [and a gay Christian friend said] I've never realized how important it was to have gay friends until now. She said, you always said to me that you need to have friends that are like you. You need to have people to support you, that you can talk about and that know what you are and what you are going through. She said until now, I've not realized that. She said, these people are so cool and it's so good to part of a community of women. That's what it feels like and even when you are there [at church] and there are people you don't know, you still feel part of something you share together. It's nice.

[Communion is] really nice. It's nice to go up there and hold somebody's hand and take communion, and be with people. I like it when whoever's in front says everybody's welcome, and nobody's different from anybody else. Wherever you come from or where you are going, even if you don't feel right with God, you are welcome – [you] can come to him. I think that's the most important message of MCC – it's okay. No matter where you are on your journey God will accept you, God loves you and you're welcome here. And I think that's so special, because where can you get that in any church? You never get that.

It's great to have to people to hang out with. I love going to the pub [after church]. When I first started going we used to go to the pub before and we'd have communion at this big table. It was so much fun – it was so cool. It was almost like being back in biblical times. It was really cool. But then they changed it because it was a bit too long [taking too much time]. So they were just having communion at the church and hanging out there for a bit. [At another time there were] little Bible study groups we used to do afterwards. They stopped doing that because church was getting too long. It was like three hours.

There's a few people who come and go, and I just get introduced to them and they don't come back for months and I've forgotten who they are. It's getting a bit like that.

[Interviewer: So looking back on it, do you think (being Christian) made it easier or harder for you to (understand) your sexuality, than if you hadn't have been brought up a Christian?]

Do you think it would have been easier for me to come to terms with my sexuality if I had been non-Christian? I can't even imagine being non-Christian. Maybe it would have been easier for me to tell my family. But both sides of my families are so steeped in Christianity that I can't imagine my life without [it] – to be honest with you. But I don't necessarily think it's always easier when you are not a Christian. I know a lot of people who said my family would disown me if I was gay – and they are not religious at all.

I think coming to terms with my sexuality has made my faith stronger in a way: 'cause you realize how much he loves you, what a plan he must – like he throws these curved balls at you but it's always, obviously for a reason.

Introduction

You've got these five boys running the show, right, and you don't have any females, but the girls can get together and have retreats,[1] they've had retreats for the last fourteen years and the males don't even get one off … It's quite interesting really, they are quite willing to be top dog when it comes to the board, but they are not willing to submit, I guess, and go on a retreat! (Annie)

Inclusivity provides a safe place and acceptance but it does not address that question of who am I … Regardless of how inclusive they are, even MCC is going to fail. Church cannot get away from ties with the notion of family. The church is predicated on family. (Sylvia)

Subverted heteronormative practices queer Christianity in the MCC. These subverted Christian practices accommodate alternative sexualities. The MCC's space invokes 'a radically inclusive God' (Shore-Goss 2013: 2) in practice and enables LGBT Christians to worship. It provides a safe space where 'healing and wholeness' can be attained, and where the authentic self can be lived. However, there are questions about the extent to which the MCC provides 'radical inclusive love of God' and how far Christianity is queered. This chapter focuses on the limits of inclusivity and the extent of queerness in the MCC. Annie, for example, quoted above, expresses her frustration at continuing inequalities in the MCC. She also reveals a binary understanding of masculinity and femininity commonly expressed within the MCC. Sylvia, a transgender participant, also articulates that conceptually, however hard individuals may wish to express inclusivity, the normative foundations will inexorably lead to failure.

As a Christian organization, the MCC upholds the basic theological premise of Christianity, that the triune God is 'omnipotent, omnipresent and omniscient' and 'every person is justified by grace to God through faith in Jesus Christ'. It is only through 'God's gift of grace [which] is not earned, but is a pure gift from a God of pure love, that we are saved from loneliness, despair and degradation' (MCC 2013b). God and Jesus are greater than human beings, who should 'seek genuine forgiveness for unkind, thoughtless and unloving acts; and commit [to] a life of Christian service'. This premise leads to the conclusion that, as Ken Plummer asserts (1995: 148): 'queer fundamentalists have no way of reconciling differences with Christian fundamentalists'. Radical feminists similarly cannot reconcile the premise of patriarchal Christianity with their fundamental principles of gender equity (Raphael 1999; Kirkman 2001; Christ 2004).

The findings of our research indicate that the traditional hierarchical construction of relationships within the institution of Christianity remain largely untroubled. Traditional understandings of gender and family underpinned by Christian doctrine exclude queer forms of being. Sylvia highlights the struggle of transgendered individuals to 'find a place at the table'. As she expresses it: 'The church is predicated on family'. The ambiguity and complexity of her experience was not easily encompassed even in the context of the inclusivity of the MCC. The MCC challenges heteronormativity but, as will be shown, reinforces gendered binaries and traditional family structures.

Bisexual individuals are often treated with suspicion within both the LGBTIQ community and the MCC (Daniels 2010; Toft 2010). Not only does bisexuality present an ambiguous and problematic non-dichotomous view of sexuality that is 'not quite formed', it also carries with it the stigma of non-monogamy even though this is in most cases inaccurate (Klesse 2005: 365; Daniels 2010: 46). The MCC (2013a) overtly and covertly encourages a normative expectation of family, privileging monogamy over other structures of sexual relationships and thus reproducing a new normative way of being, a homonormative ideal. Homonormativity is 'the assimilation of heteronormative ideals and constructs into homosexual culture and individual identity. It refers to politics that do not contest dominant heteronormative assumptions and institutions such as monogamy, procreation and binary gender roles' (Duggan 2002; *Positive Space Network Resource Person Manual* 2010: 26).

Although the congregations we visited consciously challenge stereotypes of gender and sexuality, deeply embedded traditional normative understandings of gender and family are present to a greater or lesser degree. This chapter analyses the responses to ambiguity in the MCC. On one hand, space is queered through rituals and practices that subvert normative expectations of sexuality, and to a lesser extent, gender. Inclusivity through the radical love of God is practised. On the other, gendered and other normative distinctions continue to be reproduced for three main reasons. First, the participants are driven by the desire to be authentic to a gendered and sexed body. This essentialist understanding of sexuality and gender enables individuals to begin with the premise that they as individuals are essentially 'good'. Second, adherence to a normative Christian habitus forms the basis for distinctions between what is right, and what is considered wrong. Third, practising according to a renewed shared religious habitus fosters a deep sense of belonging, upon which individuals build their legitimacy as LGBT Christians and as valuable human beings.

Gender

A policy of gender-inclusive language is practised in two MCC churches and to a limited extent in the third. Each congregation and each individual apprehends this policy in different ways. The pastors of two MCC churches articulate strong support for the use of gender-inclusive language to enable the inclusion of men and women. The third pastor is more flexible with its use, declaring: 'At [our MCC congregation] we don't care if you are male or female', concluding that gender-inclusive language is unnecessary.

One pastor sees gender inclusivity as a practical tool, to encourage, empower and include as many people as possible. He explains:

> It's not about whether God's a man or a woman or whatever, but it's about removing barriers. So that everyone can feel and touch and experience God in a way that is empowering for them. So when it comes to inclusivity and gender issues, that's [removing barriers] our driving force, to the best of our ability.

There are two major theological arguments underlying this practice: one that the nature of God is binary, containing both male and female characteristics, and second that the nature of God is 'beyond gender', a 'queer' God without boundaries or delineations. On the whole, from the interview content and Bronwyn's experience as a participant/observer, the theological premise that a binary God creates essential male and female characteristics was most prominent in these congregations.

One pastor, for example, explains how valuable it is to 'preach and teach the various faces of God, balance the beautiful wisdom imagery – the spirit of God that blows through people and is always feminine, and the masculine of God, God the father'. His use of gender-inclusive language stems from his belief in a dichotomous and gendered God, a balance between a God the father and the loving spirit of God, the feminine. This God is an inclusive God. While a masculine judging God excludes and separates, a comforting feminine God accepts and embraces. This is a common belief among participants who understand God as a duality of distinct masculine and feminine aspects. This God is not a queer God. However, this is a God that includes and welcomes both male and female genders.

On the other hand, Peter describes his understanding of gender-inclusive language as stemming from a queer God, saying: 'The case of inclusive language is trying to make God appear bigger than just a man, greater than, all encompassing.' Liz also appreciates both understandings of God. While on one hand she believes 'male and female come from God, so God's got as many feminine attributes as masculine', on the other hand she also says that 'God isn't male or female, God is God.' This is a 'queer' God, a God that goes beyond the duality of male and female. Arthur illustrates vividly how he understands God in a similar way:

> You can't stuff God into a label or into a concept without something being left over. It's like the mad hatter's tea party where he tried to stuff the mouse into the teapot. It's impossible to define God because in doing so you are confining God and my God is too big to be confined.

A God who is not confined is a God that doesn't judge. Luke also explains that for him 'the experience of God is something that removes all boundaries'.

Peter, who has always been scathing towards anyone preaching against homosexuality, says: 'Look at Galatians 3: 6–9 – there's not a Jew nor Greek, there's no slave nor free, or a male or female ... or gay or straight.' For him no boundaries exist, thus no judgement comes from God, only though ignorance of God. Based upon this understanding of God, Peter supports the use of gender-inclusive language as 'something we should embrace' from the theological perspective that 'God is greater than male', but adds vehemently, not because 'lesbians don't like God referred to as male'! His response illustrates one of many tensions clustered around gender in the MCC related to the use of gender-inclusive language.

The use of gender-inclusive language enables inclusivity. The responses of the LGBT participants in this study to this stated policy of UFMCC is a gauge to measure gendered attitudes within the MCC. The response towards its use is strikingly mixed and ranges from gratitude and empowerment, to reluctant and condescending acceptance, to dismissal, even resentment. Surprisingly, responses do not necessarily follow gendered lines.

Language does have an impact on the understanding of and relationship with God. For some women this is a successful strategy. As Judith explains:

> Inclusive language has been really good for me. I never realized it, that male patriarchal system. I look back and my father beat me up ... the ungendered

language was making a difference. But it wasn't something I really noticed. At first, it was a bit weird, but then I realized, when it was all masculine, it was like there was a closed heaven.

This is similar to Liz, who says; 'My relationship with God – I'm very glad we use inclusive language, I think because I had an abusive Dad, it would be very hard to marry the idea of God being a loving God and God being a father figure.'

Both women could begin to relate to God differently and recognize that God was not necessarily masculine in the same way that they had experienced masculinity. Without this, they would both relate God to their childhood experiences of their own fathers, who had abused and disempowered them. Three other women find the gender-neutral language important for their personal religious development, while many remain ambivalent.

Several men support the use of gender-inclusive language but find it unimportant for their religious growth. However, Michael draws on his 'early Christian experience with the heavy masculine wording' to fully support inclusive language, saying:

It's very much a carry-over attitude that the woman's place is in the kitchen and should not be heard. And to me that's a put-down. It's an inclusive language in whichever form it is, to my mind, exactly what it should be. It encompasses both genders and reflects the attitude of this day and age rather than something out of the 19th century.

A large number of men and women are ambivalent about its use; some are hostile. Paul explains the contention it provokes:

I can really understand women being uncomfortable with the whole emphasis on the maleness of God, which by the way is not scriptural. But at the same time I do understand that there are some people for whom the maleness of God is very, very important. So we have to try and balance all of those things so that everyone can experience a relationship with God that is relevant for them in their life journey. Now, if you are a woman who's been raped and beaten by your father, sitting here and saying, 'Our father in heaven' is going to close down maybe any chance of hearing anything positive about God ... so we take away a word that can simply be a barrier.

Although Paul's desire is to include women, from a feminist point of view his attitude reproduces a traditional patriarchal response to women that is regularly evident in the interviews. Women are pathologized as being in need of assistance in order to experience God. Although the use of language is embracing and inclusive, the implications are that women are pathologically in need of concessions from a patriarchal institution.

This is also illustrated by the attitude of some male participants, who accept its use as a necessary but tiresome appeasement for women. One male MCC congregant explains:

> I am a little amused sometimes by the concern for changing the words in stuff, it's like, if it makes you happy, but really at this point we have more important things to be worried about. That's my attitude as a man. I try to be sympathetic and it's good to be inclusive ... but when you start putting awkward words into replacing 'he' in a classic song, is this just going too far?

Although he does not articulate what is more important, he implies that this use of language is unnecessary and pedantic compared with more 'important things to be worried about'. It is not clear if he is criticizing the over-use of gender-inclusive language used without thought for its purpose, which often overshadows the real issue, the gendered nature of Christianity.

Approximately half the interviewees, both men and women, resist the use of gender-inclusive language. One female congregant, for example, expresses her difficulty, saying: 'I don't like it! ... Like the Lord's Prayer. They have inclusive language for that! I just find I can't do it ... there's no way.' She further explains: 'This is the one I know, this is the one I stick to, in saying that I don't like it, I respect it at the same time.'

While many of the men and women support its use on principle, they also express feeling strange using gender-inclusive language. May explains: 'Even the old hymns have been de-gendered much to the extent they can be and I really like that, but in my head, the 'hims' and 'hes' are still there.' Some articulate that they could only understand God as 'he': 'I was brought up with *him* as *he*.' This is illustrative of the deeply embedded nature of the religious habitus in which God has always been related to as he. Despite being cognitively aware of the value of the change, the religious habitus generates an emotional response that resists the change in language. In this way the 'sticky' emotion of the pronoun retains its patriarchal power. The destabilizing or queering of gendered Christian culture only occurs within the bounds of what is comfortable. The institution of Christianity is deeply imbued with patriarchy, patriarchal language and heterosexism. The religious 'habitus' with its deeply ingrained patriarchal language, concepts and divinities, meant many participants struggled to use gender-inclusive language.

In general the younger participants found gender and the use of gender-inclusive language less of an issue than many of the older participants. Natalie, the youngest participant, says: 'Gender never affected me. And the fact that MCC is very gender-sensitive about saying God is a he and stuff ... I don't get offended that people refer to God as he.' One congregation used little gender-inclusive language. As one young woman comments dismissively: 'That gender language, [this congregation] is a bit less hung up on that.' To her, gender-inclusive language is restrictive. Another woman explains:

> What I find hard is the inclusive language – it's just strange to me. I've never had issues calling God Father or anything like it. I guess [this congregation] is a lot more laid back about this than other MCC churches and I really appreciate that ... at [this congregation] I don't feel any patriarchy at all. It's quite even in my feeling.

These women indicate that the feeling of being included equally as a woman within the MCC congregational culture does not require gender-inclusive language. In saying that the congregation is 'less hung up on that', and 'is more laid back', these women indicate that to them gender-inclusive language, with its awkwardness, is unnecessary and restrictive. There was a 'laissez-faire' attitude towards patriarchal Christianity, which indicates that the women feel empowered within their group and, second, there is a belief that the congregation is making an impact upon gendered attitudes, dissolving gender divisions. The younger individuals held fewer emotional sticky attachments to the masculine pronouns.

The intention of gender-inclusive language is to enable and empower women. Its use is underpinned by either a dichotomous conception of God with both masculine and feminine aspects, or a queer God who cannot be defined. These strange bedfellows, the dichotomous and queer God, while seemingly at odds with each other, go hand in hand to create a space of inclusivity and acceptance that has meaning for the LGBT Christians in this study. Despite this, the emphasis on the dichotomous God facilitates a continuation of power inequalities within the MCC as an institution, with the privileging of masculinity over femininity. The following sections focus on the ascription of gendered characteristics, specifically in relation to leadership and relations between men and women.

Ascribed gender characteristics – self and others

Gender in the MCC is challenged. Individuals transgress the normative expectation of consistent sex/gender roles and expose the socially constructed nature of gender. The MCC in this sense queers gender boundaries. However, responses to leadership issues, to ambiguities in relationships between men and women (such as transgender and bisexuality) expose deeply entrenched normative understandings of ascribed gendered characteristics – towards both self and others.

Women and men in leadership are fairly evenly represented across all three of the churches visited. However, in one of the congregations men make up the majority of leadership positions. The congregation with predominantly male leadership elicits mixed responses, all of which ascribe binary gender characteristics to men and women. One of the more active women in this congregation, Alice, was complicit in male-dominated leadership of her congregation, explaining that this was due to the dichotomous nature of men and women: 'I'd love to see more women on the board but I think it's within the nature … so I'm too sensitive to be on the board, I thrive with congregational care.' She ascribes leadership characteristics to males and in doing so enables the reproduction of patriarchal structural values.

As Alice explained the gender binary in the interview, she realized that perhaps there were fuzzy borders, saying: 'I sometimes think God suits men, and Jesus suits softer beings – I shouldn't just say women – God as an authority figure suits people who look for an authority figure and where Jesus suits people who want the close relationship, perhaps.' Alice says that her role is aligned with Jesus, who exhibits feminine qualities that she feels she can exemplify.

Later Alice continues to describe the nature of women and men as distinct: 'Well, I think the evening service suits the nature of women, it's soft, gentle, the lights are down … I think the evening is a lot closer to what Jesus would've instigated.' In contrast, the morning service with 'marching songs and strict ritual' is accepting of authority. Alice reiterates the emphasis on Jesus, saying that Jesus was 'more embracing of females as anyone else at the time', and is 'a liberator of females'. Her understanding of the role of Jesus is in line with Carter Heyward's (1999) feminist theological approach to Jesus as a Jesus who struggles for equality and justice, a far more egalitarian Jesus, a non-authoritarian Jesus.

Alice's traditional, dichotomous understanding of gender is shared by one minister, who understands God to have clear masculine and feminine characteristics. He contrasts the strong 'God the father', and the feminine, soft and gentle 'spirit of God that blows through people and is always feminine – the beautiful wisdom imagery of Sophia, the wonderful Old Testament thing'. He respects the two women who are deeply involved in the church, describing them as 'matriarchs' without whom 'the church couldn't work'.

Many of the women understand that a change of attitudes towards women within the church is necessary. The majority suggest that 'change comes slowly', as Victoria says. She continues: 'Church reflects society ... I think it's about strong women standing up, I believe, with love in their hearts and leading through love.' She explains that for her, as a positive person, she believes change will come for women (and has already occurred) through 'patience, persistence and perseverance', that 'I know if I wait long enough [change] will be even sweeter when we get there.' Her assimilationist attitude ascribes stereotypical feminine characteristics to women as 'waiting and being patient', and of being 'loving'. She also exhibits a realistic understanding of the inertia of change.

There is a high degree of separation between men and women in one of the MCC congregations. Alice describes initially coming to a service which consisted of all men: 'The service was wonderful, but after the service, no-one spoke to us over a cup of tea. We were the only women there but no-one, not even the pastor, spoke with us.' She and her partner, far from being discouraged, recognized the need for women: 'offering that softness, that love, that openness, that welcoming, nurturing nature of women in a church of men who don't necessarily experience that a lot'. The feminine characteristics of 'softness, love and welcoming' are considered to be natural to women in general, reflecting the essential understanding of God-given dichotomous gendered characteristics.

Ascribing masculinity as being 'more suited to being on the board' as Alice does, becomes problematic when issues of power are attached to this difference. Annie, for example, is not patient and at times is less forgiving. She expresses frustration at the gender imbalance, saying: 'I would like to see, not that I would personally do it, but I would like to see a woman on the board, and I think, a lot of the decisions ... on the board – they are men, so they are male focused, and there is a lot of controversy.' She adds that despite men being in leadership positions, in contrast to the women, they cannot 'get it together' to organize a retreat as 'they are not willing to submit'. Annie expresses a binary view of masculinity and femininity, revealing her understanding of masculinity to be dominating and individualistic, where men were unable or unwilling to work together to organize a retreat.

The response to women in leadership is mixed. There are tensions surrounding the issue of leadership in the MCC, with two men expressing frustration at women. Peter, for example, comments that despite 'a congregation of gays and lesbians [being] fairly refreshing', the past female leadership of the church was 'a mob of fairly vicious women'. Luke too, who at this time attends a congregation with little tension between men and women, explains that in the past he had felt there was a bitter division between 'gay politics' and 'lesbian politics' and recalls how 'each wanted him on their side'. For him what was initially empowering for women, 'taking our place at the table', becomes an 'angry, aggressive thing'. Women are pathologized for expressing 'masculine' characteristics of anger and aggression.

Others are extremely positive towards having women in leadership assigning positive feminine characteristics; for example, William exclaims:

> Women make better leaders than men. I think they've got warmth, more so than a man, and a man tries to keep his position. But a woman is more relaxed, more gentle, and that keeps the group together.

William understands that the ascribed feminine characteristics of gentleness and warmth together with group thinking enable women to be good leaders. Others resist assigning gender characteristics to women, with one male interviewee suggesting: 'It is the person and what they are saying that is important to me', and another male saying: 'I've worked with men, I've worked with women … There have been difficult men, and difficult women … I have trouble with difficult people.'

Queering relationships

One MCC congregant describes his congregation as having fluid gender expression: 'Well, you see it here in [this congregation]; Karen is the epitome of the handy woman. She'll climb on the roof and fix something electric … you'll find one of the guys baking for supper … there's a certain freedom there.' He explains the benefit is that 'there's a blend of talents that might otherwise not be known'. He also articulates that enabling more fluid gender expression means that in MCC: 'People can be themselves without any concern for being ostracized.' He makes conscious efforts to challenge gender stereotypes, to fuzzy the edges of the masculine/male, feminine/female expectations by, for example, wearing sarongs to church or beads at work.

Others experience freedom in their relationships through lack of distinction between male and female, facilitated by a queering of gender expectations and norms within the LGBT community. Nickie explains: 'There's no difference with gay people. There's five women in the church and about twenty men. And yet I feel like one of the boys and they feel like one of the girls.' She continues: 'I always feel they're my brothers and sisters. It just feels the same gender to me.' While she still distinguishes between 'the boys and the girls', she feels the borders are fluid or permeable, and she feels 'like one of the boys'. This leads to a certain freedom of expression, and a freedom in relationships, which enables her to feel as close as 'brothers and sisters'.

The pastor of one congregation explains: 'When [this church] started we were at a church where it's not just about women taking their place at the table and not putting women down either, it's just about, we don't care if you're male or female.' He continues: 'God removes all divisions ... the gender stuff; I don't really have to think about it ... I shrug it off. It doesn't matter to me.' This is echoed by another male member of the congregation: 'Gender is not important [in this congregation] ... women can serve Christ just as well as any man and can be the hands and feet and part of the body.' This sentiment is supported by the women. As one woman described when asked about gender in her congregation: 'They treat men and women equally and you will notice that men and women will take an equal part in each service ... and I think there is a strong feminine identity in that church.' Two women discuss leadership, one saying: 'It's not about gender, it's about who has the gifts to do the job, who's called.' The other said: '[This MCC] showed no distinction between male and female in leadership. Females can preach, females can have the same input. I think MCC is different.'

Four of the six interviewees from the same MCC congregation insisted that 'gender didn't matter'. Their assertion was strengthened ironically by their lack of interest in gender-inclusive language, or in fuzzying the gender boundaries through emphasized expressions of, for example, dress or gesture. One member of the same congregation said: 'Physically I am male, I have always identified as male, but when I was very little I knew I was a girl, and when I dream I'm always actually a woman in my dreams.' He adds that 'it has never been something that has caused me trouble or distress ... it doesn't matter to me'. While he is one of the only participants who describes his gendered identity so clearly (with the exception of the two transgendered interview participants), younger congregants express a similar sentiment, that they were disinterested in gender distinctions.

The youngest interview participant explains: 'I don't think gender bothers God, and I don't think gender should bother humans.' In the MCC services we observed in which young people predominate, leadership is shared between the sexes. In addition, men and women socialize easily, and don't feel the need to exaggerate and/or bend gender identity. As one female congregant said: 'I think for my Christian journey, whether I am gay, straight or bisexual, a man or a woman, I think that wouldn't matter in [this congregation] ... because they're cool.'

Response to ambiguity

The response to the transgendered congregants is illuminating of the understanding of gender roles at the MCC. Fellow MCC congregants tend to define and delineate, and at times 'Other' those who don't fit easily into binaried gender identities, despite being themselves excluded by the heterosexual majority. Anthony describes his initial discomfort with transgender:

> Something interesting ... we had the transgender day the Sunday before and I'm as guilty as a lot of people are, I've met but I don't know any transgender people. And I realize how challenged I was by that. And I took that as a good lesson that we are a marginalized group so we've got to be really careful we don't marginalize people within our group, because otherwise we are guilty of what some of the other larger faiths to do to us. That takes a transgender person or the other individual that's a bit more unique within our community to help us do that too. It's got to be a two-way street.

He reflexively interrogates his own response with the desire to be inclusive. Anthony recognizes the tendency to judge, and responds positively to the challenge, to use the challenge of difference to become better as a Christian. His desire to live non-judgementally is challenged by the gender-queer expression of transgender. Michael also describes the confusion felt by members of the congregation at a time when a transgender woman was preaching, exclaiming: 'You never knew whether you are going to be preached to by Bill or Betty.' He continues to describe how difficult it was for both the preacher and the congregation due to the unclear gender distinction, yet explains how this gave the congregation 'the opportunity to just gently accept people as they are – it's important for their spiritual well-being'.

Others are less reflexive in their attitudes to transgender, as illustrated by one female congregant:

> When that last retreat was on I got asked to do some leading the small groups up there, and the sessions. And I got put in with – there was a married lady, and there was a transgendered person, and just the 'motley crew'. And you really couldn't get anything going – discussions – because the transgender would just say the answer is yes, or no. You know like blokes do.

This attitude expresses the commonly held (mis)understanding that while being a transwoman, she is 'really a man'. In this case, the transwoman's gender is not recognized as being legitimate. Again masculine and feminine traits are identified and used to legitimize and delegitimize, to create boundaries. The congregant identifies with 'the motley crew' by which she means her lesbian friends, separating herself from the 'married lady and the transgendered person', creating renewed 'hierarchies of worthiness' (Stryker 2008). The 'motley crew' however signifies belonging and safety that cultivates the feeling of love for the self, and the development of legitimacy as same-sex attracted Christians.

This attitude to the transgendered individual illustrates how difficult it is to actually live 'queer' and the entrenched nature of gender and sexuality in individual and group identity. It also indicates a dichotomous understanding of gender roles – in this case the idea that men are unable to discuss and cooperate, but simply see issues in terms of 'yes or no'.

Bisexuality also challenges binary thinking. According to Rebecca, bisexual individuals 'don't really belong in either camp. Even though it's LGBT it's never really'. Rebecca was the only participant who identifies positively as bisexual. Two women say that they could identify as bisexual but don't, considering there to be a biased negative attitude towards it.

The discomfort felt by others towards transgender and bisexuality is indicative of the emotional investment in normalcy and coherence. Even Nova explains how bewildering it is for her: 'Now I wake up and I don't know if I'm Arthur or Martha! And I think it's okay, but it's bewildering for me.' The transwomen disrupt gender roles and expectations, creating discomfort. From birth, gendered characteristics and roles are culturally reinforced repetitively and continuously. Transgender individuals transgress these clearly defined boundaries, doing gender differently, unsettling themselves and others. The response from the members of MCC is either reflexive, eliciting inclusivity, or reactive, reproducing normative binaries.

Being transgender

Gender roles and ascribed binary characteristics are also ironically reinforced by the transgendered individuals themselves. The two transgender participants illustrate the power of gender as a defining factor of identity, challenging queer ways of being. While both transwomen transgress the consistent sex/gender role boundaries and expectations, they reproduce normative gendered understandings. For example, femininity for these women is highlighted and emphasized in dress and behaviour. They both dress in elegant frocks and apply large amounts of makeup, emphasizing their femininity. Feminine characteristics are also highlighted, with both women expressing sensitivity and gentleness. Both also understand their femininity as essential – as a previously undiscovered aspect of their essential and God-given self.

For example, in the vignette that opens Chapter 6, Sylvia explains: 'I read an article on men who cross-dress … Words like gentleness were used. And I thought, hang on a minute. That's describing me.' She also describes the moment she bought her first wig:

> I … went, "Oh shit." It feminized my face. It was a long haired wig. And the face I saw, there was a recognition there. It was like, that's me … And so quite literally, yes, seconds, life was not going to be the same again.

She goes on to describe how: 'Twenty, thirty years of things that just didn't make sense now began to make sense.' The confusion of not understanding, of being alone with contradictory gendered impulses, such as buying feminine hygiene products, began to be slowly resolved.

Nova also identified from an early age an essential feminine within herself. She was seeking a femininity that resonated with her. She explains: 'I see that lesbians and drag queens can sometimes be so aggressive. I cannot accept that particularly in drag queens. I find that they are very attractive but when they started to speak, I find that repelling. I'm not that person.'

Both Nova and Sylvia describe clear pivotal moments when they recognize or have a glimpse of their 'true' gendered selves. On the one hand, gendered expectations are challenged; on the other hand, the essentially understood traits of femininity or masculinity are propagated, albeit in differently sexed bodies. This also raises the question of authenticity. The transwomen recognize their 'true gendered selves' in pivotal moments that evoke the desire to discover and explore their authentic self. In pursuit of the authentic essential self, both Nova and Sylvia queer space and to a degree queer Christianity. As Sylvia exclaims: 'I took God seriously from day one. And that's been the driver for my transitioning.' Her Christian God is empowering her to transition, to transgress the binary of sex/gender. Her enacted queer Christianity is driven by the search for an authentic God-created self. For Sylvia, it is a moral imperative to discover that essential queer self. This reveals an unresolvable tension between the desire to discover an authentic self and the means to attain this.

Patriarchy, monogamy and family in the MCC

Attitudes to patriarchy, monogamy and family in the MCC further underline the ongoing significance of normative Christian understandings of gender and sexuality. Essentialist understandings of gender and sexuality are bound up with Christian understandings, emotional orientations, and relational practices of gender and sexuality. Relationships with God and Jesus and emotional attachments within the congregations nurture the feeling of belonging and take precedence over cognitive objections to patriarchal practices. Practising Christianity is deeply fulfilling for many of the participants, and this takes precedence over more progressive or queer understandings of gender and sexuality.

Very few participants in this study understand Christianity as explicitly patriarchal. In fact, one woman explicitly rejects the suggestion: 'I don't feel any patriarchy at all.' Another, however, comments upon the content of the sermons in her congregation. Despite the best efforts of the pastor who, in his words, 'preaches and teaches on the various faces of God', Anthea explains that as opposed to Catholicism where 'they talk more about the female characters, you don't hear that here. You are always hearing about the disciples.' She muses on the lack of women in the congregation, exclaiming: 'Some of those readings are fiery! … They seem to have a lot of anger. Maybe that's why women don't go to it … Especially that [biblical] Paul; the language is a bit aggressive almost.' Anthea recognizes the patriarchal nature of the MCC she attends, ascribing masculine gendered characteristics to it. She equates angry, fiery and aggressive with masculinity. Anthea, however, loves the MCC, finding a sense of belonging in the inclusivity and solace in the friendships. The relationships she has developed take precedence over her cognitive objections.

Those women in MCC who attempt to modify Christianity by changing it from within, do so by expressing the need for ascribed feminine characteristics of love and patience. They experience the love of God and Jesus, and the support of community that enables them to find comfort in the church. The fact that some women in the MCC recognize the patriarchal attitudes within it, yet remain steadfastly Christian, also underlines the centrality of emotions and relationships, of habitus, to religious commitment and religious experience.

Although the interviews did not focus on the organization of relationships, there was a consensus that monogamy is preferable. While polyamory did not enter the discussion, promiscuity is mostly understood as incompatible with the church teachings. The bylaws of UFMCC (MCC 2013a) articulate that 'the rite of holy union/matrimony is the spiritual joining of two persons'. Most participants are in long-term committed monogamous relationships. Matt, for example, reports with pride that this year he and his partner are celebrating their 21st anniversary together. Two participants explicitly describe promiscuity as immoral. According to Anthea:

> I mean, it sounds judgemental, but I struggle a bit with some of this gay scene where they are, particularly the men, with their promiscuity and yet they go to church. I don't understand that part. But that's just, I think, that's the male, particularly the male gay scene. And I think anything goes. I don't always understand how they can do that with Christianity. I would feel a bit of conflict about going to church being that kind of person that I believe God wants me to be, and then I'm going out there, you know, sleeping around and doing things that maybe I don't think for me are morally right. It would be hard to come to church asking for forgiveness. It is all right to ask forgiveness, but you go out and do the same thing again.

Anthony too, having at one time lived fairly promiscuously, explains:

> I'm in a monogamous relationship and I don't need any of that stuff [promiscuity] anymore and it never satisfied myself anyway ... But ultimately I think most people are looking for intimacy with someone. And that's not about the five minutes of pleasure, that's about something more ... It's commitment and the things that come with that.

This commitment to 'normalcy' is common, not only in terms of sexual relationships, but also expressed in the desire to celebrate services traditionally. As one older congregant reported explaining proudly to her heterosexual friend:

> I could blindfold you and take you in there and you'd hear the sermon and you wouldn't know you were in a gay congregation. Because they never say: 'Not like those, straight people' or anything like that. You'd never know. If she didn't see the people, she wouldn't know where you were.

The normative nature of the Christian practices at the MCC reinforce a feeling of legitimacy. The commitment to monogamy, also a normative Christian practice, excludes and 'Others' those who do not live according to this practice. Monogamy is closely related to the family, a contested and changing institution (Blumstein and Schwartz 1983). For the participants of MCC, family was generally understood as based upon monogamous relationships. The institution is constrained within normative Christian expectations. 'Family' is also central to the feeling of belonging, and the reworking of a religious worldview which included alternative sexualities. Within 'family' space, religious habitus could be transformed through the building of new significant relationships, as discussed in Chapter 3 and illustrated in Chapter 6. However, 'family' is also a contested word, a word and concept that can exclude.

'Family' is also an example of a sticky word that elicits powerful emotional responses. There are continual references to 'brothers and sisters', to 'coming home' (discussed in Chapters 5 and 6), and the importance of family to the building of inclusive spaces in order to discover and live according to the authentic self. These words, however, exclude some forms of being, and reinforce gendered binaries of those who belong and those who do not belong. As Sylvia reports:

> Church cannot get away from ties with the notion of family. The church is predicated on family. There are people out in the community for whom family is just too painful. They've [the church] got to address questions of how do we keep family and reach out to people to whom family is just too painful and do it in a way that is meaningful.

Sylvia underlines the importance of, and desire for, family. She is, however, critical of the exclusions the word 'family' engenders. Family as she understands it also excludes ambiguity. It excludes non-monogamous relationships. For Sylvia, relationships are complex and ambiguous, and at times a fluid mix – which is not encouraged or understood within the normative space of the MCC.

Conclusion

Despite the queering of heteronormative space in all the four congregations and a fluid expression of gender across sexed bodies, a dichotomous gender construction appears resistant to change. Gender is understood as a God-given essential characteristic for the majority of the same-sex attracted Christians we interviewed. This understanding holds that both male and female characteristics are necessary to express the fullness of God's nature. Ironically, the transgendered individuals who challenge gender dichotomies also understand gender in essentialist terms, displaying 'emphasized femininity' (Connell 1995). Gender is understood as an essential and substantive reality that is performed in order to live an authentic existence. There is a strong emotional investment in this essentialist understanding of gender. This is illustrative of the tension between the queering of Christianity and the search for the authentic self.

Power issues associated with the gender dichotomy in the church spaces were evident. This is especially apparent in one congregation where a patriarchal leadership is upheld by the more traditional Christian representation of gendered difference. Masculinity is privileged, being understood as suited to leadership and to guiding others, and is valorized. Femininity is constructed as caring, as gentle and healing, in a supporting role. At the intersection with Christianity, the dichotomous construction of male and female leads to a greater or lesser degree the maintenance of power imbalances. Both institutional and individual habitus reproduce gendered stereotypes, despite institutional efforts such as the use of gender-inclusive language. Gender clearly mattered, and is a powerful and deeply meaningful social characteristic that still remains attached to hierarchy, position and power.

Further, the response to ambiguity in the MCC is indicative of the deeply entrenched nature of the normative Christian habitus upon which these individuals create meaning. Romantic monogamous relationships are prioritized. The essentialist understanding of an authentic sexuality leads to bisexuality being viewed as an 'immature' state. Ambiguity disturbs individuals. Ambiguity threatens the safe spaces that are created in the MCC. Individuals feel safe in spaces that are unsurprising and in some sense 'normative'. The queering of religious space occurs insofar as the individual and group needs are met in the desire to live an authentic life. This does not occur if the queering violates existing 'horizons of significance' that are a product of a Christian normative habitus. Despite challenging heteronormative mainstream Christianity, the MCC creates its own 'homonormative' space.

Discussion and Conclusion

Introduction

The lived experience of committed LGBT Christians is at times traumatic and painful, yet is also transformed into experiences that are deeply rewarding. LGBT Christians are often treated with hostility by members of most Christian denominations and by the wider LGBTIQ community. LGBT Christians act according to moral mandates based upon an ethic of authenticity (Taylor 1991), seeking to discover and express their 'true' sexuality and/or gender. The desire to be 'authentic' derives from both contemporary culture and from their religiosity. Some individuals struggle with the integration of their sexual, gendered and religious identities. The transformation of a deeply embedded religious habitus to include LGBT sexuality and gender is a complex and difficult process, driven by emotions formed within relationships and new religious practices, in conjunction with cognitive transformations in belief and understanding.

A form of queer Christianity is produced through LGBT Christians living according to an ethic of authenticity in the context of a transformed religious habitus. Safe spaces within which LGBT Christians worship are central to making this possible. Queer Christian practices enable LGBT Christians to find fulfilment in an authentic life. However, there are limits to the queering. Structural and cultural processes within the institution of Christianity resist change. Resistance to change is produced and reproduced within the congregations of the Metropolitan Community Church (MCC). While heteronormativity is subverted and queered, gender and other normative Christian structures remain relatively unchallenged.

The ethic of authenticity

LGBT Christians are motivated by an 'ethic of authenticity' to express their 'true', sexual, gendered and religious selves. This desire is amplified by their religiosity, which positions their sexuality and gender as 'God-given'. This theme was explored in detail in Chapter 4. According to Charles Taylor (2007: 475), 'each of us has his/her own way of realising our humanity'. For the LGBT Christians in this research, realizing their unique humanity is bound up with the essentialist argument of some gay theologians (Comstock 1993), that God created each person in his own image, just as 'He wanted them'. Warner (2005) suggests that this emphasis on essentialism is a finding common to most ethnographic and sociological studies of LGBT Christians, in particular those which concentrate on men (Thumma 1991; Yip 1997a; 1997b; 1999; Rodriguez and Ouellette 2000; Lukenbill 2005; Primiano 2005; Wolkomir 2006; Gross and Yip 2010). Whether this is applicable to women is debatable, but according to Wilcox (2002: 504), among religious lesbians 'essentialism reigns supreme'. Our research supports her assertion that essentialism and the connected desire to express the 'true' gendered and sexual self is common to both males and females.

Coming out, both to self and others, as a 'true gendered and sexual self', is experienced as a moral mandate when living according to an ethic of authenticity. Coming out is also understood as a religious rite. The majority of participants in this study maintain that in order to be 'a true Christian' they are compelled to express their 'true' sexuality, first to themselves and then to others. 'Coming out' in Christianity is a central theme of much of the literature in this field. Drumm (2005) and Wilcox (2002) recognize the importance of coming out in the lives of LGBT Christians. Shallenberger (1998) articulates coming out as a spiritual journey. Comstock (1993), Gorman (1997) and O'Brien (2004) describe how 'coming out' for a Christian magnifies the religious experience, relating intimately with Jesus's suffering. According to O'Brien, this becomes a 'raison d'être'. These sentiments are expressions of living an 'authentic Christianity'. Our research supports the conclusion drawn by Speakman (2009) who links the coming-out process and the integration of a sexual and religious self for Christian lesbians with authenticity. Speakman ascribes the qualities of 'uncompromising' and 'genuine' to the way lesbians express their Christian faith. For Abes and Kasch (2007), the intra-sections of these separate but fused strands of identity are also arguably the expression of a 'queer' self.

To express the 'true' religious self, individuals act according to an ethic of authenticity, in that they are guided by 'horizons of significance' (Taylor 1991), based upon their Christian habitus. This means their practices are guided by moral mandates, such as to love God and Jesus, to love others and to love the self. Religiosity motivates the individual's desire to resolve any internal conflicts they may have in integrating their sexuality, gendered self and religious self.

Internal conflicts

Being same-sex attracted and/or gender-questioning is a profound dilemma for LGBT Christians, given their religious upbringing and societal attitudes to same-sex attraction. In order to express the 'true', original self, the participants in this study act as agents to create conditions that enable them to integrate their sexuality with a renewed Christian worldview, a new religious habitus. This process was examined in Chapter 5.

All LGBT Christians in our research are aware of the tension between their sexuality and their Christian worldview; however, not all experience this as internal conflict. For eleven of the twenty-eight interviewees, the sense of self was not affected upon becoming aware of their alternative sexuality or gender, nor were they driven away from their faith. Those who were not internally conflicted were guided by a religious habitus that provided ready-made tools to negotiate their same-sex attraction. These tools could be cognitive in nature, such as 'theological capital' as suggested by Yip (2005: 49). However, cognitive factors typically operated in combination with relational and emotional experiences through which they could recognize and experience God's love for them. This love was translated into a love for their own authentic self, including their sexuality. These people felt a moral mandate to express their God-given sexuality. This finding also supports understandings of religion as less driven by cognitive understandings and more fundamentally emotional, experiential and relational (Riis and Woodhead 2010; Harvey 2013; Ezzy 2014).

The remainder of the LGBT Christians in our study (n=17) experienced internal conflict between their sexuality and/or gender and their Christian worldview. All but one had resolved this conflict at the time of the study. The internal conflict individuals experience varies in intensity and duration, depending on the person's religious background. Those who come from fundamentalist and orthodox churches experience more internal conflict, consistent with the findings of Barton (2010). For those who were conflicted, the moral dilemma was based upon a religious worldview and habitus that did not encompass their same-sex attraction. Their religious habitus excluded same-sex attraction as a possibility.

The younger participants in our research are more likely to experience a higher degree of conflict than the older participants. The reason for this is probably that the younger participants came from more fundamentalist and charismatic Christian backgrounds and were drawn to MCC congregations that offered a modern, charismatic approach. The intensity of conflict is therefore connected with the fundamentalist Protestant Christian worldviews of their upbringing, rather than their age. Those from liberal Protestant backgrounds experience far less internal conflict than those from extremely conservative or fundamentalist charismatic backgrounds. This finding is supported by Fitzpatrick (1993), whose research into prejudice indicates that fundamentalism is associated with less acceptance of homosexuality. LGBT Christians who grow up with a fundamentalist religious habitus are enculturated into an internalized homophobia.

There is little difference between women and men in our research with respect to the experience of internal conflict. Other studies of LGBT Christians have found that women experience less conflict than men (Rodriguez and Ouellette 2000; Shokeid 2005; Speakman 2009). Rodriguez and Ouellette postulate that women are less directly affected by the biblical verses that condemn homosexuality. However, in our research, upbringing is more influential on the intensity of the experience of conflict. The women who came from conservative backgrounds initially felt more troubled by their own sexuality than those from liberal religious backgrounds.

For the transgender participants, internalized conflict is exacerbated by the complex intersectionality of gender identification and sexuality. However, both transgendered participants expressed the vital importance of religion to their transitioning and their daily life. Their faith is a stabilizing factor that is deeply integrated into their sense of self.

Whether or not they experience internal conflicts, the individuals in our research seek to express their true sexuality, gender and faith. LGBT Christians act to create the conditions that enable them to integrate their sexuality and/or gender with a renewed Christian worldview and a new religious habitus. This transformation process involves a combination of changes in emotions, theology, relationships and practices.

Transformation

The transformation of religious identity is enmeshed with the transformation of religious habitus. Religious habitus are resistant to change as they are deeply embedded in dispositions, ways of thinking, relating, feeling and doing. However, a habitus can be changed, notably in 'unexpected situations' (Navarro 2006: 16). For the individuals in our research, their 'unexpected situation' is the awareness of their alternative sexuality or gender. Chapter 6 described the process of building a renewed life of faith for LGBT Christians.

Religious habitus are developed dialogically over time, and therefore cannot be changed in isolation. Theorists such as George Herbert Mead (1934) and Charles Taylor (1991) underline the dialogical nature of identity as it is created in relations with 'significant others'. Identity is thus always changing as relationships and particular 'significant others' become more or less important. The religious habitus of individuals can only be changed relationally, associated with concomitant transformations in emotions, interpretations and religious practices. While it is possible to express religiosity alone, practising ritual as a group focuses and empowers the religious experience. Group experiences cannot be divorced from individual identity.

Before some individuals can begin to integrate their sexuality and/or gender and their religious worldview, they experience a 'catalytic moment', a term borrowed from Levy and Reeves (2011). A 'catalytic moment' is a sudden recognition of the need to change or a recognition that their previous worldview may not be God's will. It is an empowering moment. Relationships are crucial for the creation of emotional 'catalytic moments'. In some cases, theological interpretations are altered in conjunction with newly formed significant relationships or though the breakdown of old relationships. Rather than 'new knowledge' alone, as postulated by Levy and Reeves (2011), our research suggests that new theology alone cannot effect change. Theological interpretations are bound up with changed relationships. Theology that accepts LGBT sexuality and/or gender is understood as legitimate, or rejected as illegitimate, as it is interwoven with relationships with significant others and communities.

The relative importance of shared ritual versus individual agency is debated in the literature. Some argue that individual agency is central to the process of integrating religious worldview and alternative sexuality (Thumma 1991; Primiano 1993; Gorman 1997; Kirkman 2001; Wilcox 2003; and Yip 1999; 2005). These researchers argue that institutions, rituals, relationships and socialization are not primary, but simply support this process, or are the last step in a long individual process. They argue that individual identity integration and transformation occur independently from these group processes.

In contrast, other studies suggest that the gay-affirming congregation with its ritual is crucial to the process (Rodriquez and Ouellette 2000; Brumbaugh 2007). Our research supports this argument, as detailed in Chapter 6. Although individual agency is important in the transformation, this is always done within the context of the transformation of significant relationships and the enactment of ritual within the group. The experience of belonging and of being part of a community is powerful and enabling and, over time, alters religious habitus.

Queer Christian spaces?

The institution of Christianity is arguably queered in the spaces of the MCC as a product of the pursuit of authenticity and LGBT transformations of religious habitus (Browne 2010). Religious practices unique to LGBT Christians unsettle the heteronormative structures of Christian practice. This is particularly evident in the ritual of communion. Stacy Brumbaugh (2007) focuses on the transformative power of communion in her research on the MCC. Both Melissa Wilcox (2003) and Bernard Lukenbill (2005) describe how heteronormative discourse is changed through the use of ritual and liturgy, including gender-inclusive language. Group spaces, practices and ritual are unequivocally effective and empowering for many of the LGBT Christians.

The safe 'queer' space of the MCC is healing and nurtures a sense of belonging for many of the participants. The sense of belonging is critical to the building of a new religious habitus (Wise, Harris and Watts 2005). The space is queer in that it disrupts the heteronormative constraints that exist in most Christians spaces. Ritual, in particular communion, is also 'queered' and is effective in legitimating alternative sexuality within the Christian sphere. Individuals report the importance of this space and the ritual for feeling accepted and legitimate as Christians in front of God.

However, MCC spaces are limited in the 'queering'. The queering of Christianity is irregular, inconsistent and, at times, resisted. In some respects, the MCC congregations remain steadfastly within normative Christian boundaries. Unresolved tensions are prominent in the MCC, in particular between the role of men and women. This is more pronounced in older congregations where patriarchal practices are reproduced and overtly supported by both men and women. Gender-inclusive language, for example, often causes discomfort, and is deemed by some as unnecessary. The resistance to gender-inclusive language is evidence of the inertia of traditional Christian habitus. Gendered distinctions are reproduced in three of the four congregations, despite the reflexive desire to be inclusive. Often the inclusivity is a understood as a patriarchal 'duty of care' in which women are either understood to be in need of appeasing, or are pathologized for responding with less than feminine composure.

From its inception, the MCC has been reflexive about these tensions. Bisexual and transgender individuals both create tension and unsettle the normative order. The response to bisexuality in the MCC is indicative of the continual tension between the queer transgressing of normative boundaries through religious practice and liturgy, and the upholding of normative Christian order. Bisexuality challenges the 'homonormative' essentialist understanding of sexuality. The knowledge that 'God made me this way' is central to the legitimation of self for LGBT Christians and critical to enabling a change of religious habitus. Bisexuality also appears to violate the Christian values of the monogamous family and structured faithful relationships, although such interpretations derive from a misunderstanding of bisexuality.

The situation in the MCC is similar to that observed by Elizabeth Dinnie and Kath Browne (2011), who conclude that sexual fluidity is an unsustainable position in the heteronormative environment of a new-age religious group. This does not take away from the unique contribution to the lives of LGBT Christians that the MCC has made worldwide. The denomination is also in a process of reflexive interrogation of the extent to which it demonstrates the 'dynamic inclusive love of Jesus' (Shore-Goss 2013). Thomas Bohache (2013), for example, is a minister in the MCC who questions the extent of 'queering of the MCC' in his article 'Unzipping Church: Is There Room for Everyone?'

Understanding religion

Religious experience is integrally relational and emotional. Theology informs, but does not drive participation in religious practice, nor does it drive resolution of internal conflict. This is demonstrated by the experiences of the LGBT Christians in this study. Moving away from cognitive and theologically oriented theoretical understandings of religion is important. Religious experience is embedded in culture, experience, relationships and emotion. There are complex contextual, relational, practice and emotional factors that are integral to religion. Emotion has often been ignored as a factor (Ahmed 2004). This has enabled hierarchical relationships based on deeply embedded emotions to remain unchanged. The nature of emotion within religion is entwined with the politics of power, notably for people with alternative sexualities and gender identities.

Religious worldviews and habitus are often resistant to change. Religious habitus can be transformed but this is a complex relational and practical process.

Emotions and relationships are central to creating, sustaining and transforming religious habitus. Habitus is embodied and is the basis upon which an individual builds 'horizons of significance'. These, in turn, shape moral judgements and choices about how to act. It is also through actions and through relationships that a habitus and moral 'horizons of significance' can be transformed. This can be an uncomfortable phase, where morality is contested. Critics of Charles Taylor such as Noumena (2007) have suggested that 'horizons of significance' refer to 'demands that come from beyond our own desires ... from history, tradition, society, nature or God' (Taylor 1991: 58), and that as such Taylor's theory precludes personal agency in social change. Noumena argues that such external demands often go hand in hand with oppression. Our research suggests that 'horizons of significance' can change as part of a broader transformation of habitus. Habitus is altered over time through transformations of relationships, practices, cognitions and emotions. Individuals exercise personal agency and resist oppressive constraints, but this is not a revolution. In our research, LGBT Christians 'mingle cultural norms with personal agency' (Rappaport 2000: 11).

Conclusions

The concept of the 'ethics of authenticity' (Taylor 1991) provides a unique lens through which to analyse the experience of LGBT Christians. We have argued that religiosity drives the desire of LGBT Christians to exercise their agency as they seek an authentic life that encompasses sexuality, gender and religiosity. This is accomplished by living according to moral mandates that are based upon horizons of significance that give meaning beyond the self. The deeply personal struggles of LGBT Christians to integrate previously separate aspects of their identities demonstrates the critical importance of emotion, relationships and ritual practices to the transformation of identity. We draw on Ahmed's (2004) theory of emotion, Butler's (1990) concept of performativity, and Bourdieu's (1977) concept of habitus to interpret this theoretically.

Safe spaces, such as those of the MCC, are crucial to LGBT Christians because they enable and empower individuals. Within the safe spaces of the MCC, a new religious habitus is forged. However, even within the MCC, there remain tensions between Christianity and 'queer'. As individuals enact queer Christian practices, and strive to express the 'true' authentic self, spaces are queered. Yet the queering is constrained by Christian normative boundaries. The LGBT

Christians in this study and the spaces of the MCC remain in permanent tension, as there is a foundational inconsistency between the core principles of 'queer' and 'Christianity'.

The lives of LGBT Christians matter. Through detailing the aspirations and struggles of these individuals to live authentic lives, true to their sexuality, gender and religion, we hope to unsettle the walls of prejudice, promoting better understanding, within both wider LGBTIQ communities and religious communities. Many LGBT Christians feel profound social exclusion, as a consequence of the perception that belonging to the LGBT community excludes the possibility of being Christian. The 'messiness of real life' (Yip 2010: 45), is 'outed' by LGBT Christians.

The lived experience of religion is complex, individualized and unique, yet also shared and structured. Each individual who participated in this study provides an insight into the nature of religious experience. Although this is a small detailed study, the processes observed have significant implications for broader theoretical understandings of religion and religious transformation.

Methodological Considerations

The book is based on empirical research conducted by Bronwyn Fielder, which investigated the way in which a group of LGBT Christians negotiated their seemingly disparate identities. The book has been co-authored by Douglas Ezzy, and ethics approval for the project was provided by the University of Tasmania Human Research Ethics Committee (HREC Ref: H0012415).

The research included the use of in-depth interviews, participant observation, and self-reflection. Bronwyn conducted twenty-eight interviews, including four with key informants (the pastors of each congregation) as well as with congregants – male and female – in each of four congregations of the Metropolitan Community Church (MCC) in Sydney and Melbourne, a LGBT-affirming Christian denomination. In addition, two interviews were conducted with members of the Uniting Church in Sydney. Quotations from the interviews are indicated by the use of a pseudonym. Quotations have been edited for clarity. Repeated words are deleted, as are repetitive phrases such as 'sort of' and 'you know'. These deletions and some minor changes are not indicated in the quotations. Where extended sections have been deleted, this is indicated by '…'. Where we have added words for clarity, these are included in [square brackets]. Potentially identifying information has been deleted, or changed. Bronwyn also participated in services and other activities such as group meals and other social occasions. Through participation, she was able to gain an appreciation of the group dynamics and hierarchy, the symbols and rituals either shared or unique to each congregation, and external emotional and bodily responses to these rituals.

Initial contact with the MCC congregations was by way of an introductory email with an information sheet attached, requesting meetings to introduce the project and its aims, as well as an interview. In consultation with the pastor/ministers, the project was introduced to the congregation. Over a period of seven months, Bronwyn visited the four MCC congregations five to six times each.

Individual interviews were dispersed throughout the seven-month period of visits and revisits to the MCCs. This allowed Bronwyn to engage reflexively with her field experiences through questions in interviews, and to have her observations informed by the information she gained in the interviews.

Observation and participation give Bronwyn distinct experiences and empirical information that would not otherwise have been available. Observation of services enabled the gathering of data relating to overt and shared interactions (Tolich and Davidson 1999), such as external signs and symbols and religious and gendered practices.

Participation also laid the groundwork for immersive engagement with the MCC and enabled a better understanding of the emotional world of the individuals and groups (Zablocki 2001). Religious experience is often beyond articulation and is not necessarily easily expressed in words (Riis and Woodhead 2010; Harvey 2013; Ezzy 2014). In order to better represent the participants' world view, Bronwyn considered participation to be a requirement. Tosh (2001) and Zablocki (2001) similarly argue that only through being open and vulnerable to the experience of the participants of religious groups is it possible to come close to understanding their lived experience. Participation serves to inform and strengthen ethical considerations and to enhance the methodological veracity of the research.

Participation and observation can also complement interviews. Participant observation allowed Bronwyn to observe interactions which then provided context for stories related in the interviews (Tolich and Davidson 1999). As a consequence of observing services, Bronwyn was later able to visualize details that were discussed during interviews, for example when interviewees described ritualized behaviours such as communion. Observation also provided a different perspective on gendered and/or hierarchical interactions between the congregants themselves, or between pastors and congregants, which were discussed in interviews. In cases where behaviours in services departed from the expected norms of the group, such as the use of gender-inclusive language, this was noted and followed up in interviews.

Each of the vignettes are based on a participant interview. They have been edited with a view to creating a narrative that is easy to read. We have deleted significant portions of text without indicating this. We have also rearranged the order of the paragraphs so that they flow in a more logical sequence. All words added by the authors are indicated in [square brackets].

Notes

Chapter 1

1　We use the acronym LGBT rather than LGBTIQ because we did not interview, and therefore cannot discuss the experiences of intersex and queer identified Christians. Their experiences are important and we would have liked to have included them, but none of the people who volunteered to participate in the study identified as queer or intersex.

2　All references to the Bible are to The Revised Standard Version [RSV].

Chapter 3

1　UFMCC refers to the worldwide association of the Universal Fellowship of the Metropolitan Community Churches. When referring to specific churches and congregations, the shorter acronym MCC is used.

2　The Apostolic and Nicene creeds state theological principles common to most Christian churches.

Chapter 5

1　While overall it has been shown that the majority of people who are brought up Christian leave on becoming aware of same-sex attraction (Couch et al. 2008), our study is concerned with those who remained active Christians.

2　Then the Lord God said: 'It is not good that the man should be alone; I will make a helper fit for him … and the rib which God had taken from man he made into the woman … therefore the man leaves his father and his mother and cleaves to his wife and they become one flesh' (Gen. 2:18, English Standard Version).

3　A Christian evangelist who preaches to young people to not have sex before marriage, and that homosexuality is against God's wishes and that you can be healed if you are gay.

Chapter 6

1   Gay theology argues that interpretation of the Bible has traditionally been influenced by patriarchal cultural and historical factors, which it exposes, offering an interpretation that affirms loving homosexual relationships as legitimate.

2   Congregants are encouraged to take communion together with their partner and/or friends. They approach the communion table together, and often pray as a couple or group with the minister or acolyte.

3   Open table means that everyone, member or not, is invited to communion, to be together at the table.

Chapter 7

1   MCC Australia has held women's retreats every year since 1999. Till the time of the research, however, no men's retreats had been organized.

Glossary of Terms

Alternative sexuality   Refers to any form of sexual activity or orientation that does not conform to the heterosexual norm.

Gender identity   As gender is socially constructed; this term refers to the way any person identifies – male, female or other.

Heteronormativity   Refers to the social constraints enforced by institutions, their structures, understandings and practices that privilege heterosexuality by making it appear natural and coherent, culturally desirable and appropriate (Berlant and Warner 1998: 548).

LGBT   On the whole, this book concentrates on the experiences of lesbian women and gay men as they negotiate tensions between their sexual and religious identities. However, the experiences of the small number of bisexual and transgender Christian participants are critical in the analysis and justify the use of the acronym LGBT when referring to the participants.

LGBTIQ   Lesbian, Gay, Bisexual, Transgender, Intersex, Queer. The book refers to the non-heterosexual and gender-questioning wider community as LGBTIQ. The authors resist using the term homosexual (or gay as an umbrella term) because of the ambiguity of both (Steffens and Wagner 2004).

Queer theory   Questions natural assumptions about stable identities, such as sexuality and gender. It questions the 'natural' nature of heterosexuality and aims to expose how both gender and sexuality are constructed through performativity – embodied actions of individuals (Lovaas, Elia and Yep 2007).

Sexual identity   As distinct from sexual behaviour, refers to how people place themselves in sexual categories such as lesbian, gay, bisexual and queer.

Universal Fellowship of Metropolitan Community Churches   Is generally referred to as MCC, a Protestant Christian denomination founded in 1968 by a gay minister, the Rev. Roy Perry (Enroth and Jamison 1974; Warner 2005). The church has grown from the original congregation of twelve men to 250 congregations in over twenty-five countries, and although totally inclusive, attracts mostly LGBTIQ individuals.

Bibliography

Abes, Elisa and Kasch, David (2007). Using Queer Theory to Explore Lesbian College Students' Multiple Dimensions of Identity. *Journal of College Student Development*, 46(6): 619–36.

Adam, Barry (2003). The Defense of Marriage Act and American Exceptionalism: The 'Gay Marriage' Panic in the United States. *Journal of the History of Sexuality*, 12(2): 259–76.

Adams, Bert and Sydie, R. (2002). *Classical Sociological Theory*. Thousand Oaks, CA, London and New Delhi: Sage Publications.

Ahmed, Sara (2004). *The Cultural Politics of Emotion*. New York: Routledge.

Andries, Jan (2007). *Het Homohuwelijk en de Kerk* (in Dutch). Retrieved 3 December 2016 https://web.archive.org/web/20160310025908/http://janandriesdeboer.nl/?p=41.

Armour, Ellen (2010). Blinding Me with (Queer) Science: Religion, Sexuality and (Post?) Modernity. *Journal of the Philosophy of Religion*, 68: 116–18.

Atkinson, P. and Delamont, S. (2008). (eds) *Representing Ethnography. Reading, Writing and Rhetoric in Qualitative Research*. Four Volume Set. London: Sage Publications.

Australian Broadcasting Commission (2012). Radio interview. Accessed 13 October 2014. mpegmedia.abc.net.au/rn/podcast/2012/11/rer_20121128_1745.mp3.

Australian Bureau of Statistics (2013). Same Sex Couples. Accessed 13 October 2014. http://www.abs.gov.au/AUSSTATS/abs@.nsf/Lookup/4102.0Main+Features10July+2013#religious.

Bailey, Derrick (1955). *Homosexuality and the Western Christian Tradition*. London: Longmans Green.

Barton, Bernadette (2010). 'Abomination' – Life as a Bible Belt Gay. *Journal of Homosexuality*, 57: 465–84

Bates, Aranya (2005). Liberation in Truth: African American Lesbians Reflect on Religion, Spirituality and Their Church. In Scott Thumma and Edward Gray (eds) *Gay Religion*. New York and Oxford: Altamira Press: 221–38.

Baunach, Dawn (2011). Decomposing Trends in Attitudes toward Gay Marriage, 1988–2006. *Social Science Quarterly*, 92(2): 346–63.

Beckstead, Zachary (2010). Commentary: Liminality in Acculturation and Pilgrimage: When Movement Becomes Meaningful. *Culture Psychology*, 16: 383.

Bell, Catherine (1992). *Ritual Theory, Ritual Practice*. New York and Oxford: Oxford University Press.

Bell, Daniel (1976). *The Coming Of Post-industrial Society*. New York: Basic Books.

Bell, David and Binnie, Jon (2004). Authenticating Queer Space: Citizenship, Urbanism and Governance. *Urban Studies*, 41(9): 1807–20.

Berger, Helen and Ezzy, Douglas (2007). *Teenage Witches*. New Brunswick, Canada: Rutgers University Press.

Berlant, Lauren and Warner, Michael (1998). Sex in Public. *Critical Inquiry: Intimacy*, 24(2): 547–66.

Berlinerblau, Jacques (1999). Ideology, Pierre Bourdieu's Doxa, and the Hebrew Bible, *Semeia*, 87: 193–214.

Bible, Revised Standard Version (1962). Cleveland and New York: World Publishing.

Blumstein, Philip and Schwartz, Pepper (1983). *American Couples: Money, Work, and Sex*. New York: William Morrow.

Bohache, Thomas (2013). Unzipping Church: Is there Room for Everyone? In Robert Shore-Goss, Thomas Bohache, Patrick Cheng and Mona Faye-West (eds) *Queering Christianity: Finding a Place at the Table for LGBTQI Christians*. Santa Barbara, Denver and Oxford: Praeger: 271–92.

Boswell, John (1979). The Church and the Homosexual: An Historical Perspective (keynote address at Dignity's 4th Biennial Convention). In Kathleen Leopold and Thomas Orians (eds) *Theological Pastoral Resources: A Collection of Articles on Homosexuality from a Pastoral Perspective*, 6th edn. Washington, DC: Dignity: 16–20.

Boswell, John (1992). Categories, Experience and Sexuality. In Edward Stein (ed.) *Forms of Desire: Sexual Orientation and the Social Constructionist Controversy*. New York and London: Routledge: 133–73.

Boswell, John (2009). *Christianity, Social Tolerance, and Homosexuality: Gay People in Western Europe from the Beginning of the Christian Era to the Fourteenth Century*. Chicago: University of Chicago Press.

Bouma, Gary (2006). *Australian Soul*. Melbourne: Cambridge University Press.

Bouma, Gary (2007). Book Review. The Existential Jesus: A Fresh Encounter with Mark's Gospel Impresses with Its Unbiased Approach. *The Age*. 30 March 2007. Retrieved 3 December 2016. http://www.theage.com.au/news/book-reviews/the-existential-jesus/2007/03/30/1174761732548.html.

Bourdieu, Pierre (1977). *Outline of a Theory of Practice*. Cambridge: Cambridge University Press.

Bourdieu, Pierre (1990). *The Logic of Practice*. Stanford, CA: Stanford University Press.

Bourdieu, Pierre (2000). *Pascalian Meditations*. Trans. Richard Nice. Stanford, CA: Stanford University Press.

Brady, Anita and Tony Shirato (2011). *Understanding Judith Butler*. London: Sage Publications.

Brown, Andrew and Woodhead, Linda (2016). *The Church that Was: How the Church of England Lost the English People*. London, Oxford, New York, New Delhi and Sydney: Bloomsbury.

Browne, Kath (2010). Queer Spiritual Spaces. In Kath Browne, Sally Munt and Andrew Yip (eds) *Queer Spiritual Spaces*. Farnham, UK: Ashgate: 231–45.

Browne, Kath, Munt, Sally and Yip, Andrew (2010). *Queer Spiritual Spaces*. Farnham, UK: Ashgate.

Brumbaugh, Stacy (2007). *The Use of the Communion Ritual for the Process of Identity Congruence among Lesbian, Gay and Bisexual Christians*. Master of Arts Dissertation, Graduate College of Bowling Green State University, OH.

Bullough, Vern (1976). Untitled Review. *The American Historical Review*, 81(2): 352–53.

Butler, Judith (1990). *Gender Trouble: Feminism and the Subversion of Identity*. New York and London: Routledge.

Butler, Judith (1993). *Bodies That Matter*. New York and London: Routledge.

Carroll, John (2007). *The Existential Jesus*. Melbourne: Scribe.

Cass, Vivian (1979). Homosexual Identity Formation: A Theoretical Model. *Journal of Homosexuality*, 4: 219–35.

Christ, Carol (2004). *Rebirth of the Goddess: Finding Meaning in Feminist Spirituality*. London and New York: Routledge.

Comstock, Gary (1993). *Gay Theology Without Apology*. Cleveland, OH: Pilgrim Press.

Comstock, Gary and Henking, Susan (eds) (1997). *Que(e)rying Religion: A Critical Anthology*. New York: Continuum.

Connell, Raewyn (1995). *Masculinities*. Sydney: Allen and Unwin.

Connell, Raewyn and Dowsett, G. (eds) (1992). *Rethinking Sex: Social Theory, Sexuality Research*. Melbourne, Melbourne University Press.

Connerton, Paul (1989). *How Societies Remember*. Cambridge: Cambridge University Press.

Couch, Murray, Mulcare, Hunter, Pitts, Marian, Smith, Anthony and Mitchell, Anne (2008). The Religious Affiliation of Gay, Lesbian, Bisexual, Transgender and Intersex Australians: A Report from the Private Lives Survey. *People and Place*, 16(1): 1–11.

Crossley, Nick (2005). *Key Concepts in Critical Social Theory*. London, Thousand Oaks, California, New Delhi and Singapore: Sage Publications.

Csordas, Thomas (1990). Embodiment as a Paradigm for Anthropology. *Ethos*, 18(1): 5–47.

Daniels, Martha (2010). Not Even on the Page: Freeing God from Heterosexism. *Journal of Bisexuality*, 10(1–2): 44–53.

Davie, Grace (1994). *Religion in Britain since 1945: Believing Without Belonging*. Oxford, UK and Cambridge, MA: Blackwell Publishers.

Dickson, Curtis (2012). *There's a Place for Us: LGBTIQ People's Experiences of Belonging and Participation in Christian Community in Sydney, Australia*. Unpublished Honours Dissertation, University of Sydney.

Digoix, Marie, Franchi, Marina, Galán, José Ignacio Pichardo, Selmi, Giulia, de Stéfano Barbero, Matias, Thibeaud, Matthias and Vela, Jose (2016). Sexual Orientation, Family and Kinship in France, Iceland, Italy and Spain. *Families and Societies: Working Paper Series*. 54.

Dinnie, Elizabeth and Browne, Kath (2011). Creating a Sexual Self in Heteronormative Space: Integrations and Imperatives amongst Spiritual Seekers at the Findhorn Community. *Sociological Research Online*, 16(1): 7. Accessed 25 April 2012. http://www.socresonline.org.uk/16/1/7.html.

Dowd, Chris (2011). (http://www.youtube.com/watch?v=3R7nKXr7t_
    Q&feature=related).

Driver, Tom (1991). *The Magic of Ritual: Our Need for Liberating Rites that Transform
    our Lives and Communities.* San Francisco: Harper.

Drumm, Rene (2005). No Longer an Oxymoron: Integrating Gay and Lesbian Seventh-
    Day Adventist Identities. In Scott Thumma and Edward Gray (eds) *Gay Religion.*
    New York and Oxford: Altamira Press: 47–66.

Dubowski, Sandi Simcha (Director) (2001). *Trembling before G–D.* USA: Produced by
    Sandi Simcha Dubowski and Marc Smolowitz.

Duggan, Lisa (2002). The New Homonormativity: The Sexual Politics of Neoliberalism.
    In Russ Castronovo and Dana Nelson (eds) *Materializing Democracy: Toward a
    Revitalized Cultural Politics.* Durham and London: Duke University Press: 175–94.

Durkheim, Emile (1963). *Incest: The Nature and Origin of the Taboo.* Trans. Edward
    Sagarin. New York: Lyle Stuart.

Edser, Stuart (2012). *Being Gay, Being Christian: You Can Be Both.* Wollombi,
    NSW: Exile Press.

Eichberg, Rob (1991). *Coming Out: An Act of Love.* New York, London, Ringwood,
    Toronto and Auckland: Plume.

Enroth, Ronald and Jamison, Gerald (1974). *The Gay Church.* Grand Rapids,
    MI: William Eerdmans Publishing.

Epstein, Steven (1994). A Queer Encounter: Sociology and the Study of Sexuality.
    Sociological Theory, 12(2): 188–202.

Erlanger, Steven (2013). *Hollande Signs French Gay Marriage Law,New York Times,*
    18 May. Accessed 4 December 2016. http://www.nytimes.com/2013/05/19/world/
    europe/hollande-signs-french-gay-marriage-law.html.

Ezzy, Douglas (2014). *Sex, Death and Witchcraft: A Contemporary Pagan Festival.*
    London: Bloomsbury Academic Press.

Fitzpatrick, Lee (1993). Fundamentalism, Christian Orthodoxy, and Intrinsic Religious
    Orientation as Predictors of Discriminatory Attitudes. *Journal for the Scientific Study
    of Religion,* 32(3): 256–68.

Foucault, Michel (1990). *The History of Sexuality, Volume 1: The Will to Knowledge.*
    Trans. Robert Hurley. London, New York, Ringwood, Australia, Toronto and
    Auckland: Penguin.

Frame, Thomas (2007). *Anglicans in Australia.* Sydney: University of New South
    Wales Press.

Gahan, Luke (2013). From the Embers of Religion a New Spirituality Grew. In Luke
    Gahan and Tiffany Jones (eds) (2013) *Heaven Bent: Australian Lesbian, Gay,
    Bisexual, Transgender and Intersex Experiences of Faith, Religiosity and Spirituality*
    [electronic edn]. Melbourne: Clouds of Magellan: 51–60.

Gahan, Luke and Jones, Tiffany (eds) (2013). *Heaven Bent: Australian Lesbian, Gay,
    Bisexual, Transgender and Intersex Experiences of Faith, Religiosity and Spirituality*
    [electronic edn]. Melbourne: Clouds of Magellan.

Giddens, Anthony (1992). *The Transformation of Intimacy: Sexuality, Love and Eroticism in Modern Societies*. Cambridge: Polity Press.

Gillies, Val (2003). *Families and Intimate Relationships: A Review of the Sociological Literature*. Accessed 24 April 2014. www.lsbu.ca.uk/families/workingpapers/familieswp2pdf.

Glaser, Chris (1998). *Coming out as a Sacrament*. Louisville, KY: Westminster John Knox Press.

Goffman, Erving (1974). *Stigma: Notes on the Management of Spoiled Identity*. Middlesex, UK: Penguin Books.

Gorman, Michael (1980). *A New Light on Zion: A Study of Three Homosexual Religious Congregations in Urban America*. PhD Dissertation, Department of Anthropology, University of Chicago.

Gorman, Michael (1997). A Special Window: An Anthropological Perspective on Spirituality in Contemporary US Gay Male Culture. In Gary Comstock and Susan Henking (eds) *Que(e)rying Religion: A Critical Anthology*. New York: Continuum: 331–37.

Gorman-Murray, Andrew, Waitt, Gordon and Johnston, Lynda (2008). Guest Editorial: Geographies of Sexuality and Gender Down Under. *Australian Geographer*, 39(3): 235–46.

Gray, Edward and Thumma, Scott (2005). The Gospel Hour: Liminality, Identity and Religion in a Gay Bar. In Scott Thumma and Edward Gray (eds) (2005) *Gay Religion*. New York and Oxford: Altamira Press: 285–302.

Grimes, Ronald (2000). *Deeply into the Bone: Re-inventing Rites of Passage*. Berkeley: University of California Press.

Gross, Martine and Yip, Andrew (2010). Living Spirituality and Sexuality: A Comparison of Lesbian, Gay and Bisexual Christians in France and Britain. *Social Compass*, 57(1): 40–59.

Grosz, Elizabeth (1994). *Volatile Bodies: Toward a Corporeal Feminism*. Bloomington: Indiana University Press.

Hansen, Jennifer and Lambert, Serena (2011). Grief and Loss of Religion: The Experiences of Four Rural Lesbians. *Journal of Lesbian Studies*, 15(2): 187–96.

Harvey, Graham (2013). *Food, Sex and Strangers: Redefining Religion*. London: Acumen.

Heelas, Paul and Woodhead, Linda with Seel, Benjamin, Szerszynski, Bronislaw and Tusting, Karin (2005). *The Spiritual Revolution. Why Religion is Giving Way to Spirituality*. Malden, MA, Oxford, UK, Carlton and Victoria: Blackwell Publishing.

Heyward, Carter (1999). *Saving Jesus from Those Who are Right: Rethinking What it Means to Be Christian*. Minneapolis: Fortress Press.

Hillier, Lynne, Dempsey, Deborah, Harrison, Lyn, Beale Lisa, Matthews, Lesley, and Rosenthal, Doreen (1998). *Writing Themselves In: A National Report on the Sexuality, Health and Well-Being of Same-Sex Attracted Young People*. Melbourne: National Centre in HIV Social Research, La Trobe University.

Hillier, Lynne, Turner, Alina and Mitchell, Anne (2004). *Writing Themselves in again 6 Years on: The 2nd National Report on the Sexual Health & Well-Being of Same Sex Attracted Young People in Australia*. Melbourne: Australian Research Centre in Sex, Health and Society, La Trobe University.

Hillier, Lynne, Mitchell, Anne and Mulcare, Hunter (2008). I Couldn't Do Both at the Same Time: Same Sex Attracted Youth and the Negotiation of Religious Discourse. *Gay and Lesbian Issues and Psychology Review*, 4(2): 80–93.

Hillier, Lynne, Jones, Tiffany, Monagle, Marisa, Overton, Naomi, Gahan, Luke, Blackman, Jennifer and Mitchell, Anne (2010). *Writing Themselves in 3: A Third National Study on the Sexual Health and Well-Being of Same-Sex Attracted and Gender Questioning Young People*. Australian Research Centre in Sex, Health and Society, La Trobe University.

Holpuch, Amanda (2015). Some Alabama Counties Refuse Marriage Licenses to Gay Couples Despite Ruling. *The Guardian*, 9 February. Accessed 20 February 2015. http://www.theguardian.com/us-news/2015/feb/09/some-alabama-counties-refuse-marriage-licences-gay-couples.

Hookway, Nicholas (2013). Emotions, Body and Self: Critiquing Moral Decline Sociology. *Sociology*, 47(4): 841–57.

Iyer, Malathy (2014). Homosexuality Is Unnatural, Leading Psychiatrist Says. *The Times of India*, 21 January. Accessed 22 February 2014. http://timesofindia.indiatimes.com/india/Homosexuality-is-unnatural-leading-psychiatrist-says/articleshow/29126819.cms.

Jakobsson, Kotsadam and Jakobsson (2013). Attitudes toward Same-Sex Marriage: The Case of Scandinavia. *Journal of Homosexuality*, 60(9): 1349–60.

Jagose, Annamarie (1996). *Queer Theory: An Introduction*. New York: New York University Press.

Jordan, Mark (1997). *The Invention of Sodomy in Christian Theology*. Chicago: University of Chicago Press.

Kertzer, David (1988). *Ritual, Politics and Power*. New Haven, CT and London: Yale University Press.

Kirkman, Alison (2001). Ties that Bind. *Journal of Lesbian Studies*, 5(1–2): 211–27.

Klesse, Christian (2005). Bisexual Spaces: A Geography of Sexuality and Gender. *The Sociological Review*, 53(2): 365–68.

Kosofsky Sedgwick, Eve (1990). *Epistemology of the Closet*. Berkley and Los Angeles: University of California Press.

Lasch, Christopher (1979). *The Culture of Narcissism: American Life in an Age of Diminishing Expectations*. Berkeley: University of California Press.

Levy, Denise and Reeves, Patricia (2011). Resolving Identity Conflict: Gay, Lesbian, and Queer Individuals with a Christian Upbringing. *Journal of Gay & Lesbian Social Services*, 23(1): 53–68.

Lipovetsky, Gilles (2005). *Hypermodern Times*. Cambridge, UK and Malden, MA: Polity Press.

Lovaas, Karen, John Elia and Gust Yep (2007). Shifting Ground(s). *Journal of Homosexuality*, 52(1–2): 1–18.

Lukenbill, Bernard (2005). Pluralism and Diversity: Music as Discourse and Information in a Gay and Lesbian Congregation. In Scott Thumma and Edward Gray (eds) *Gay Religion*. New York and Oxford: Altamira Press: 167–80.

MacCormack, Carol (1980). Nature, Culture and Gender: A Critique. In Carol MacCormack and Marilyn Strathern (eds) *Nature, Culture and Gender*. Cambridge, UK, and New York: Cambridge University Press: 1.

Maddox, Marion (2005). *God Under Howard: The Rise of the Religious Right in Australian Politics*. Sydney: Allen and Unwin.

Maddox, Marion (2011). A Secular Cancellation of the Secularist Truce: Religion and Political Legitimation in Australia. *Annual Review of the Sociology of Religion*, 2: 287–308.

Mahaffy, Kimberly (1996). Cognitive Dissonance and Its Resolution: A Study of Lesbian Christians. *Journal for the Scientific Study of Religion*, 35(4): 392–402.

Maliepaard, Emiel (2015). Bisexuals in Space and Geography: More-Than-Queer? *International Journal of Geography*, 193(1): 148–59.

Marriage Amendment Act 2004. Accessed 28 June 2011. www.comlaw.gov.au.

Masterson, Anthony (2006). Review: Epistemology of the Closet by Eve Kosofsky Sedgwick. *International Gay and Lesbian Review*. Los Angeles: University of California Press.

McKinney, William and Tolbert, Mary (2005). Foreword. In Scott Thumma and Edward Gray (eds) (2005) *Gay Religion*. New York and Oxford: Altamira Press: ix.

Mead, George Herbert (1934). *Mind, Self, and Society*. Chicago: University of Chicago Press.

Merleau-Ponty, Maurice (1962). *Phenomenology of Perception*. Trans. Colin Smith. London and New York: Routledge and Kegan Paul.

Metropolitan Community Church, website (n.d.). Accessed 21 July 2013. http://mcchurch.org/overview/.

Metropolitan Community Church, North London (n.d.). *About Us: History of MCC*. Accessed 10 February 2014. http://mccnorthlondon.org.uk/aboutus/history-of-ufmcc/.

Metropolitan Community Churches (2013a). *Governance*. Accessed 20 February 2015. http://mcchurch.org/how-we-work/governance.

Metropolitan Community Churches (2013b). *Statement of Faith*. Accessed 28 February 2015. http://mcchurch.org/commission-on-the-mcc-statement-of-faith/statement-of-faith.

Moon, Dawne (2005). Discourse, Interaction, and Testimony: The Making of Selves in the U.S. Protestant Dispute over Homosexuality. *Theory and Society*, 34 (5/6): 55–177.

Morrow, Deana (2003). Cast into the Wilderness: The Impact of Institutionalized Religion on Lesbians. *Journal of Lesbian Studies*, 7(4): 109–23.

Munt, Sally (2010). Queer Spiritual Spaces. In Kath Browne, Sally Munt and Andrew
    Yip (eds) *Queer Spiritual Spaces*. Farnham, UK: Ashgate: 1–33.

Murphy, Katherine (2015). Same-SexMarriage: A Reform that Would Put
    the Icing on the Cake. *The Guardian*, 9 April, Australian edn. Accessed 7
    December 2016. https://www.theguardian.com/australia-news/2015/apr/09/
    same-sex-marriage-a-reform-that-would-put-the-icing-on-the-cake.

Navarro, Z. (2006). In Search of a Cultural Interpretation of Power: The Contribution of
    Pierre Bourdieu. *Institute of Development Studies Bulletin*, 37(6): 11–22. Accessed 1
    June 2015. http://www.powercube.net/wp-content/uploads/2010/02/Navarro.pdf.

Noumena (2007). *Charles Taylor's Horizons of Significance*. Accessed 24 February 2015.
    http://staffofra.blogspot.com.au/2007/02/charles-taylors-horizons-of.html.

O'Brien, Jodi (2004). Wrestling the Angel of Contradiction: Queer Christian Identities.
    Culture and Religion, 5(2): 179–202.

Paris, Jenell and Anderson, Rory (2001). Faith-Based Queer Space in Washington, DC:
    The Metropolitan Community Church-DC and Mount Vernon Square. *Gender,
    Place and Culture*, 8(2): 149–68.

Perry, Troy (2004). History of the MCC. Accessed 18 April 2017. http://mcchurch.org/
    overview/history-of-mcc/.

Perry, Troy and Swicegood, Thomas (1990). *Don't be Afraid Anymore: The Story
    of Reverend Troy Perry and the Metropolitan Community Churches*. New York:
    St Martin's Press.

Plummer, Ken (1995). *Telling Sexual Stories: Power, Change and Social Worlds*.
    London: Routledge.

Plummer, Ken (2005). Critical Humanism and Queer Theory: Living with the Tensions.
    Queer Studies. Accessed 17 August 2011. http://what-when-how.com/social-
    sciences/queer-studies-social-science/.

Positive Space Network Resource Person Manual (2010). University of Victoria, Canada.
    Accessed 23 February 2015. http://web.uvic.ca/psn/wp-content/uploads/PSN-
    Resource-Person-Manual.pdf.

Primiano, Leonard Norman (1993). I Would Rather Be Fixated on the Lord: Women's
    Religion, Men's Power and the Dignity Problem. *New York Folklore*, 19: 89–103.

Primiano, Leonard Norman (2005). The Gay God of the City: The Emergence of the
    Gay and Lesbian Ethnic Parish. In Scott Thumma and Edward Gray (eds) *Gay
    Religion*. New York and Oxford: Altamira Press: 7–30.

Raphael, Melissa (1999). *Introducing Thealogy: Discourse on the Goddess*. Sheffield:
    Sheffield Academic Press.

Rappaport, Julian (2000). Community Narratives: Tales of Terror and Joy. *American
    Journal of Community Psychology*, 28(1): 1–24.

Rey, Terry (2008). *Bourdieu on Religion: Imposing Faith and Legitimacy* [electronic edn].
    London: Equinox Publishing.

Rich, Adrienne (1980). Compulsory Heterosexuality and Lesbian Existence. *Journal of
    Women's History*, 15(3): 11–48.

Riis, Ole and Woodhead, Linda (2010). *A Sociology of Religious Emotion*. New York: Oxford University Press.

Ritter, Kathleen and O'Neill, Craig (1996). *Righteous Religion: Unmasking the Illusions of Fundamentalism and Authoritarian Catholicism*. Abingdon, UK and New York: Routledge.

Rives, Belinda (2005). A Model for All? Religious and Sexual Identity Integration in Homosexual Persons. *Religion, Culture and Society*, 19.

Robnett, Belinda (1997). Spontaneity and Emotion in Social Movement Theory. In Kathleen Blee (ed.) *No Middle Ground*. New York: University Press: 65–95.

Rodriguez, Eric (2009). At the Intersection of Church and Gay: A Review of the Psychological Research on Gay and Lesbian Christians. *Journal of Homosexuality*, 57(1): 5–38.

Rodriguez, Eric and Ouellette, Suzanne (2000). Gay and Lesbian Christian: Homosexual and Religious Identity Integration in the Members and Participants of a Gay-Positive Church. *Journal for the Scientific Study of Religion*, 39(3): 333–47.

Roseneil, Sasha (2000). Queer Frameworks and Queer Tendencies: Towards an Understanding of Postmodern Transformations of Sexuality. *Sociological Research Online*, 5(3). Accessed 10 November 2013. http://www.socresonline.org.uk/5/3/roseneil.html.

Rycenga, Jennifer (2004). Roundtable Discussions: What is the Future of Lesbian, Gay, Bisexual, Transgender and Queer Studies in Religion? *Culture and Religion*, 5(2): 267–81.

Salih, Sara (2007). *Judith Butler*. London and New York: Routledge.

Shallenberger, David (1998). *Reclaiming the Spirit: Gay Men and Lesbians Come to Terms with Religion*. New Brunswick, NJ and London: Rutgers University Press.

Shokeid, Moshe (2005). Why Join a Gay Synagogue? In Scott Thumma and Edward Gray (eds) *Gay Religion*. New York and Oxford: Altamira Press: 83–98.

Shore-Goss, Robert (2013). Introduction: Queering the Table. In Robert Shore-Goss, Thomas Bohache, Patrick Cheng and Mona Faye-West (eds) *Queering Christianity: Finding a Place at the Table for LGBTQI Christians*. Santa Barbara, Denver and Oxford: Praeger: 124.

Sixsmith, Andrew (1986), Independence and Home in Later Life. *Dependency and Interdependency in Old Age: Theoretical Perspectives and Policy Alternatives*. 338–47.

Speakman, Cynthia (2009). *Christian Lesbians and Their Spiritual Journeys*. Master of Social Work Dissertation, California State University, Long Beach. Accessed 25 February 2013. http://gradworks.umi.com/14/66/1466153.html.

Spong, John Shelby (1991). *Rescuing the Bible from Fundamentalism: A Bishop Rethinks the Meaning of Scripture*. New York: Harper Collins.

Steffens, Melanie and Wagner, Christof (2004). Attitudes toward Lesbians, Gay Men, Bisexual Women, and Bisexual Men in Germany. *The Journal of Sex Research*, 41(2): 137–49.

Strudwick, Patrick (2014). Gay Life in Northern Ireland is Under Threat – Time to Act. *The Guardian*, 12 December, Australian edn. Accessed 25 March 2015. http://www.theguardian.com/commentisfree/2014/dec/11/gay-life-northern-ireland-human-rights-stormont-lgbt.

Stryker, Sheldon (2008). From Mead to Structural Symbolic Interactionism and Beyond. *Annual Review of Sociology*, 3: 15–31.

Sullivan, Harry (1940). *Conceptions of Modern Psychiatry*. New York: Norton.

Sumerau, J. Edward (2012). That's What Men Are Supposed to Do: Compensatory Manhood Acts in an LGBT Christian Church. *Gender & Society*. 26: 461–87.

Supreme Court of the United States (2015). *Obergefell et al. v. Hodges, Director, Ohio Department of Health, et al.* Accessed 4 December 2016. https://www.supremecourt.gov/opinions/14pdf/14-556_3204.pdf.

Taylor, Charles (1991). *The Ethics of Authenticity*. Cambridge, MA and London: Harvard University Press.

Taylor, Charles (2007). *A Secular Age*. Cambridge, MA and London: Harvard University Press.

Thompson, Roger (1994). *Religion in Australia: A History*. Melbourne: Oxford University Press.

Thumma, Scott (1991). Negotiating a Religious Identity: The Case of the Gay Evangelical. *Sociological Analysis*, 52(4): 333–47.

Thumma, Scott and Gray, Edward (eds) (2005). *Gay Religion*. New York and Oxford: Altamira Press.

Toft, Alex (2010). *Bisexual Christian Identity: A Sociological Exploration of the Life Stories of Female and Male Bisexual Christians*. PhD Dissertation, University of Nottingham.

Tolich, Martin and Davidson, Carl (1999). *Starting Fieldwork: An Introduction to Qualitative Research in New Zealand*. Auckland: Oxford University Press.

Tosh, Nancy Ramsey (2001). Mirror Images: Wicca from the Inside Out and Outside In. In David Bromley and Lewis Carter (eds) *Toward Reflexive Ethnography: Participating, Observing, Narrating*. Oxford: Elsevier Science: 197–222.

The Uniting Church in Australia (2015). *About the Uniting Church in Australia*. Accessed 15 May 2015. https://assembly.uca.org.au/about/uca.

van Geest, Fred (2007). Changing Patterns of Denominational Political Activity in North America: The Case of Homosexuality. *Review of Religious Research*, 49(2): 199–221.

van Gennep, Arnold (1909/1960). *The Rites of Passage*. Chicago: University of Chicago Press.

Veith (2013). *Charismatic Sacrament, Charismatic Liturgy*. Accessed 27 October 2014. http://www.patheos.com/blogs/geneveith/2013/12/charismatic-sacrament-charismatic-liturgy/.

Wacquant, Loïc (1995). Review: Towards an Archaeology of Academe: A Critical Appreciation of Fritz Ringer's 'Fields of Knowledge'. *Acta Sociologica*, 38(2): 181–86.

Walton, Gerald (2006). Fag Church. *Journal of Homosexuality*, 51(2): 117.

Warner, Michael (1991). Introduction: Fear of a Queer Planet. *Social Text*, 29: 317.

Warner, Stephen (2005). *A Church of Our Own: Disestablishment and Diversity in American Religion*. New Brunswick, NJ: Rutgers University Press.

Whitehead, Andrew (2010). Sacred Rites and Civil Rights: Religion's Effect on Attitudes toward Same-Sex Unions and the Perceived Cause of Homosexuality. *Social Science Quarterly*, 91(1): 63–79.

Wilcox, Melissa (2002). When Sheila's a Lesbian: Religious Individualism among Lesbian, Gay, Bisexual and Transgender Christians. *Sociology of Religion*, 63(4): 497–513.

Wilcox, Melissa (2003). *Coming Out in Christianity: Religion, Identity and Community*. Bloomington and Indianapolis: Indiana University Press.

Wilcox, Melissa (2007). Outlaws or In-laws? *Journal of Homosexuality*, 52(1–2): 73–100.

Wilcox, Melissa (2009). *Queer Women and Religious Individualism*. Bloomington and Indianapolis: Indiana University Press.

Wilcox, Melissa (2010). Book Review: How the Religious Right Shaped Lesbian and Gay Activism. *Sociology of Religion*, 71(2): 251–53.

Wise, Michael, Harris, Catherine and Watts, Velma (2005). Cultural Capital, Habitus and Sense of Belonging: The Impact of Ascribed and Achieved Status. *Paper presented at the annual meeting of the American Sociological Association*, Marriott Hotel, Loews Philadelphia Hotel, Philadelphia. 12 August. Accessed 02 February 2015. http://citation.allacademic.com/meta/p20435_index.html.

Wolkomir, Michelle (2006). *Be Not Deceived: The Sacred and Sexual Struggles of Gay and ex-Gay Christian Men*. New Brunswick, NJ and London: Rutgers University Press.

Woo, Hoon (2013). The Understanding of Gisbertus Voetius and René Descartes on the Relationship of Faith and Reason, and Theology and Philosophy. *Westminster Theological Journal*, 75(1): 45–63.

Yang, Guobin (2000). *China's Red Guard Generation: The Ritual Process of Identity Transformation, 1966–1999*. New York: New York University Press.

Yip, Andrew (1997a). Attacking the Attacker: Gay Christians Talk Back. *The British Journal of Sociology*, 48(1): 113–27.

Yip, Andrew (1997b). Dare to Differ: Gay and Lesbian Catholics' Assessment of Official Catholic Positions on Sexuality. *Sociology of Religion*, 58(1): 165–79.

Yip, Andrew (1999). The Politics of Counter-Rejection. *Journal of Homosexuality*, 37(2): 47–63.

Yip, Andrew (2005). Queering Religious Texts: An Exploration of British Non-Heterosexual Christians' and Muslims' Strategy of Constructing Sexuality-Affirming Hermeneutics. *Sociology*, 39: 47–65.

Yip, Andrew (2010). Coming Home from the Wilderness: An Overview of Recent Scholarly Research on LGBTTQI Religiosity/Spirituality in the West. In Kath

Browne, Sally Munt and Andrew Yip (eds) *Queer Spiritual Spaces*. Farnham, UK: Ashgate: 35–50.

Ysseldyk, Renate, Matheson, Kimberly and Anisman, Hymie (2010). Religiosity as Identity: Toward an Understanding of Religion from a Social Identity Perspective. *Personality and Social Psychology Review*, 14(1): 60–71.

Zablocki, Benjamin (2001). Vulnerability and Objectivity of the Sacred. In David Bromley and Lewis Carter (eds) *Toward Reflexive Ethnography: Participating, Observing, Narrating*. Oxford: Elsevier Science: 223–45.

Index